REINVENTING THE CHINESE CITY

REINVENTING THE CHINESE CITY

RICHARD HU

Columbia University Press   *New York*

Columbia University Press
Publishers Since 1893
New York   Chichester, West Sussex
cup.columbia.edu

Library of Congress Cataloging-in-Publication Data
Names: Hu, Richard, author.
Title: Reinventing the Chinese city / Richard Hu.
Description: New York : Columbia University Press, [2023] |
Includes bibliographical references and index.
Identifiers: LCCN 2023003480 | ISBN 9780231211000 (hardback) |
ISBN 9780231211017 (trade paperback) | ISBN 9780231558693 (ebook)
Subjects: LCSH: Urbanization—China. | City planning—China. |
China—Economic policy.
Classification: LCC HT384.C6 H82 2023 | DDC 307.1/2160951—
dc23/eng/20230407
LC record available at https://lccn.loc.gov/2023003480

Cover design: Milenda Nan Ok Lee
Cover photo: Richard Hu

CONTENTS

ABBREVIATIONS

AI	artificial intelligence
APEC	Asia-Pacific Economic Cooperation
CBD	central business district
CCTV	China Central Television
CCTV	closed-circuit television
CDB	China Development Bank
CNETDZ	China National Economic and Technological Development Zone
CNHIDZ	China National High-Tech Industrial Development Zone
CNKI	China National Knowledge Infrastructure
CPC	Communist Party of China
FDI	foreign direct investment
GDP	gross domestic product
IoT	internet-of-things
LegCo	Legislative Council
NDRC	National Development and Reform Commission
NPC	National People's Congress
PRC	People's Republic of China

R&D	research and development
RoC	Republic of China
SAR	special administrative region
SEZ	special economic zone
SOE	state-owned enterprise
SUSTech	Southern University of Science and Technology
USTC	University of Science and Technology of China
WHO	World Health Organization

REINVENTING THE CHINESE CITY

1

A NEW URBAN ERA?

*It is a truth universally acknowledged, that a single politician
in possession of good power, must be in want of a new era.*

This well-known opening sentence from Jane Austen's
Pride and Prejudice is adapted here to analogize the current "new era" of China. This new era is not the first of
its type, nor will it be the last. Xi Jinping claimed a new era to
delineate and define his time in office, which began in late 2012.
It was clearly meant to differentiate his rule from those of his
predecessors—and probably also from those of his successors—
signaling his wish to put his own imprint on the future writing
of Chinese history. When will this new era end? It is presumed
to be the middle of the twenty-first century; by then, China will
have become "a great modern socialist country in all respects"
and achieve "the rejuvenation of the Chinese nation on all
fronts" through "a Chinese path to modernization."[1]

That is the "Chinese dream" that Xi Jinping first outlined in
October 2012 when he came into power. In October 2022, achieving these goals was identified as the "central task" for the new era
at the twentieth National Congress of the Communist Party of
China (CPC), the most important platform for setting national

development strategies and at which Xi secured a historic third term in office. The new era is articulated in a set of development visions, aspirations, and ambitions, though its "newness" is debatable and questionable, depending on one's perspective and the contexts of its narrative. Today, "new era" is a key concept in both political and nonpolitical discourses in China and is likely to remain so as long as Xi is in office or the power of his influence remains.

In 2017, Xi and his ideologues formulated a "thought" for himself and the new era: Xi Jinping Thought. In Chinese ideological orthodoxy, a "thought" carries more weight than a "theory." For example, Mao Zedong Thought and Deng Xiaoping Theory indicate the difference in each leader's level of importance in the construction of the national ideology as well as the writing of national history. Creating a thought for Xi seems to suggest a desire to draw parallels between Xi and Mao. But thematically, this Xi thought is more similar to Deng's. The thought has a clumsy full title, "Xi Jinping Thought on Socialism with Chinese Characteristics for a New Era," which lacks brevity, freshness, and originality. The key concept of "socialism with Chinese characteristics" was invented and promulgated by Deng Xiaoping. Xi seemed to simply rebadge it for his new era. Xi's thought was enshrined in the charter of the CPC in 2017 and the constitution of the People's Republic of China (PRC) in 2018. Being credited with a thought bearing his name in the charter and constitution marked the establishment of Xi Jinping as a paramount leader of his time, both institutionally and symbolically.

Xi Jinping Thought is basically a collage of visions and guidelines concerning almost every dimension of national development: it is broad, grand, and aspirational. This fundamental attribute signifies that the thought is evolving, incorporating newly arising issues and proposed notions. It also means the thought is open to interpretations and justifications. No matter how elusive it may be, Xi thought must be legitimized within the framework of Marxism—the nation's paramount ideological orthodoxy—to represent a form of Chinese contemporary Marxism, or "a new breakthrough in adapting Marxism to the Chinese context and the needs of our times."[2] Articulating a Chinese leader's thought (or equivalent) following Marxism to establish his ideological legitimacy and authority has been applied to every leader from Mao Zedong to Xi Jinping, and this approach is likely to continue with future leaders.

This new era—as a political discourse and a contemporary backdrop—contextualizes this book's interest in a new urban era that is emerging in China. This new urban era is both political and apolitical. It is political in the sense that it is integral to the new era as a political discourse. All the visions, agendas, strategies, and policies of the new era apply to and influence, first and foremost, Chinese cities while the nation is rapidly transforming into an urban society. The new era discourse is influencing an urban discourse, ushering in a new urban era in terms of agenda-setting for planning, policy, and development.

The new urban era is also apolitical in the sense that China's urbanization is reaching a critical stage, forging a new urban discourse in its own right. This new urban discourse, though not completely independent of the predominant political discourse, has its own "urban" logic and context. Further, the new urban discourse has played a major role in shaping the political discourse of the new era, given the importance of cities in national development. This political-apolitical dichotomy reveals the connection and interaction between the new era and the new urban era, a two-layered setting for the book's central concern with the reinvention of the Chinese city: the nation is transforming, so is its city, and so is the writing of its city.

GROWTH AND POST-GROWTH

The state of the Chinese city is in question for good reasons. Both China's urban growth (figure 1.1) and economic growth (figure 1.2)—two interwoven processes and two major indicators of the nation's rapid transformation—are phenomenal. As is commonly known, the year 1978 represents a dividing line for understanding contemporary China, not only in a political sense but also in a socioeconomic sense. From that year on, China has embarked on Deng Xiaoping's modernization agenda of "reform and opening up" (*gai ge kai fang*) centered on economic development, departing from the Maoist era of class struggles, political movements, and socioeconomic stasis.

Xi Jinping's new era discourse tries to integrate the Maoist era before 1978 and the Dengist era after 1978 into a holistic narrative of the CPC's leadership, and further into a justification that his new era is as distinct—and as important—as the previous two eras on the path of China's progress. This discourse sounds more a propagandic maneuvering than an evidenced observation. In any sense, the year 1978 witnessed a swerving of the direction of China, transforming and remaking the nation to this day and into the foreseeable future. Figures 1.1 and 1.2 illustrate urban growth and economic growth of China in comparison with the world to show so.

First, China is transitioning from a rural to an urban society. Its urbanization rate—the percentage of urban population—was 17.9 percent in 1978, far below the world's then average of 38.5 percent.[3] China was largely a rural society before 1978. Further, it was a dual society of urban-rural separation through a strict *hukou* system that links household registration with access to services and opportunities. The *hukou* system was formally established in 1958. It has been loosened in both practice and

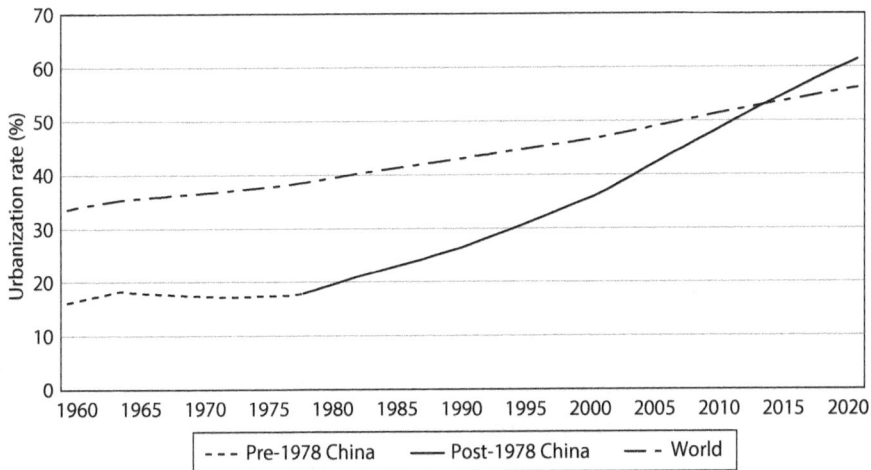

FIGURE 1.1 Urbanization rates of China and the world, 1960–2020

Source: Created by the author using data from World Bank, "Urban Population (% of Total Population)," accessed January 19, 2023, https://data.worldbank.org /indicator/SP.URB.TOTL.IN.ZS.

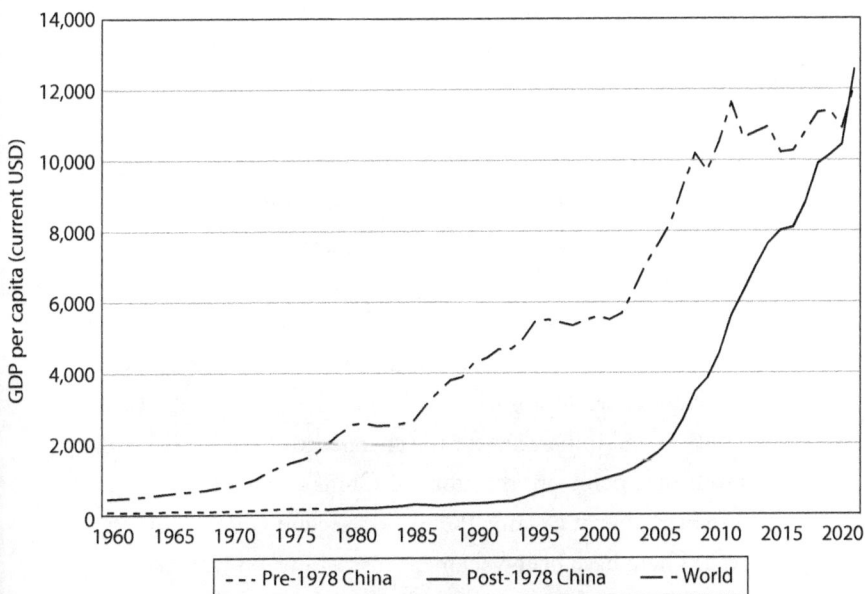

FIGURE 1.2 GDP per capita of China and the world, 1960–2021

Source: Created by the author using data for 1960–2020 from World Bank, "GDP per Capita (Current USs)," accessed January 20, 2023, https://data.worldbank.org/indicator /NY.GDP.PCAP.CD; and data for 2021 from Tianyu Wang, "2021: China's GDP Growth Beats Expectations with 8.1 Percent, Fastest in 10 Years," *CGTN*, January 17, 2022, https://news.cgtn.com/news/2022-01-17/China-s-GDP-tops-114-36-trillion-yuan -in-2021-16T64Jtona8/index.html.

policy in recent decades, but it remains a major institutional factor hindering urban transformation, urban-rural integration, and regional coordination of development.

Now, with more than 60 percent of the population residing in cities, China is becoming a highly urbanized society. In 2011, China's urbanization rate passed 50 percent. For the first time in the society of an ancient agrarian civilization, more people lived in cities than in the countryside. Just two years later, China's urbanization rate (at 53 percent) surpassed that of the world. While the urbanization rates of both China and the world have continued to increase, the gap between them continues to widen (see figure 1.1). The annual growth rate of China's urbanization (measured by the growth of urban population) has been constantly and significantly higher than that of the world's average since 1978. This explains how China's urbanization rate has steadily chased and overtaken the world's within a short time frame of several decades.

Second, China is transitioning from a low-income to a high-income country. In 1978, its gross domestic product (GDP) per capita was just 7.8 percent of the world's average.[4] This extreme poverty put the world's most populous nation in crisis; it also put in crisis the legitimacy of the CPC, which had promised Chinese people a prosperous life and had ruled the country since 1949. These crises to a great extent propelled and justified the necessity of and imperative for the changes to come.

From that point on, the story of China's economic rise has been remarkable: it became the world's second largest economy in 2012. There have been vehement discussions on whether and when China would become the largest economy. What is an even more remarkable economic story is how China has caught up with the world's average in GDP per capita. That has been probably the hardest task in the nation's development given its

very low level of economic output in 1978 and very large population size. Recent data (in 2021) showed that China's GDP per
capita was US$12,551, surpassing the world's average, estimated at
US$12,100.[5] These latest economic data also put China very close
to the threshold of joining the club of high-income countries,
defined by the World Bank as those with a gross national income
(GNI) per capita of more than US$12,695 as of July 1, 2021.[6]

China accounted for 22 percent of the world's population in
1978 and 18 percent in 2020.[7] Overtaking the world's average
in either urbanization rate or GDP per capita—which are, of
course, interlinked—has been a mission of tremendous national
and human development. Because of China's sheer size, it is also
a race in which China is chasing itself. This China-world race
has remade not only the nation but also the world: today's world
is an urban one; more than 800 million Chinese people (and
human beings) have been lifted out of poverty. If China becomes
a high-income country in 2023 as predicted,[8] it would double the
world's high-income population.

The picture just painted is an old story of the Chinese city
updated with some of the latest data; it is a story of growth.
This book focuses on the most recent period of the 2010s and
onward to retell a new story of the Chinese city—a story of
"post-growth." There are a number of important reasons for this.
China's urban development has entered a critical phase in this
period, by itself and in comparison with the world, as measured
by the aforementioned quantitative indicators. At the same time,
debates about China's urbanization being at a crossroads and
advocacy for inclusive growth and sustainable development have
been surging.[9] A new urban discourse is emerging in China, pursuing so-called new-type urbanization (*xin xing cheng zhen hua*)
that prioritizes quality over quantity. This discourse is resetting
the Chinese urban agenda from growth to post-growth.

It should be noted that this shift is not unique to the urban transformation in China; it is a common theme in the transformations of numerous Asian and Pacific cities.[10] However, the theme particularly stands out in China because of the shift's massive scale and profound influence in the country. Nurtured in the previous decades of rapid urbanization, this shift has been dominating the urban discourse and practice in much of the 2010s; it is likely to shape the trajectory of Chinese urban planning and development until the middle of the century.

THE QUANTITY-QUALITY CONTRADICTION

There is nothing that does not contain contradiction; without contradiction nothing would exist. . . . There are many contradictions in the process of development of a complex thing, and one of them is necessarily the principal contradiction whose existence and development determine or influence the existence and development of the other contradictions.[11]

—Mao Zedong, 1937

Mao Zedong wrote *On Contradiction* (*Mao dun lun*) in August 1937. The essay was based on Mao's lectures for his communist cadres, drawing from the writings of Karl Marx, Friedrich Engels, and Vladimir Lenin and elaborating on them with references to the practice of the CPC and in China at that time. Mao wrote this essay not just out of his intellectual interest in philosophy but with broader political aims. Grafting some Marxist elements onto the political agenda of the CPC, Mao theorized his own thought to justify both its correctness and the incorrectness of the thoughts of his rivals, and ultimately to solidify his leadership, which was being challenged. This classic writing has been one of the keystones of Mao Zedong Thought—the earliest homemade orthodox ideology of the CPC and, later, the PRC.

As a result, "contradiction" has been a frequent, central concept in Chinese political discourse. A major change in the national development direction must be preceded and underpinned by a shift in the "principal contradiction" identified for the nation. Thus, what constitutes the principal contradiction to be tackled is of the utmost importance in setting national development agendas. However, the principal contradiction has not always been identified according to the Marxist theory of dialectical materialism and historical materialism, as Mao expressed in his essay. It could be highly politicized or personalized, depending on the dominant power relations and power struggles of the time, as had happened before and after the establishment of the PRC in 1949.

During much of Mao's rule, which began in 1949, he continued to hold his revolutionary mindset and insisted that the principal contradiction of the nation was one of class struggle between the proletariat and the bourgeoisie. This mistaken principal contradiction—arising from Mao's misreading of social reality, intraparty struggles, or simply his personal whim—had underlain the political turmoil, social crisis, and economic stagnation until Mao's death in 1976.

To change China's direction in the post-Mao era and legitimize his agenda of reform and opening up, Deng Xiaoping needed to reidentify the principal contradiction, which was formalized in 1981 as "the ever-growing material and cultural needs of the people vs. backward social production."[12] This new principal contradiction determined that the central task of the party and the people was economic development and growth rather than class struggle—that was how it was argued and justified during the transition from the Maoist to the Dengist era. The rest is history: Deng Xiaoping's reform and opening-up agenda, centered on addressing the redefined principal contradiction, has profoundly transformed China.

Following those historical steps, Xi Jinping's new era demanded a new principal contradiction, both of which were endorsed at the nineteenth CPC National Congress in October 2017. The new principal contradiction is defined as "unbalanced and inadequate development vs. the people's ever-growing needs for a better life."[13] Addressing this principal contradiction would run through the whole process of China becoming "a great modern socialist country" by the middle of the twenty-first century, as stated earlier. After that, a new principal contradiction is expected to emerge, since the current one is expected to be solved. This is the general roadmap that has been desired, proposed, and justified for the new era. The new principal contradiction was identified, among other purposes, to capture a transformative stage of national development after China had experienced rapid growth for four decades.

As noted, China has been rapidly transitioning from a rural to an urban society. With more than 900 million people now living in cities,[14] the new era—as a reality or an imaginary—is primarily about a new urban era. In a previous publication in 2008, I bookended an urban age for China of half a century, from 1980 to 2030, during which the annual urban population growth rate would be consistently more than the world's average, based on historical data and future estimates.[15] After China's urbanization rate increases to a certain high level—say, 80 percent—the annual growth rate of its urban population will naturally decrease to a constant low level. If China is entering a new urban era, what differentiates it from the old one? The new principal contradiction identified for Chinese society, if it is a valid one, should apply to its cities.

The rapid growth that has characterized China's urbanization is giving way to the pursuit of new-type urbanization characterized by quality—an urban discourse that was on the rise in the 2000s and became established in the 2010s. In March 2014, the Chinese government released the *National New-Type Urbanization Plan (2014–2020)*—China's first national urbanization plan—to set the tone for urban transformation. This plan marked a "qualitative transition" in national urbanization policy.[16] A new version of the *National New-Type Urbanization Plan* for the period 2021–2035 was prepared, but it had not been publicized as of March 2023. This shift in urban discourse is built on a quantity-quality contradiction confronting China's urbanization and its cities, aligning to the principal contradiction of the nation in a general sense.

The quantity-quality contradiction has underpinned the emergence of a new urban discourse, which has accelerated in the recent decade and suggested the coming of—or an aspiration for—a new urban era. This contradiction is premised on two basic understandings. First, the speed of China's urbanization will not persist; it is already slowing down. Second, its rapid and massive urbanization has mixed outcomes; it has come with both great achievements and grave problems.

Arising from the quantity-quality contradiction, a new urban era is quintessentially defined by a shift from quantitative growth to qualitative upgrading, which is dominating the debates about China's urban transformation. Despite the fact that this shift reflects a consensus of cognition and knowledge among stakeholders and interest groups, translating it into policy making and planning, and, most importantly, action and desired outcomes involves a process of complexity, uncertainty, and contention.

NEW NORMAL OR OLD PATH?

The term "new normal" has increased in popularity in recent decades, triggered by waves of global crises and domestic changes. Used to refer to new financial and economic conditions after the 2008 global financial crisis, the term has become exponentially more popularized since COVID-19; it is often applied to descriptions of the pandemic's disruption and impact. However, the term's use in China has special political and economic contexts; the Chinese version, *xin chang tai*, is integral to the new era discourse. After it was "invented" and endorsed by the new generation of leaders headed by Xi Jinping, who came into power in late 2012, it instantly became a buzzword in policy discussions, media reportage, and academic publications.

The backdrop for the term's emergence was that in the years after 2012, the Chinese economy slowed to an annual growth rate of around 7 percent. This "moderate" growth rate—as far as the Chinese economy was concerned—presented something of a shock to people who were used to observing and enjoying double-digit economic growth rates in the previous decades. At the time, there was a debate about whether the future economy would bounce back to create a V-shaped trajectory or if it would flatten to follow an L-shaped path.

Said to be masterminded by Liu He, Chinese vice premier (in office in 2018–2023) and Xi Jinping's then primary economic adviser, "new normal" was first used by Xi in May 2014 on an inspection visit to Henan Province. On November 9, 2014, in a keynote speech at the Asia-Pacific Economic Cooperation (APEC) CEO Summit, Xi elaborated on new normal as the government's evaluation of and expectation for the future economy. The term's use seemed to suggest that the "old" high economic growth rate was neither possible nor desirable. It signified an anticipation of a moderate and stable economic growth rate in the future. The term also implied a significant shift in policy goals of the Chinese economy from quantitative growth to qualitative upgrading through structural economic reform and innovation. As of March 2023, the State Council dedicated a webpage to the topic of "new normal, steady growth," promoting the concept and its policy implications. Accordingly, "high-quality development" (*gao zhi liang fa zhan*) is the new strategic development goal, differentiating itself from the previous one marked by the quantity of growth, speed, and scale.

In a China Development Forum in March 2015 in Beijing, Angel Gurría, then secretary-general of the Organisation for Economic Co-operation and Development (OECD), remarked, "As China's economy shifts to a 'New Normal,' GDP growth will become increasingly reliant on domestic consumption, efficient and sustainable resource use, and rising productivity. This demands a 'New Normal' for urbanisation, with city policies that reflect the shift of gear."[17] Certainly, the new normal concept has generated some excitement and expectations among outside observers who are concerned about China's transformation and its implications for the world. The concept has also been seamlessly incorporated into the discourse of new-type urbanization.

The new normal or new-type urbanization discourse now dominates Chinese planning and development; it seems to be shaping the way the Chinese city will be imagined, planned, built, and managed from the 2020s until the mid-twenty-first century, the time frame of a likely new urban era. Much is known about how China has changed from a rural to an urban society through rapid urbanization in only four decades. That urbanization is now shifting in scale and speed. Further, it is shifting in thinking, approach, and practice in pursuit of a new normal for the Chinese city.

In this book, I investigate the contemporary transformation of the Chinese city—its drivers, rationale, patterns, and outcomes. In doing so, I aim to develop a cohesive narrative of the new Chinese city to inform a critical understanding and reflection of the new-type urbanization being advocated and pursued. This aim is intentionally different from the writing about the Chinese city that has focused on its rapid growth since the late twentieth century. Rather, I rewrite and retheorize the Chinese city in terms of the newness in its post-growth imaginary and reality.

I have selected three keywords—"green," "smart," and "innovation"—that underpin the new urban discourse and use them as prisms through which to reveal the very nature of the urban transformation that is under way, including enabling factors, transformative processes, emerging trends, and fundamental paradoxes. I borrow the Maoist terms "revolution," "movement," and "great leap forward" to pair with the keywords to describe three prominent, interlinked phenomena—"green revolution," "smart city movement," and "great innovation leap forward"— that are spreading across Chinese cities. These Maoist terms, albeit somewhat outdated, are revived not just for rhetorical effects; they are used, metaphorically and analogically, to capture and highlight the "Chineseness" of these new urban phenomena.

The investigation is guided by a central question: is the current urban transformation leading to a new normal or following an old path? Through addressing this question, I establish a dialogue between the new and old Chinese city to reveal the continuity and change between them. I decouple the urban imaginary and the urban reality to differentiate them and, further, to ascertain the relationship between them—how they are functioning and interacting to shape the urban transformation. I draw on historical and contemporary materials and data from primary and secondary sources to analyze, interpret, and develop insights into the urban phenomena.

For each of the phenomena, I use the experience of one city to further showcase the issues of concern: Beijing for the green revolution, Hangzhou for the smart city movement, and Hefei for the great innovation leap forward. I include the top city, Beijing, because it is the most symptomatic of China's urban transformation, though it has already attracted much attention in Chinese urban studies. The emerging star cities Hangzhou and Hefei are included, as they have traditionally received less attention in research and debates than top cities. But they are rapidly rising in the national urban system and are more illustrative of the dynamics in China's urban transformation than the top-tier cities.

I conduct a focused examination of Xiong'an, the newest city, to demonstrate many of the propositions around China's urban transformation in action. Xiong'an is a bold, ambitious urban experiment, being planned and built from scratch. As imagined, it aims to explore and pioneer a new way of planning and developing a "utopian" city to address the "dystopian" problems and challenges confronting Chinese cities. It was initiated and supported by a strong political will to spearhead a paradigm shift in China's urban development model. I use the Xiong'an case to reveal how the new urban discourse is shaping, as well as being shaped by, the imperative of new-type urbanization. I also examine the structural paradox underlying the Xiong'an experiment, which poses critical questions and uncertainties about this new city as both a political initiative and an urban imaginary.

I also write about the latest situations in Hong Kong. While Hong Kong is not included as a case for examining any of the foregoing aspects of China's urban transformation, being the most "un-Chinese" Chinese city, it presents a unique perspective from which to understand China's contemporary governance and urban transformation. Hong Kong has experienced profound changes in recent years and is becoming increasingly integrated into the regional and national urban systems and into the national development strategy. This integration is being driven in contexts and by factors that are more external than internal to the city. The recent reorientation of Hong Kong is injecting new issues and angles into approaching the Chinese city in the new era, especially in terms of the relationality of city making and nation building—an enduring thesis in understanding China's urbanization and modernization.[18]

OVERVIEW OF THE BOOK

This chapter sets the contexts, raises the questions, and introduces the methods for understanding the latest development of the Chinese city. China's urbanization is entering a new stage of transformation in discourse, policy, and practice. While a political new era has been proclaimed to map out a national development vision until the mid-twenty-first century, a new urban era also seems to be emerging, shaping the transformation—and the reading—of the Chinese city during the 2010s and onward. Established on a principal quantity-quality contradiction underlying many aspects of China and the Chinese city, a new-type urbanization is being pursued, shifting the focus of urban development from quantitative growth to qualitative upgrading to achieve high-quality development.

This shift defies an old reading of the Chinese city in terms of growth and calls for an investigation of the essence of the post-growth Chinese city. Guided by a central question of whether this shift constitutes a new normal or simply extends an old path, this book penetrates three urban phenomena—green revolution, smart city movement, and great innovation leap forward—together with other aspects of contemporary urban transformation, aiming to update and advance an understanding of the Chinese city.

Chapter 2 addresses the green revolution. Both growth and pollution are the hallmarks of many Chinese cities. State-led developmentalism has created massive urbanization and great economic recovery within just a few decades. However, this growth has been achieved at the grave cost of environmental degradation. Now a state-led green revolution is emerging, aiming to counter the environmental consequences of growth. The environmental challenge had been long recognized and debated from the end of the twentieth century, but it did not come to the fore of policy making and enforcement until the early twenty-first century. Environmental concerns are priori- tized in the political agenda to such an extent that the pursuit of an "eco-civilization" is incorporated into the national modern- ization strategy.

However, paradoxes exist at both strategic and operational levels. An ecotopia with Chinese characteristics—a mixture of neoliberalism and greenism—is essentially a type of "greenized" prodevelopment in the new circumstance of an environmental imperative. A fundamental sustainability paradox of "grow- green" challenges China's ambitious dual agendas of modern- ization and decarbonization by the mid-twenty-first century. While some progress has been made in improving the environ- ment in recent years, the way ahead for China's green revolution is challenging and contingent. This chapter uses Beijing's envi- ronmental challenges and progress to illustrate the revolutionary efforts of "blueing" the city's sky in the recent decade.

Chapter 3 addresses the smart city movement. China was a latecomer in the global smart city movement, but now, in a way it is a leader. China has the largest number of smart city programs in the world. It is also the most passionate about developing and employing new technology to build smart cities and further a smart society. Behind these drives is a smart city coalition comprising the endorsement of the government, the advocacy of high-tech giants and professional consultants, dissemination by academia, and acceptance—conscious and unconscious—by the community.

An explicit technocentrism characterizes the smart city movement, prioritizing the achievement of efficiency and productivity in operating and managing urban systems through capitalizing on smart technology. This technocentrism, while meeting the critical demands of economic transformation, environmental challenges, and urban governance and services, has generated social concerns and played into political interests. Smart authoritarianism—the marriage between smart technology and rising authoritarianism—is "smartizing" the state's capacity for censorship and surveillance, exposing the worrying side of the smart city movement, which is marching ahead uncritically. This chapter uses Hangzhou, a city conventionally known for its beauty, to show the recent smartization of a city's imaginary, economic base, and urban management.

Chapter 4 addresses the great innovation leap forward. In a process taking several decades, China has been transitioning from a preindustrial to an industrial and postindustrial economy, which has taken many developed countries hundreds of years. There has been a strong aspiration for an intensive transformation from "made in China" to "innovated in China." China has made a long-term commitment and consistent investment to build up its innovation capacity and become an innovative nation, an integral part of its modernization strategy. Innovation is injecting new dynamics and dimensions into China's urbanization, including both "planned innovation" through top-down designated high-tech development zones and "unplanned innovation" through bottom-up e-urbanization.

However, China's strategic innovation pathway faces both international and national challenges. Internationally, the escalating innovation-centered geopolitics—"inno-politics"—exposes China's disadvantage in the global innovation race and further bolsters its determination to pursue so-called indigenous innovation and self-reliance in advanced technologies. Nationally, the innovation drive is encountering growing illiberalization in governance and social management, testing how far the great innovation leap forward will reach. This chapter uses Hefei, an obscure inland city, to demonstrate how a city can integrate local innovation assets with a dedicated innovation strategy to achieve new growth opportunities.

Chapter 5 critically examines Xiong'an, the newest Chinese city and the latest urban experiment. Xiong'an was initiated at a critical moment in China's transformative urbanization, with the aim of exploring and advancing a new paradigm of urban thinking and development with a strong Chinese hallmark. The notion was triggered by an imperative to address the Beijing syndrome—unlimited urban growth and associated urban problems and sustainability challenges—through moving its noncapital functions elsewhere and, further, to coordinate the development of the Beijing-Tianjin-Hebei region. The imagining and planning of Xiong'an has used all the buzzwords—like green, smart, and innovation—that might forge a contemporary urban utopia.

However, Xiong'an is more than an urban experiment; it is also a political initiative. It is commissioned with the goal of becoming an urban flagship to commemorate Xi Jinping's new era. For this reason, it has received unreserved state support in political endorsement, planning, and resources. It is essentially a state project with limited nonstate participation and free from the involvement of market forces. Will bold vision and political will suffice to sustain to fruition the long duration and large scale of such a future city? The answer to this question has yet to be considered and in the long run seems uncertain.

Chapter 6 examines the recent governance and planning changes in Hong Kong and the contexts and rationale for them. It explores the historical and cultural roots that have defined the uniqueness of the city as an East-West connector. However, since its return to China in 1997, the city has experienced escalating economic frustration, social division, and political unrest, which were the most exposed in the 2019 street movement. The chapter unpacks the city's internal problems and external geopolitics, which together have placed Hong Kong in a position that has called for the central government's forceful intervention.

The "one country, two systems" policy is being profoundly reinterpreted and reconstructed at a critical midpoint of the policy's fifty-year tenure for the city. In doing so, the city is being reoriented toward a closer integration with the regional development of the Greater Bay Area and the national development trajectory. The latest development blueprint by the Hong Kong government maps out an ambitious Northern Metropolis initiative to build a new city along the border with Shenzhen to embrace the spillover of technology and innovation. All the recent transformations seem to suggest the second return of Hong Kong to its motherland.

Chapter 7 employs a futuristic perspective on the imaginary of the Chinese city. China will achieve its modernization basically and fully, by 2035 and 2050, respectively; this is how the national development roadmap for the new era envisions. This national strategy is refreshing and reshaping the way the Chinese city is being imagined and planned. China is reforming its planning system as an integral part of the modernization of its governance system and governance capacity. A new planning system is being established to streamline the planning process, implementation, and governance. Emerging regionalization is redefining the spatial representation of and planning response to transformative urbanization. "City cluster" and "metropolitan circle" become new spatial scales for planning integrated, coordinated regional development.

A comparison of the latest master plans of Beijing, Shanghai, and Shenzhen, which all set ambitious development goals for 2035 and 2050, illustrates the influences of the new national development strategy and new planning system on the newest urban imaginaries. However, despite the grandeur of narratives and visions, the macro urban transformation is generating new winners and losers involving urban-rural disparity, intracity inequality, and intercity unbalance. Policy and planning interventions for these urban challenges and issues have had mixed outcomes.

Chapter 8 concludes the book. It responds to the question of "new normal or old path," which governs the inquiry into the recent transformation of China's urbanization. It critically examines the historicity of the "newness" of the new (urban) era to unravel the era's continuity and change. It further delves into the government-market relationality: although the market has been firmly established in the Chinese orthodox discourse of ideology and policy, how the relationality has functioned has demonstrated strong path dependence in terms of the instrumentalization of the market by and for the state. This relationality captures and explains many aspects of China's (un)transformation, including its cities, in recent decades.

The traditional oriental wisdom of "essence-function" (*ti-yong*) is employed to make sense of the nature of the Chinese city.

It highlights the "Chineseness" and a meta-thesis in understanding the Chinese city: urbanization is integral to modernization; city making is instrumental to nation building. This meta-thesis breaks through historical phases and regime changes, aligning the urban transformation in the early twenty-first century backward to the genesis of modern planning in the early twentieth century and forward to an urban imaginary toward the mid-twenty-first century.

2

THE GREEN REVOLUTION

Wendy Yang is a friend of mine in Beijing. She is a typical middle-class Beijinger: educated and open-minded, with a happy family, a decent job, and an enviable lifestyle. Around 2015, she expressed an interest in migrating overseas and raised the idea with me. It was a bold idea from an outsider's perspective, given the fact that her family, life, and career were all established in a booming city and country. Many people would dream of migrating to Beijing. For her, the only factor propelling the idea of relocating overseas was the city's worsening air pollution—it had reached a nearly unbearable level, and it was not certain when and how this problem could be solved. Her biggest concern was the health of her son, who was three years old then; she was seeking a cleaner environment for the future generation.

Interestingly and ironically, a middle-class Beijinger would turn into an environmental refugee. Wendy and her family did not migrate in the end—Beijing has many other attractions that would offset its polluted air and hold them there. But many Beijingers did emigrate. As I will further discuss in this chapter, there are clear correlations between environmental pollution and migration choices in China.

In September 2021, when I was writing this chapter, I recalled with Wendy our exchanges of years ago. I asked her how she felt about the air quality in Beijing now. She indicated that it had significantly improved and that air purifiers—a household necessity in many Chinese cities—are seldom used anymore.

Indeed, I have other anecdotal indications of the improvement of Beijing's air quality. I have many friends in Beijing linked on WeChat—the most popular social media app among the Chinese community. At least five years ago, air pollution had been a frequent topic in the posts by friends in Beijing, demonstrating both its severity and the level of concerns about it. The city's pollution could be instantly spotted in many photos, which were posted to illustrate other features of the area but in which a gray background of air or sky was visible. Somehow, the number of such posts has been declining, almost unconsciously. They have been replaced gradually by posts that often show—unintentionally—the city's cleaner air and bluer sky compared with previous photos. Air pollution has not disappeared, but its frequency and severity have lessened, explicitly and impressively. It is not as topical in social media as it was years ago. This change seems to be happening, quietly but remarkably.

Beijing is not the most polluted city, nor is it the only Chinese city that has seen impressive air quality improvement in recent years. Its status as the capital city has attracted more attention to its pollution than similar problems in other cities. Major cities like Beijing, Shanghai, Chengdu, Guangzhou, Chongqing, and Shenzhen have all improved their air quality to various degrees. As measured by their annual average levels of fine particulate matter (PM2.5), in 2015–2020, they all improved from "unhealthy" to "moderate" or "unhealthy for sensitive groups."[1]

However, this improvement reflects only the progress in cities within China, not in comparison with non-Chinese cities. In the international context, the air pollution in most Chinese cities does not meet the PM2.5 target of 10 μg/m³ set by the World Health Organization (WHO).² China ranked fourteenth in the 2020 world ranking of air pollution as measured by annual average PM2.5 concentration weighted by population.³ In air quality, Chinese cities are making progress, but they are also facing challenges.

> Overall, air quality in cities across China has been improving. In 2020, 86 percent of Chinese cities observed cleaner air than the previous year, and average pollution exposure by population fell 11 percent. . . . Only 2 percent of the 388 Chinese cities included in this report achieved the WHO annual PM2.5 target of < 10 μg/m³, while 61 percent of cities met China's national Grand II annual standard of < 35 μg/m³ (in line with the WHO interim target 1). China remains the world's largest producer and consumer of coal, a principal contributor to PM2.5 pollution nationally. Although China is achieving the largest growth of any country in renewable energies, these sources account for just 23 percent of China's energy consumption, while coal accounts for 58 percent.⁴

China's environmental challenges involve more than air pollution, although it is the most observable, detectable, and measurable of these challenges. Many types of environmental degradation have been widespread: pollution of water and soil as well as air, resource waste, deforestation, desertification, and climate change. Almost all areas of human and natural environments have been affected. This damage is generating negative effects and externalities, some known and some yet unknown, in nearly every aspect of daily living and well-being: health, livability, disasters, and social and economic costs.

In his report to the twentieth CPC National Congress in October 2022, Xi Jinping boasted of the environmental achievements in the past ten years of his new era: "This has led to historic, transformative, and comprehensive changes in ecological and environmental protection and has brought us bluer skies, greener mountains, and cleaner waters."[5] While some progress has been made, the changes are yet far from "historic, transformative, and comprehensive."

China's rise has been characterized not only by rapid industrialization and urbanization but also by massive environmental problems, all of which have emerged within a short time frame of several decades. The levels of its economic achievement and environmental damage are both remarkable, and they are manifestly correlated. While pundits propose a so-called China model to summarize its best practices of economic development and success in lifting most of the population out of poverty, they also have to acknowledge the environmental challenges that the China model has incurred, which have affected the sustainable well-being of current and future generations in the nation and the world.

While the contradiction between "grow" and "green" is a global challenge, it is most conspicuous in China. First, this conspicuousness is about scale: the scales of both China's growth and associated environmental sacrifices are breathtaking, given the size of its population, land, and economy. Second, this conspicuousness is about timing: the timings of China's modernization and the sustainability imperative have simply coincided.

Unlike those developed societies that had industrialized and modernized their economies mostly before the 1980s, China has been a latecomer. Its modernization process—through rapid industrialization and urbanization—started in the late twentieth century and has gained momentum, in part thanks to accelerated globalization and technological advances, in the early twenty-first century. This has also been a period of escalating environmental challenges and climate change confronting human beings across the globe.

China has had to tackle the missions of both modernization and sustainability simultaneously. Its modernization agenda of reform and opening up is a revolution in the same sense as those "red" revolutions that established the nation, as claimed by the agenda's inventor, Deng Xiaoping, in the early 1980s.[6] Its sustainability agenda is also a revolution—a "green" revolution.

UNDER THE DOME

Chai Jing was a journalist at China Central Television (CCTV) in 2001–2013. In contrast to the stereotype of journalists working for the state mouthpiece, Chai's programs about people and social issues were compassionate, direct, and (modestly) critical. Chai's fresh interview style and her humanistic, investigative journalism won her more popularity—and sometimes controversy—among Chinese audiences than many of her colleagues at CCTV and her other peers in the Chinese official media. She was also labeled as a "public intellectual" (*gong zhi*)—a term of mixed respect and disrespect in the Chinese discourse as a result of social differences in political and social stances and opinions—for her proliberal writing and comments about public affairs.

It was not surprising that Chai ultimately resigned from CCTV, presumably to pursue an independent life and freedom of expression. Her finale as a journalist came two years after her departure from CCTV: she produced and presented an environmental documentary, *Under the Dome* (*Qiong ding zhi xia*), which is probably her best-known and definitely her most controversial program.

Under the Dome was an investigative documentary on China's pollution. Presented by Chai herself, it combined Chai's experiences and interviews, reportage on environmental deterioration and power relations behind the scenes, criticism of environmental policies and state-owned fossil fuel giants, and reflections on the national development model. The issues covered were not new, and some data were not rigorous. But the film's refreshing narrative and presentation style, Chai's charisma, and a well-orchestrated communication campaign made it a textbook success in terms of dissemination and impact.

The timing of the documentary's public release on February 28, 2015, was deliberate: the day before, China's new environmental minister, Chen Jining, had been appointed. On March 3, 2015, China's annual rubber-stamp national conferences for legislation and political consultation would be held in Beijing.

The documentary became an instant sensation in social media and official online media. On March 1, the new environmental minister sent a text message to Chai expressing gratitude for her contribution to the enhancement of public awareness of environmental issues. On March 2, a day before the national conferences, the documentary and all articles about it were censored online. But the film's short existence was long enough to have an impact. Within forty-eight hours of its release, it had more than 200 million views. During the subsequent national conferences, despite its online censorship, the documentary—and environmental issues generally—were hot topics among the delegates. One delegate equated its impact on environmental awareness in China to that of Rachel Carson's *Silent Spring*, published in 1962.

Under the Dome was more than a sensational media phenomenon. Its popularity, and the debates and controversies it generated, struck a chord with people who had concerns about China's environmental situation at the time. The documentary was produced in 2014. In 2013, east China had experienced the most severe smog with the longest duration in its history, covering one-quarter of the country and impacting a population of nearly 600 million.[7] "Fog and haze" (*wu mai*), a result of air masses of pollutants and lack of air flow, was voted as the "Chinese term of the year." It remains a term frequently used in reportage, discussions, and policy documents about pollution in Chinese cities. In *Under the Dome*, Chai Jing approached the degrading of the environment and its hazards for health and livability from the perspectives of a journalist, a resident, and a mother. The 2013 east China smog was an immediate backdrop and a triggering factor for many of Chai's observations in the documentary and for people's sympathy with her efforts.

Debates on the documentary even encroached on Chai's personal life: rumors emerged that she had given birth to a daughter in the United States in 2013 and that her family migrated there after the documentary's sensational release. These unconfirmed rumors touched on Chai's privacy. They stirred some popular interest because environmental migrants have become a new phenomenon in the concurrent context of China's economic rise and environmental degradation.

Contrary to our traditional perceptions of environmental refugees, Chinese environmental migrants are people from the middle and upper classes who decide to emigrate—often overseas—to pursue clean air and a better lifestyle. While these people have benefited from China's rapid economic growth, they have also decided to escape its environmental externalities. This is the paradox confronting national development pathways

and individual choices. A member of the Chinese elite migrating overseas can easily arouse nationalistic responses or criticism in public discourse, especially from the less well-off. This
explains why rumors might merge Chai Jing's private and personal migration choices with the debates about her documentary on environmental issues.

Indeed, pollution is becoming, among other things, an important factor in people's decision to move into or out of a city in
China, or to leave the country. Some empirical studies have
testified to this. One study of Chinese cities showed that an
increase in its air quality index (indicating worsening air pollution) on one day would cause an increase in online searches
of "emigration" the next day; this positive correlation was more
pronounced for days when pollution was particularly heavy.[8] Air
pollution does not just push out a city's residents; it also makes
it harder for cities to attract new residents. Another study of
Chinese counties revealed that air pollution could reduce inward
migration—especially of educated people at the early stage of
their professional careers—and result in net outward migration
and total population decline.[9]

Migration preferences, decisions, and patterns are more complicated than air pollution alone can explain, although it is an
increasingly important factor, particularly for better-off groups
in society. The pollution-migration equation has multiple socioeconomic variables. I earlier discussed the anecdotal experience
of my friend Wendy Yang in Beijing. Despite her initial interest
in migrating overseas to flee Beijing because of concerns about
air pollution, other factors have led her to remain in the city.
Pollution is a common concern; its impacts on individuals' decisions and actions differ. Pollution is influencing socioeconomic
restructuring in China. However, it has also been related to the
nation's adamant pursuit of socioeconomic progress.

DEVELOPMENT IS THE
ABSOLUTE PRINCIPLE

Deng Xiaoping and his predecessor, Mao Zedong, were different, or opposite, in personalities and styles. Mao was utopian, imaginative, and romantic—these terms used sometimes as a euphemism for his irrationality and recklessness. He was an eloquent speaker as well as a prolific writer and poet. Deng was down-to-earth, pragmatic, and straightforward. Unlike Mao, Deng did not produce many literary or political writings. The legacies of Deng's political visions and doctrines are mostly in his talks or conversations. As a result, Deng's political sayings are often colloquial, plain, and to the point. One of his best-known sayings is "development is the absolute principle" (*fa zhan cai shi ying dao li*).

Deng said this in early 1992 during the so-called Southern Talks (*Nan fang tan hua*), when he visited several cities in south China and made a series of remarks—informal but strategic—to advocate his prodevelopment stance.[10] That was not the first time Deng expressed such a stance on development. He had consistently prioritized development—mainly in terms of economic growth—in his agenda for China's modernization from the late 1970s when he became the nation's paramount leader. He urged that this agenda should not waver for one hundred years—in a metaphorical sense.

Development has remained on China's priority agenda to this day. It will continue to be so in the coming decades, as outlined in its long-term strategies until the mid-twenty-first century, though in the name of high-quality development (see chapter 1). The connotations of "development" have been evolving, but economic growth has been a central component of it: economic growth is integral to development and provides the base for other forms of development—a notion that integrates Deng's pragmatism and certain elements of Marxian materialistic principle of "base" and "superstructure."[11] In its advancement of this development discourse at home, the Chinese government has emphasized the "right to development" (*fa zhan quan*) as a human right and the legitimacy of pursuing "development interest" (*fa zhan li yi*) in its diplomatic, and sometimes geopolitical, discourses.

Since the turn of the century, a notion of "latecomer advantage" (*hou fa you shi*) has been emerging in China, envisioning the nation's development trajectory in the new century. To put it simply, this notion holds that China, as a latecomer in the course of modernization, can benefit from the experiences of the forerunners (the West) through learning their successes and avoiding their mistakes, and thus it could possibly achieve a faster and better development trajectory than the West.[12] This is a crude notion: it is a hotchpotch of aspiration, optimism, and imagination that appeals to the nation's growing confidence and nationalism.

This appeal in political and public discussions has oversimplified the complexity of national development in terms of historical, cultural, and social attributes and environmental, economic, technological, and political settings—both domestically and internationally. Certain aspects of China's development are often interpreted as a sort of representation of the latecomer advantage, like its infrastructure construction, innovation advancement, urbanization, and industrialization. A critical question is, to what extent are they representative of the advantage bestowed on a latecomer or simply of an established pattern advanced by a latecomer in a different setting?

Indeed, China has learned much from the West and has adapted those lessons to local settings to achieve a sort of indigenous progress, or development with Chinese characteristics.

However, China has also encountered the same pitfalls as experienced in the West's development, like social inequality, environmental degradation, and institutional path dependence. For example, there is no convincing evidence that the latecomer advantage has materialized in China in its balance of economic growth and environmental protection.

It seems that the environmental dimension of China's development has followed an approach of "pollute first, clean up later" (*xian wu ran, hou zhi li*),[13] as is often criticized at home and overseas. This approach has never been a purposeful policy design. However, the term captures important aspects of the formation of the environmental challenges confronting China. Here are two broad explanations for how that has come out.

First, under an overwhelmingly prodevelopment discourse, economic growth has consistently prevailed over environmental protection in the economy-environment relationality, which has been more a contradiction than a balance in China's rapid transition from an agrarian to an industrial society. Governmental entrepreneurialization has been a global neoliberal trend since the late twentieth century; it has been especially salient at all levels of Chinese government during the nation's transition from a planned economy to a market economy. Different levels of government converge on pursuing economic growth in terms of setting strategies and policies; governments at the same level compete for opportunities and resources for economic growth.

Leaders and officials are rewarded in recognition and promotion according to their performance in growing local GDP. They are given every incentive to grow the local economy, often at the cost of the environment should the economic growth incur it. As a result, environmental protection is rhetoric that lacks incentives and enforcement to translate it into action and outcomes.

Second, China has faced a learning curve in environmental awareness and policy design for its rapid industrialization and resultant pollution. For several decades before environmentalism was accepted as a norm, factories with chimneys emitting fumes were welcoming images of the advanced economy and social progress that the nation was pursuing. In the 1950s and 1960s, numerous state-owned factories were planned and constructed in many areas without sufficient consideration for their environmental impacts. In the 1980s, mushrooming "township and village enterprises" (*xiang zheng qi ye*) were pioneers of Deng Xiaoping's prodevelopment strategy, experimenting with privatization and marketization in driving China's early economic growth. However, many of these small, rudimentary enterprises were polluters, generating resource waste and environmental hazards.

Enhancing environmental awareness has been a gradual process, and such is the case for environmental policy and governance as well. The design and enforcement of environmental standards are complicated processes requiring increased awareness, knowledge, and action; further, they involve competing power relationships and contentions among stakeholders and among government departments. When the environmental pressure is reaching almost its maximum level, it challenges the legitimacy as well as sustainability of the development principle. The environmental challenge, among other growth-related challenges, has pressed for the new discourse of high-quality development.

ECOTOPIA WITH CHINESE CHARACTERISTICS

China's environmental challenges seem to have created a wonderland of opposites that could coexist in interdependence.

Its massive and rapid industrialization and urbanization have produced an ecological dystopia, as seen in the environmental damages and challenges. They have also led to the imagining of an ecological utopia—ecotopia—as the antithesis of the ecological dystopia.

"Eco" was the new buzzword emerging from the late twentieth century in China; its buzziness has been growing along with the escalating environmental degradation in the nation and the world. Along with their imagery as heavy polluters, Chinese cities are also seen as emerging "urban sustainability laboratories."[14] Eco has triggered a suite of new imaginaries—some imported and some homegrown—of Chinese cities and society, such as garden city, green city, sustainable city, low-carbon city, eco-city, and sponge city. These ecotopian aspirations have grown out of an environmental imperative. But they have instantly established a dialogue with the aforementioned prodevelopment discourse, fusing into the dominant economic and political agendas.

Eco is being reinvented and repackaged with new meanings and connotations that go beyond environmental concerns. Ecotopia articulates the old prodevelopment pathway under a new branding that reads as trendy, appealing, and futuristic. Thus, it is widely welcomed and accepted, serving various purposes. The popularity of the ecotopia reflects, on the one hand, the severity of environmental challenges in China and a strong aspiration to respond to them. On the other hand, the ecotopia also provides a ready tool that can be used to "greenize" the operationalization of the doctrine "development is the absolute principle." The ecotopia is reshaping the discourse—rhetoric, policy, and practice—of China's urban and national development, mixing promises, uncertainties, and pitfalls.

Expo 2010 in Shanghai was the first to be located within a city area and had a focus on the city theme, as its slogan—"better city, better life" (*cheng shi rang sheng huo geng mei hao*)—told. It became a "city" expo for considered reasons. Shanghai bid for this mega event—an idea nurtured from the 1980s–1990s—to showcase not only Shanghai's rise as a global city but also China's rise as a global power.[15] For these purposes, no other theme was more suitable than the city's in showing (off) the nation's progress in urbanization in its prime city. Eco was surely one of the key concepts underpinning the city theme when China's urbanization had just reached a critical turning point from quantitative growth to qualitative upgrading (see chapter 1).

An umbrella notion of "eco+" was invented by Wu Zhiqiang—the expo's chief planner and a planning professor at Tongji University, Shanghai—to advocate a paradigmatic sustainable urban development that was centered on ecological concerns. This notion, despite its breadth and vagueness, also echoed the political catchphrase "harmony society" (*he xie she hui*), an invention of then Chinese president Hu Jintao. Largely for these reasons, the eco+ notion found favor with the state. Expo 2010 was a holistic expression of the ecotopia dominating the Chinese urban development discourse at the time. This expression was visionary, aspirational, futuristic, and highly technocentric. It made no attempt to address or concern the social and cultural complexity and the economic and political factors that have often constrained an eco-city imaginary. Instead, it seemed to exclusively focus on a connection between ecology and innovation, assuming a technological determinism on the pathway to ecotopia.

In the years leading up to Expo 2010, "the world's first eco-city" was imagined and marketed in Dongtan, on Chongming Island in Shanghai. An area of agrarian land on the tip of the alluvial island at the estuary of the Yangtze River, Dongtan ignited all the imaginings about an eco-city in the early years of the new century. It was ever planned to be one of the Expo 2010 projects, with expectations that its early phase would be completed and in use by then. Consultancy firm Arup was the master planner. When it was just in the drawing stage, project director Peter Head acclaimed, "Dongtan is a step in a new direction. Although historically it may be a small step, it feels like a big step. It is a much more logical use of resources and we hope that it will inspire others to evolve something quite radically different in the future. We hope it will be like the Industrial Revolution but in a more sustainable direction."[16]

However, no "small step" was ever taken for this project except for planning drawings, media reportage, interest from professionals, and diplomatic exchanges. It attracted several British politicians' visits to the site, which endorsed it as an exemplary case of Sino-British collaboration in eco-city expertise and investment. Before any substantial action and construction were undertaken, the Dongtan eco-city project was terminated several years ahead of Expo 2010, which the project echoed in theme and coincided with in timing. Its legacy was only some fanfare about the eco-city. While it could stimulate some initial political and professional interest, it would have to face commercial reality and technological feasibility. Another legacy of the project could be intellectual or professional. Despite its failure, Dongtan helped diffuse the eco-city concept in China: some lessons learned from its strategic approach and planning seemed to live on through informing subsequent eco-city projects in China, like the Sino-Singaporean eco-city project in Tianjin, and overseas.[17]

Numerous projects of diverse nature and scale—including new district development, urban renewal, property development, and periurban or rural tourism projects—bear the name of eco-city or its equivalent in China. By 2012, the Chinese government, via the Ministry of Environmental Protection, awarded

38 "eco-cities" (or counties) and 1,559 "eco-towns"—an explicit endorsement at the national government level.[18] These projects have fared differently and ended up with mixed eco outcomes. Many have demonstrated some eco elements through employing certain eco planning and design approaches—imported or indigenous—and utilizing some technological innovations in building, materials, energy, community management, and environmental protection. Some simply self-claimed to be eco.

These "eco" aspirations and brandings have merged with "smart" and "innovation," all the latest representations of the neoliberal urbanism that has influenced the Chinese city since the late twentieth century. Eco, as a green brand, is often marketed with smart and innovation brands to win these projects state support and market recognition. In essence, these eco-cities and similar green urbanism projects are new entrepreneurial, experimental cities of "green capitalism," building on a bias toward economic growth and technological fixes to environmental challenges, as well as a failure to concern broader social sustainability.[19] Many eco-cities have become vanity projects of property development in which the government, developers, and consultants—mostly international consultants—find a common green opportunity while excluding broader public interests and social concerns.

"Eco-civilization" is a term with a strong flavor of "Chineseness" for the political endorsement it has received and its promotion as a national strategy. A coined term that elevates the contemporary concern with ecology to the level of a new type of civilization, it assumes and maps a simplistic, linear trajectory of evolutionary human civilization from primitive to agrarian, industrial, and now ecological. It is presented as a Chinese version of modernity that purports to decouple economic development from environmental degradation.[20] The term's meaning and implication are open to debate, including its propagation as a theoretical advancement of socialism with Chinese characteristics under the new era discourse (see chapter 1). A burgeoning body of Chinese literature has been published about the term in the twenty-first century, responding to its political endorsement and elevation to national strategy. In 2000, only 78 newspaper articles and 10 academic papers were published in Chinese on eco-civilization; in 2017, they increased to 5,816 and 6,412, respectively.[21]

The term has gradually come to occupy a central position in the Chinese political discourse. In 2007, the seventeenth CPC National Congress proposed the construction of eco-civilization. At the eighteenth National Congress in 2012 and at a series of subsequent CPC conferences, eco-civilization was conceptually expanded. Politically, it was incorporated into an integrative framework for national development, encompassing economic, political, cultural, and social dimensions. The term's buzziness and importance reached a climax at the nineteenth National Congress in 2017, at which Xi Jinping outlined its importance.

> Building an ecological civilization is vital to sustain the Chinese nation's development. We must realize that lucid waters and lush mountains are invaluable assets and act on this understanding, implement our fundamental national policy of conserving resources and protecting the environment, and cherish the environment as we cherish our own lives. We will adopt a holistic approach to conserving our mountains, rivers, forests, farmlands, lakes, and grasslands, implement the strictest possible systems for environmental protection, and develop eco-friendly growth models and ways of life. We must pursue a model of sustainable development featuring increased production, higher living standards, and healthy ecosystems. We must continue the Beautiful China initiative to create good working and living environments for our people and play our part in ensuring global ecological security.[22]

In March 2018, China's constitution was amended to formally include eco-civilization. It is now a national strategy, an integral part of Xi Jinping Thought, and a hallmark of the new era. Certain elements in eco-civilization resonate with Chinese traditional wisdom about human-nature harmony. However, its surge into a national strategy has been backed by a strong political will, serving a renewed development vision and policy agenda. Eco-civilization is now rewriting the narratives, pathways, strategies, and actions toward sustainable development in and beyond China.[23] At the core is a state-led imaginary/utopia that draws on some elements of traditional wisdom and fuses them with technological instruments and political aspirations intended to achieve both economic growth and environmental protection.

The Chinese version of the phrase "lucid waters and lush mountains are invaluable assets" in the earlier quote was used by Xi Jinping in 2005, seven years before he became China's top leader. Literally meaning "mountains and rivers green are mountains of silver and gold" (*lv shui qing shan jiu shi jin shan ying shan*), this phrase is often shortened, metaphorically, into "green is gold," which is being advocated and propagated as a green version of "development is the absolute principle."

THE SUSTAINABILITY PARADOX

As commonly understood, sustainability is a paradox in a very broad sense. It is more than an environmental concern; it involves social equity and economic growth. The classic triple bottom lines of sustainable development—economy, environment, and society—are intrinsically contradictory.[24] Balancing them to create a sustainable development paradigm presents both a wicked problem confronting all human beings and possibly a wicked opportunity if the problem could be dealt with well.

Pollution is more than an environmental issue. Underlying it are a commitment to socioeconomic development on the one hand and the constraints of environmental technologies and innovation on the other. International discussions about issues like climate change often go beyond environmental challenges and technological advances. They can easily slip into debates or contentions about global inequalities, and sometimes into geopolitics—an area more of international differences than commonalities with regard to commitment to and responsibility for sustainability. Sustainability geopolitics has been escalating in the recent decade along with the restructuring of global political and economic systems.

As far as the present China is concerned, the primary sustainability paradox exists between its pursuit of economic growth and its environmental imperative. China's economic growth has clearly coupled with environmental pollution (figure 2.1). Here are some data to illustrate this, showing comparisons between economic growth and CO_2 emissions in China and the world in past decades. In 1980–2020, China's GDP per capita grew from an extremely low point of US$195 to US$10,500, a fifty-four-fold growth. Over the same period, the world's average GDP per capita increased from US$2,549 to US$10,926, a four-fold growth. China's economic miracle has not only pushed up its own GDP per capita, but it has also significantly contributed to the growth of the world's average (see chapter 1). In 1980, China's CO_2 emissions per capita were 1.5 tons, well below the world average of 4.6 tons. Since then, the former has been constantly growing, surpassing the latter around 2005 and reaching 7.4 tons in 2018.

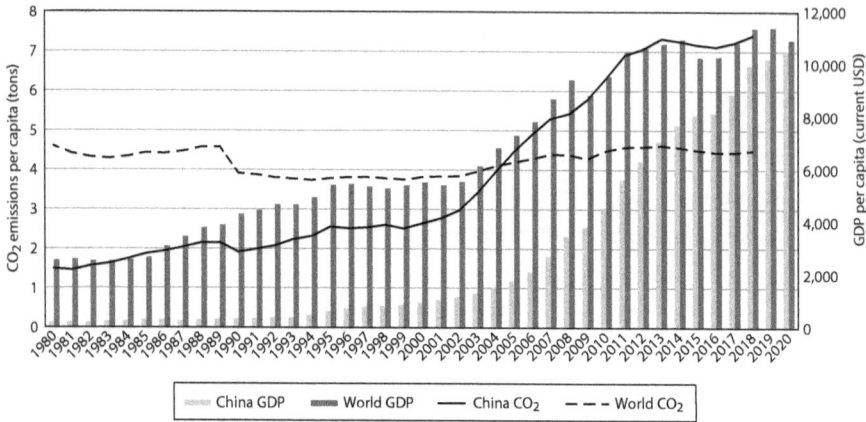

FIGURE 2.1 GDP per capita and CO_2 emissions per capita of China and the world, 1980–2018/2020

Source: Created by the author using data from World Bank, "CO_2 Emissions (Metric Tons per Capita)," accessed January 20, 2023, https://data.worldbank.org/indicator /EN.ATM.CO2E.PC; World Bank, "GDP per Capita (Current USs)," accessed January 20, 2023, https://data.worldbank.org/indicator/NY.GDP.PCAP.CD.

It is worth noting that during this period (1980–2018), the world's average CO_2 emissions per capita have been largely constant, at around 4 tons (figure 2.1). Presumably, transformation toward a postindustrial economy (in the developed countries especially), the world's total population growth, and advances in environmental technologies and renewable energy have jointly contributed to the relative leveling of the world's average CO_2 emissions per capita. For example, in the past decade, thirty-three mostly rich countries that are home to over one billion people have experienced decoupling of economic growth and rising emissions of greenhouse gases: their GDP increased while their emissions reduced.[25] This phenomenon could be one of the few optimistic signs among the escalating global environmental challenges.

By any measure, in the recent four decades, China has restructured the world's environmental landscape as an externality of its rapid economic growth (and urbanization). But historical and comparative perspectives present a holistic picture of this phenomenon and its likely trajectory in the future. From 1980 to 2019, the world's annual CO_2 emissions nearly doubled, from 19.37 billion tons to 36.44 billion tons (table 2.1), profoundly exacerbating global environmental problems. In 2006, China's annual CO_2 emissions surpassed those of the United States, making it the largest polluter. From 1980 to 2019, China's share in the world's annual CO_2 emissions increased from 7.5 percent to 27.9 percent; at the same time, the U.S. share decreased from 24.3 percent to 14.5 percent. However, measured on a per capita basis, U.S. CO_2 emissions remained at 15.2 tons in 2018—more than double those of China in the same year—despite a decrease from 20.8 tons in 1980.

TABLE 2.1 CO_2 EMISSIONS OF CHINA, THE UNITED STATES, AND THE WORLD, 1980-2018/2019

Year	Per capita emissions (tons) 1980	2018	Annual emissions (billion tons) 1980	2019	Cumulative emissions (billion tons) 1980	2019
China	1.5	7.4	1.46 (7.5%)	10.17 (27.9%)	21.98 (3.7%)	219.99 (13.7%)
U.S.	20.8	15.2	4.72 (24.3%)	5.28 (14.5%)	200.67 (34%)	410.24 (25.5%)
World	4.6	4.5	19.37 (100%)	36.44 (100%)	589.82 (100%)	1,610 (100%)

Note: The percentages in parentheses represent the shares of emissions in the world in those years.
Source: Created by the author using data from: Hannah Ritchie, Max Roser, and Pablo Rosado, "CO_2 and Greenhouse Gas Emissions," Our World in Data, last modified August 2020, accessed January 20, 2023, https://ourworldindata.org/co_2-and-other-greenhouse-gas-emissions; and World Bank, "CO_2 Emissions (Metric Tons per Capita)," accessed January 20, 2023, https://data.worldbank.org/indicator/EN.ATM.CO_2E.PC.

In an even longer historical context of measuring by cumulative CO_2 emissions (estimated from 1751), China's share in the world increased significantly from 3.7 percent in 1980 to 13.7 percent in 2019. However, in both years, China was well below the United States, although the latter decreased its cumulative CO_2 emissions share from 34 percent in 1980 to 25.5 percent in 2019. Measured by countries, China (and other developing countries) is the largest contemporary polluter; the United States (and other developed countries) has been the largest historical polluter. Measured on a per capita basis, significant gaps exist between the two countries, and further between the developing and developed countries.

The sustainability paradox of "grow-green" has characterized China's development in the past decades. This paradox could become even more prominent in the coming decades. The decoupling of economic growth and environmental degradation remains a utopianized aspiration and policy goal. According to a systematic study of China's economic and environmental indicators over forty years, along with its ardent pursuit of eco-civilization, its GDP growth has shown a trend toward decoupling with emissions of major pollutants since 2015, but strong coupling has remained with CO_2 emissions.[26]

On September 22, 2020, when addressing the General Debate of the seventy-fifth session of the United Nations General Assembly, Xi Jinping made bold promises of green plans as part of China's fulfillment of the 2016 Paris Agreement: "The Paris Agreement on climate change charts the course for the world to transition to green and low-carbon development. It outlines the minimum steps to be taken to protect the Earth, our shared homeland, and all countries must take decisive steps to honor this Agreement. China will scale up its Intended Nationally Determined Contributions by adopting more vigorous policies and measures. We aim to have CO_2 emissions peak before 2030 and achieve carbon neutrality before 2060."[27]

The promises to have "CO_2 emissions peak before 2030" and achieve "carbon neutrality before 2060" are referred to as "double carbon targets" (*shuang tan mu biao*) in the Chinese discourse. These long-term targets sound positive, but the roadmap and action plans to achieve them are not clear yet, nor is their feasibility. Set against the global targets of warming limits in the Paris Agreement, China's near-term climate and energy targets in the *14th Five-Year Plan* (2021–2025)—a strategic national social and economic development plan—were deemed as "far more modest."[28] As of January 2023, the overall rating for China's climate action was "highly insufficient," according to Climate Action Tracker, which tracks government climate action and measures it against the globally agreed long-term temperature goals set in the 2016 Paris Agreement.[29]

The milestone years of 2030 and 2060 in China's double carbon targets almost coincide with the new era's milestone years of 2035 and 2050, by which China will achieve modernization "basically" and "fully," respectively. (See chapter 7 for details about these modernization targets.) The time frames of the modernization plan and the decarbonization plan—both are grand and ambitious—overlap. How the intrinsically contradictory goals in these two plans could possibly be compatible and how they could be achieved simultaneously has raised—justifiably—inquiries and doubts. A recent study estimated that to meet the target of a less than 1.5°C temperature increase above preindustrial levels, as set in the Paris Agreement, China may need to reduce its carbon emissions and energy consumption by more than 90 percent and 39 percent, respectively, incurring accumulated economic costs of 2.8–5.7 percent of its GDP by 2050.[30]

The assumptions and accuracy of these estimates may be uncertain, depending on contingent situations and factors that may emerge in the future. However, it is certain that China is facing a severe sustainability paradox between its dual ambitions of grow and green in the coming decades. This paradox raises an important question: can China achieve both modernization and decarbonization by the mid-twenty-first century? This question is important not only for China but also for the world in terms of both enhancing socioeconomic progress and addressing environmental challenges. The answer can only await the test of time.

BEIJING: TAMING THE SKY

The State Council issued the *Action Plan on Prevention and Control of Air Pollution* on September 10, 2013, amid escalating concerns and debates on the problem and calls for resolute government intervention and regulation. This was a five-year plan, stipulating specific air quality improvement targets for cities nationwide and key city regions by 2017. For Beijing in particular, the plan specified that by 2017, the annual average concentration of fine particulate matter (PM2.5) should be kept no higher than 60 μg/m^3.[31] This target for Beijing was slightly above the bottom line of the "unhealthy" air quality standard set by the WHO,[32] but it sounded ambitious then. This special target for Beijing in part reflected the severity of its air pollution and in part the city's importance in national environmental policy.

Indeed, Beijing's air is more than an environmental concern; it is of political significance. Wang Anshun was the mayor of Beijing in 2013–2016. The Chinese media widely reported an anecdote told by Wang himself. On behalf of the Beijing government,

he signed a contract of responsibility with the central government to ensure that the city's air quality would improve, as
stipulated in the action plan, and if it did not, he would need
to come to "meet with head in hand" (*ti tou lai jian*)—so Wang
was told by the central government officials. This joke reflected
the importance of Beijing's air quality for both the central and
Beijing government; it also indicated the political will and top-
down endorsement of achieving that improvement.

Chen Jining took over Beijing's mayorship in May 2017 and
remained in office until October 2022. Prior to taking this position, Chen had been the Chinese environmental minister in
2015–2017 and president of Tsinghua University in 2012–2015.
Chen's academic background is in environmental engineering. One logic of the Chinese administrative system is to consider individuals' educational and career backgrounds in the
appointment of officials. Presumably, Chen's environmental
background was a factor in his appointment as mayor; he had
a mission to address the capital's environmental protection and
rehabilitation.

Beijing's air quality matters for wider reasons than the well-
being of local residents. Given Beijing's role as the capital, its air
is a matter of national and international importance and implication from the government's perspective. Among other things,
air pollution presented probably the most challenging issue in
the preparation for the Beijing 2008 Olympics. Compared with
infrastructure construction and event organization, air was
harder to plan and manage. But the government had a will to
"command" the air: it ordered the polluters in the city and its
surrounds—factories, construction sites, and vehicles—to pause
before and during the Olympics.

A similar command approach was employed to clean the
air for other events in Beijing, like the Asia-Pacific Economic

Cooperation (APEC) conference and military parades. During the APEC conference in November 2014, residents and visitors were impressed by the blue sky, which was in stark contrast to the smog that the city suffered at other times of the year. In 2013, the city and much of east China had just experienced the longest and most severe smog in history, as noted earlier. People coined the term "APEC blue" (APEC *lan*) to celebrate as well as mock the transience of the blue sky that had been manipulated into existence for the event. Some people celebrated it for their access—and right—to blue sky. Some mocked it because the blue sky was curated for an international event and its visitors, not necessarily for local residents.

The "event blue" of Beijing's sky is unsustainable—an elephant in the room. It reflects a command and control of the sky through forceful top-down orders and interventions, aiming to achieve a positive image of the city—or face of the state—at economic and social costs that are deemed to be of less importance than the imagery of the blue sky. It is assumed—justifiably—that the polluting enterprises that were shut down before and during the events would emit more after the event to compensate for their economic loss. But the event blue served as an experiment proving that Beijing's air quality could possibly be improved within a short time frame, depending on the political will to endorse it and the readiness to pay the necessary economic and social costs.

The central issue hinges on the enduring sustainability paradox in which environmental, economic, and social goals contradict rather than balance one another. Which goal to prioritize in decision-making around these elements of the sustainability paradox lies, then, in political will. In Beijing, political will matters the most among many factors that influence decision-making and action for environmental improvement. Next, I use another example to further illustrate this.

Capital Steel Group is colloquially called "Shougang," based on the abbreviation of its Chinese pronunciation. It was a mega steel mill in west Beijing—28 km west of Tiananmen, the city center—established in 1958 on the site of a previous small steelmaking and refining factory built in 1919. Shougang was a major project of the socialist industrialization plan for the city and the nation in the 1950s and 1960s. In retrospect, the selection of its site in Beijing was not well considered: apart from its pollution impact on the capital, Beijing was not a port city and was short of water resources. In the late twentieth century, these constraints on Shougang became much more acute than when the mega mill was established.

Despite its pivotal role in Beijing's economy as a Fortune 500 giant and an important GDP contributor, Shougang also won itself the designation as Beijing's largest polluter. Its existence was becoming increasingly incompatible with the capital's transformation toward a global city and its escalating environmental imperative. Discussions about relocating Shougang had been on and off until 2004, when the central government determined that it would be moved out of Beijing. Undoubtedly, the environmental discourse in the years leading up to the 2008 Olympics facilitated this initiative. It was certainly a hard decision: Shougang's relocation lasted from 2005 to 2010, involving an investment of RMB 50 billion and the redeployment of 60,000 staff.[33]

Shougang was relocated to Caofeidian, a coastal precinct in Tangshan, Hebei Province, a city known for its steel industry clusters. The new precinct is 285 km from Beijing and has access to port facilities and water resources from desalination that are crucial for a steel plant. Interestingly, in Caofeidian, an "international eco-city" was planned, largely on reclaimed land.[34] The Tangshan government had every incentive to develop a new area wearing an eco hat to rebrand the city, which is known for high pollution. The Caofeidian project won endorsement and support from the central government, and it was selected in 2012 as one of the demonstration projects of eco-cities.

In 2008, a master plan prepared by a joint team of Sweco, a European engineering consultancy company, and Tsinghua University was selected after an international design competition for the eco-city's development. Like the planning of similar eco-cities in China, the imaginary of the Caofeidian eco-city presented a disconnect between its green focus and the heavy pollution in its surrounds, as well as a lack of engagement with the local culture and community. The master plan imagined an urban area of 150 km² and a population of one million by 2020.[35] This is in stark contrast to the reality today.

Unlike Dongtan in Shanghai, which never progressed from plan to construction, Caofeidian had some preliminary developments completed and some incomplete property and infrastructure projects. However, it lacked people living and working there and the activities that would substantiate its urbanity, which added it to the list of China's "ghost towns" (*gui cheng*).[36] To build an eco-city in an industrial cluster of polluters requires great imagination and boldness of the (local) government driven by pursuit of political accomplishment and demonstration of vanity.

Shougang's legacy site in Beijing was replanned into a business park. A place with a strong industrial form and flavor is being regenerated into a postindustrial innovation precinct for cultural and creative activities, presenting a contrast in aesthetics and meaning. The legacy site was also designated as the only urban venue of the Beijing 2022 Winter Olympics, used for

FIGURE 2.2 Beijing 2022 Winter Olympics site at Shougang

Source: The author.

freestyle and big-air snowboarding events (figure 2.2). The venue has been kept as a permanent facility to boost the precinct's reputation and transformation.

The park's planning was masterminded by Arup and is boasted of as being "China's first climate-positive project." Unsurprisingly, the plan includes all the green visions and concepts applicable to an urban regeneration project, reflected by terms like "sponge city," "net-negative," and "sustainable way" in descriptions of the plan.[37] Reimagining the legacy site of Beijing's largest polluter as an exemplary sustainable park creates an interesting juxtaposition of the opposites in both imagery and interpretation. The park is a memory of the past; it is also an imaginary of the future.

PM2.5 did not become a measure of air quality in many Chinese cities until 2013. Prior to that, the U.S. embassy measured and released PM2.5 data for Beijing, which showed higher levels of air pollution than the official report, which used PM10 data. The different criteria created confusion and even caused diplomatic bickering: a spokesperson for the Chinese Ministry of Foreign Affairs accused the U.S. embassy of "special intentions" (*bie you yong xin*) in releasing the data. Foreign revelations of a "negative" issue in China can easily arouse nationalistic responses and accusations of evil intentions. However, ultimately, the embassy's reporting helped "educate" the Chinese government and public about the measurement of air quality. This was a learning curve for the government about the importance of using fine measurement criteria and being transparent in relation to public concerns like air quality. Since then, public access to live and accurate air quality data has become the norm, thanks to technological improvements, policy change, and (most of all) a change in the mindset of government.

This has also been a period of improving air quality in Beijing. From 2013, when PM2.5 was first monitored, the city's annual average concentration of particulates declined from 89 $\mu g/m^3$ to 58 $\mu g/m^3$ in 2017 (reaching the target set in the State Council's 2013 action plan, mentioned earlier), and further to 42 $\mu g/m^3$ in 2019 and 38 $\mu g/m^3$ in 2020.[38] Similar reduction trends were also observed in other major Chinese cities in 2013–2018 despite tentative reversals in certain years.[39] A study of seventy-four major cities in China showed a 33.3 percent decrease of annual average concentrations of PM2.5 and a significant reduction in pollution-induced deaths from 2013, when the State Council's action plan was put in place, to 2017.[40] Using other measures of air quality—like PM10, SO_2, and NO_2—for which longer historical data were available, their annual average concentrations in Beijing also decreased significantly since 1998.[41] These historical data seemed to counter the local experiences in those years around 2013. But both monitored data and residents' experiences seem to converge on a conclusion that Beijing's air quality improved considerably in the second half of the 2010s.

The annual average concentration of PM2.5 at 38 μg/m³ in 2020 was "historically" low for Beijing. However, it still left Beijing as the fourteenth most polluted capital city in the world.[42] The capital's battle with air pollution is a long way from ending or being won. In local discussions about Beijing's air pollution and its possible trajectory of improvement, the smog occurrences in Los Angeles and London from the 1940s to the 1960s have often been quoted to showcase the challenges of addressing the problem and the commitment required to do so. The factors contributing to air pollution are multiple and complicated, and thus so are the necessary solutions. They need to consider emissions, urban form, urban management and governance, meteorological conditions, and geographical settings—both human-made and natural. Beijing's location in north China and mountains in the northern windway have impacted the air flow of pollutants, which is further exacerbated by the city's ever more crowded and expanding urban form.

Beijing has grown into a size that raises questions about its strategic sustainability and its suitability as the capital. The city's problems are more than air pollution, although this is among the most apparent. There have been ad hoc discussions of relocating the capital out of Beijing, but that is a bold and unrealistic notion. An alternative idea is to relocate the noncapital functions out of Beijing to alleviate its urban pressures. This idea is being implemented, once again under a strong political will, in the context of reimagining the capital and strategic planning of the Beijing-Tianjin-Hebei region. Chapter 5 will further examine how Xiong'an—China's newest experimental city—is being planned and developed to respond to the urban problems confronting Beijing and associated reimagining of the capital.

3

THE SMART CITY MOVEMENT

I visited Shenzhen in September 2019 for a fieldwork trip to prepare for my book *The Shenzhen Phenomenon* (2020). My previous visit to Shenzhen was in December 2010. In 2019, Shenzhen was not the city it had been nearly a decade earlier. My flight arrived in Hong Kong International Airport at around 5:00 A.M. on September 19. I took a one-hour shuttle bus trip to Huanggang Port to enter Shenzhen. After passing through customs, I took a taxi to the Shangri-La hotel in Futian central business district (CBD), Shenzhen's commercial and civic center. The hotel is within walking distance of the port—I took the taxi only because of my luggage. The driver was apparently disappointed when I told him where I was going; he must have expected a better business opportunity after queuing there for passengers at that early hour of the morning. He did not realize he would be a little more disappointed in a short while.

We arrived at the hotel very quickly. When I was preparing to pay the driver, he extended his smart phone to me, anticipating a digital transfer of funds. He was surprised by the cash I handed over and asked, "Don't you have WeChat Pay?" The answer was "no." He had to give me back some change, which took him some time to search for. After he drove away, I felt a bit sympathetic toward this guy for his odd experience on that early morning: an unlucrative bit of business and an alien customer. Despite his Chinese face and Chinese language, the customer seemed to be from a different world.

Yes, I was from a different world. I have been away from China for a long time. Among many changes, China is now a cashless nation. Cash, bank card, and wallet are all obsolete; what you need to take is a smart phone. I shared the morning's experience with my local friend, Jiehai Cheng, during the lunch hour, and he had a good laugh. He immediately helped install a public transport app on my phone, showed me how to use it, and transferred some funds to my WeChat account. Jiehai said, "Without smart phone payment, you cannot travel and live in this city."

During my stay in Shenzhen, the city—and the whole nation—was awaiting the seventieth anniversary of the establishment of the PRC on October 1. Two observations impressed me as I walked around to learn about the city. One concerned the numerous red national flags that decorated the streets. One public building even had its whole façade facing the city's thoroughfare, Shennan Avenue, painted with the national flag. Indeed, the seventieth anniversary of the PRC was an important occasion worth celebrating. Meanwhile, seeing the whole city in a sea of red flags was also a reminder and indicator of the change of political culture in terms of rising nationalism and patriotism in the new era. The other was the pervasive deployment of closed-circuit television (CCTV) cameras in public spaces. CCTV cameras exist in almost every city across the world, but the numbers and density of them that I observed in Shenzhen, and in other major Chinese cities, made an impression on me.

I raised my observation of the CCTV cameras with Jiehai Cheng; he echoed my thoughts. I could still remember reading

around twenty years before about street robbery incidents—
young guys riding motorcycles behind walking women and
snatching their handbags—which often happened in southern
cities like Guangzhou and Shenzhen. Jiehai confirmed that this
sort of crime had not occurred for a long time and the city was
very safe now, largely because of the presence of the CCTV
cameras. It was very unlikely, in Jiehai's view, that a crime could
be committed in a public space in Shenzhen without being spotted and the culprits identified. A city in safety vs. a city under
surveillance—these mixed feelings accompanied me during those
days of my stay in Shenzhen.

I visited Hong Kong on one of those days. It took fourteen
minutes from Futian station in Shenzhen to West Kowloon
station in Hong Kong on a high-speed train. Geographically,
Shenzhen and Hong Kong are essentially one city. However,
they are separated by a border line; they are significantly different in many aspects of urban life and development under the
"one country, two systems" governance structure (see chapter 6).
On the Hong Kong side, I tried to purchase a metro card at
the West Kowloon train station using a credit card. The staff
declined my card, suggesting that they would accept cash only
and pointing to a nearby automated teller machine where I could
withdraw cash. This experience also made an impression, given
the contrast to the cashless Shenzhen side only a fourteen-
minute commute away.

In September 2019, Hong Kong was in the heyday of a
street movement that turned into the most disruptive crisis—
violence, chaos, and uncertainty—since its return to China in
1997. On the other side, in Shenzhen, the whole city was with
a buoyant, pre-National Day atmosphere, celebrating the great
achievements of the nation, especially since 1978, when China
had launched its reform and opening-up agenda. Shenzhen was

created to spearhead this agenda; for this reason, this new city is symbolic of the agenda and its success. On August 18, 2019, just before my visit, the central government had labeled Shenzhen a "pilot demonstration zone" (*xian xing shi fan qu*) of socialism with Chinese characteristics. Shenzhen, within its short history of forty years, has become a contemporary urban miracle. It is often dubbed as China's smartest city for various reasons.

However, the experiences of China's smartest city are mixed, like the smart city movement in the nation and around the world.

FROM SMART CITY TO SMART SOCIETY

China National Knowledge Infrastructure (CNKI) is a platform for collecting and accessing Chinese literature. I searched the theme "smart city" on its website on May 11, 2021. The website identified around 27,900 Chinese publications on it. Most of them (around 21,100) were academic journal articles, in addition to theses for academic degrees, conference papers, newspaper articles, and books. Most of these publications were dated 2010 and later. Prior to that year, only sixty-one publications had appeared in 2009, one in 2008, and two in 2005. The earliest two Chinese publications on the smart city appeared in the journal *21st Century Business Review*, introducing the Malaysian smart city projects of Putrajaya and Cyberjaya.

It is hard to say whether the term smart city was introduced to China in 2005. It sounds reasonable to conjecture, however, that smart city remained an alien term in China at the turn of the century. In the 2010s, it became an instant buzzword, especially from 2013 on. Prior to this, in November 2012, the central government, through the Ministry of Housing and Urban-Rural

Development, launched its pilot smart cities program, officially signifying and triggering the start of a nationwide smart city movement. In 2013–2015, 277 Chinese cities joined this pilot program.[1] Meanwhile, the central government departments released a series of policies and guidelines on the planning and development of smart cities. It is estimated that as of 2016, there were around 500 smart city projects in China.[2]

The smart city is both a global and a local phenomenon. But the term has particular meanings and implications in China. Smart city is a relatively new term, but its predecessor terms, like digital city, intelligent city, and innovative city, were already in common use in the 1990s. In other words, smart city is a new term, but not necessarily a completely new concept, for Chinese audiences. This conceptual familiarity could partly explain the term's instant popularity in the Chinese discourse. Its Chinese translation, *zhi hui cheng shi*, means "wise city," which is even more appealing to Chinese audiences than smart city. In English, Chinese, or any other cultural contexts, who would object to the notion of a city being smart or wise? For a nation that is experiencing the largest scale of urbanization in history, smart city provides the latest urban imaginary, one that is edgy, fashionable, and futurist. It is a ready brand for making policies and promoting cities, places, and communities. This smart brand is pervasive in Chinese cities now.

In 2014, the State Council released the *National New-Type Urbanization Plan (2014–2020)* to reorient its urbanization (see chapter 1). This plan contains one section on the smart city:

> Coordinate the utilization of physical resources, information resources, and intellectual resources in urban development; promote innovation and application of the new-generation information technology like internet-of-things (IoT), cloud computing,

and big data; achieve deep fusion of urban economic and social developments. Strengthen the construction of infrastructure such as information networks and data centers. Enhance the administrative information sharing and service coordination between departments, between sectors, and between areas; strengthen the socialization of information resources development and utilization; spread smart information application and new information services; improve digitalization of urban planning management, smart infrastructure, convenience of public services, modernization of industrial development, and sophisticated social governance. Strengthen the security and protection of key information systems and key information resources in cities.[3]

As noted, the plan suggested six directions for the development of smart cities: information network and broadband, digitalization of planning management, smart infrastructure, convenience of public services, modernization of industrial development, and sophisticated social governance. For each direction, it prescribed broad areas and general goals for smart city development. This national urban plan has now passed its final year, 2020. Since the plan was a strategic document and did not set specific, quantifiable targets to measure progress or achievement, it is hard to conclude whether it has reached its goals. Thematically, these strategic statements and directions reflected broad areas of concern in China's smart city development in the second half of the 2010s.

The smart city concept attracted the top leader's interest and imagination. In October 2017, addressing the nineteenth CPC National Congress, Xi Jinping used the term "smart society" in his elaboration on "making China a country of innovators": "These efforts will provide powerful support for building China's strength in science and technology, product quality, aerospace, cyberspace, and transportation; and for building a digital China and a smart society."[4] Both official and unofficial rhetoric has tried to interpret smart society as a new concept that has advanced smart city. These interpretations are often driven by political advocacy. Smart society, like smart city, is not a new concept per se. It is a rewording of both an emerging phenomenon and a political imaginary about using the latest digital technology to advance national development.

Smart society seems to have expanded the smart city imaginary in a vast country like China. Guizhou Province, in southwest China, is known for remoteness and poverty, and it is home to numerous diverse ethnic communities. Its local economic development has been lagging behind that of other provinces, especially coastal areas. Now Guizhou is building as well as marketing China's Big Data Valley, which it is hoped will rival Silicon Valley and Bangalore. Guizhou's well-preserved ecological environment—an indicator of its less developed status compared with other provinces—and livable climate turn out to be competitive assets for attracting the new economy. Guizhou is also speeding up its provision of infrastructure like railways, expressways, broadband, airports, electricity, and water, in addition to benefiting from favorable policies from both the central and the local governments to support big data sectors.

It is reported that Guizhou's growth rate of the digital economy ranked first in China for four consecutive years, from 2015 to 2018, and the city also topped the ranks in growth rate of employment provided by the digital economy in 2019.[5] A government-led smart project has won Guizhou the reputation of "big data center" in China. The Guizhou government also sponsored an advertisement on the CNN website promoting the province's new smart image.

> When one thinks of Guizhou, the image of its lush landscapes and ethnic customs come to mind. While the province is undeniably beautiful, most people could never imagine it being a city like Beijing or Shanghai, filled with modern buildings and high-tech firms.
>
> But that's all changing, thanks to the development of big data. Since 2014, the province has made multiple innovations and ground-breaking developments in China's big data industry. In fact, Guizhou is now home to China's first big data pilot zone. . . . Five years ago, there were less than a thousand big data companies in Guizhou; now, there are about 8,900.
>
> What happened, and how did these changes take place in Guizhou? Why are multinational companies, such as Apple, Qualcomm, Intel, Hewlett-Packard, Oracle, SAP, Alibaba, Tencent, Huawei, etc., flocking to Guizhou?[6]

This advertisement highlights a quote from Jack Ma, founder of Alibaba: "If you missed the opportunity in Guangdong and Zhejiang 30 years ago, don't miss Guizhou today."

Both Guangdong and Zhejiang are prosperous coastal provinces that have rapidly developed since the 1980s and 1990s. They showcase China's economic rise in recent decades through industrialization and urbanization. Will big data remake Guizhou into Guangdong and Zhejiang through postindustrialization and smartization?

SMART CITY COALITION

The smart city movement could not have come into being without a coalition that has shaped the power structure underpinning the movement's emergence. The smart city coalition comprises the government, business, and academia, with general community support. A similar coalition and its composition could be identified for the booming smart cities in any country. However, the coalition has distinctive features that are unique to China's political, economic, and social settings.

The government has always played a leading role in advancing the smart city, following a hierarchical structure and top-down approach. The central government's endorsement and political will at the top have propelled more interest and enthusiasm from governments at provincial and local levels. Nearly every major Chinese city has some type of smart city strategy and projects to showcase its vision of and commitment to becoming smart. Understanding of the smart city differs from place to place, however, and the outcomes of those smart city strategies and projects are mixed. The media reports on new smart city initiatives frequently. It is not uncommon to read about projects that have failed for various reasons. Many projects simply wear a smart hat; they are not significantly different from those non-smart projects, apart from some rhetoric and application of new technologies. Failure still matters, since these unsuccessful projects also contribute to the spread and popularity of the smart city concept.

In 2017, the Shanghai government released *Shanghai 2035*, a master plan setting the vision of "striving for the excellent global city" for China's most important gateway city (see chapter 7). In preparing for drawing up this plan, a community survey identified eight strategic development goals aspired to by its residents. One of them was that Shanghai should become a smart city with sophisticated information and communications technology; this goal accounted for 11 percent of responses.[7] The plan identified seven features that mark the transformative thinking for its making. One feature concerned the smart city: "Adapt to the development trends in a postindustrial age, and transform the philosophy, systems, and approaches of planning. Sufficiently consider the profound influences of the new generation of technologies represented by the internet on urban life, production, and governance; and actively respond to these influences in spatial and functional layouts. Meanwhile, establish information platforms for urban spaces and databases for urban development strategy, to provide the basis for the monitoring, evaluation, and maintenance of master planning; and to establish an infrastructure for the construction and operation of 'smart city.'"[8]

The government's role in the smart city coalition is to promote the smart city concept, produce strategies and plans, and endorse initiatives and projects. The government's interest is justifiable and legitimate: to create smart cities that are livable, productive, and sustainable for its citizens through use of the latest technology. Despite variations in different cities, the smart city discourse promoted by the government has sat mostly within this rhetoric.

Businesses will surely welcome this interest and rhetoric of the government to sell their products and services. Several Chinese high-tech firms, such as Huawei and Alibaba, have quickly become international leaders in recent decades, largely thanks to the nation's rapid growth and its integration with globalization. All these firms have embraced the new business opportunities of the smart city, creating various concepts and business models utilizing the latest advances in digital technology. Both Huawei and Alibaba are working with their home city governments of Shenzhen and Hangzhou, respectively, on smart city initiatives, demonstrating the interaction and interdependence between public and private stakeholders in fostering a coalition to transform urban governance.

Tencent is a Chinese high-tech giant established in Shenzhen in 1998. It created the WeChat app, which is now the
world's largest standalone mobile app and one of the monopo-
lizers of social media, messaging, and mobile payment in China.
In 2019, Tencent announced its WeCity project, a future smart
city concept about building a comprehensive smart solution for
digital government, urban management, urban decision-making,
and industrial interconnection. Tencent's interest in the smart
city is in more than providing technology and service; it wants to
build a smart city for itself.

In June 2020, Tencent announced its plan to build its own
132.6-hectare Net City—a miniature city within its home city.
To be built on a stretch of reclaimed land, this "city of the
future" is an urban development of 2 million m² to accom-
modate around eight thousand people and it will take around
seven years to complete.[9] Master-planned by NBBJ, an American design firm, this new city scheme has embedded so-called
interconnected planning, which is underpinned by all the
catchy words for this type of project: "car-free," "human-
focused," "organic," "ecosystem," "green," "vibrant," and so on.
In an interview with CNN, Jonathan Ward, NBBJ's design
partner, imagined the project as follows.

> It's not meant to be an isolated, secure island—it's a vibrant city.
> People will walk through it, they'll connect . . . and it will be a vital
> hub for Shenzhen. Our main goal was to provide a place where
> innovation can really flourish. Going "car-free" is still a little bit
> challenging in our world, so we spent a lot of time designing the
> city to be as low-impact as possible, removing (cars from) where
> they don't need to be and focusing on people. Traditional cities
> are very much siloed, even in the densest cities where there's more
> interaction and intermixing. But what can happen now is you can

start to blur those lines (between work and play), and bring more interaction between different parts of life. You're seeing more blurring of those lines, for better or for worse. But I think we can make it for the better as we tune this model going forward.[10]

The timing of announcing the Net City project is worth noting: during the height of COVID-19. Just a month earlier, in May 2020, Google's parent company, Alphabet, canceled its plan to build a futurist waterfront neighborhood—Sidewalk Toronto. That smart city project commenced in October 2017 and ever since has attracted global attention. Its cancellation—due to the "economic uncertainty" of COVID-19, to quote from Alphabet—has also attracted global attention and triggered debates about the utopia and dystopia of the global smart cities boom.

Huawei, another Shenzhen-based high-tech giant, is an international leader of 5G technology and other smart city technologies. It is, of course, a dominant leader in the smart city market at home. Huawei has also been very successful in overseas markets, particularly in non-Western countries. The West's distrust of Huawei and the U.S.-led targeting of it have triggered a sort of technological nationalism in China (see chapter 4). Huawei has gained unprecedented support in China, morally and commercially. For city governments and the public, supporting Huawei means supporting China in the escalating China-U.S. confrontations in geopolitical and technological arenas. This nationalistic support, which its rival firms do not necessarily receive, is further strengthening Huawei's dominance in China's smart city market.

Huawei's technology is unchallenged by any other Chinese high-tech firms. What Huawei is trying to grow is its "soft" capacity to provide solutions and services that match its leadership in "hard" technology and infrastructure. As part of growing its soft capacity, Huawei developed a so-called Maslow's smart city model, mimicking the well-known Maslow's hierarchy of needs. This model is a pyramid structure of four levels from the bottom to the top: level 1 of urban infrastructure of information and communications technology at the bottom, level 2 of urban security and level 3 of digital urban services in the middle, and level 4 of smart brain at the top. This model, which was advertised on Huawei's website as of May 2021, represents the basic understanding of the smart city by Chinese high-tech firms, and probably by the government as well.

The smart city market has also attracted into the smart city coalition business members that are not conventional high-tech firms. The Ping An Group is another local business legend in Shenzhen, specializing in insurance and finance. In 2020, the group announced the establishment of a subsidiary company, Ping An Smart City, which self-brands as a comprehensive solutions provider for smart cities. Traditional consultancy firms like McKinsey, PwC, Deloitte, and KPMG have been active proponents of the smart city, with the intention of creating a market that would demand their services. Numerous think tanks and research institutes were established to ride on the smart city movement. They publish reports, organize events, create media, and trigger debates to influence the government and engage public interest. Most importantly, they steer the direction of the smart city coalition to create and expand a market for their products and services. Estimates of China's smart city market vary: under a bullish scenario, the consulting market was valued at RMB 7.9 trillion (US$1.1 trillion) in 2018, with a 33 percent compound annual growth rate projected from 2018 to 2022.[11]

The leading roles of the government and business in the smart city coalition, in China and elsewhere, are not hard to understand. However, the role of academia in forging the coalition is often overlooked. Internationally, numerous publications have appeared, which date from the 1990s and even earlier, contributing to and riding on the popularity of smart cities. However, the international literature (published in English) has not covered Chinese smart cities to a sufficient extent, creating a gap in understanding international and Chinese smart cities.[12] This gap is being enlarged, in that China is now an international leader of smart cities: it has the largest number of smart city programs and is the most passionate about new smart city practices. Only a small number of publications on Chinese smart cities have been published in English in recent years to inform the international readership. Most of them have been published in Chinese in the same period as China's rapid transformation from a latecomer to a leader in pursuing smart cities.

I searched the subject term "smart city" on CNKI to obtain the number of Chinese journal articles published in 2010–2019 (see figure 3.1). Clearly, the number of them rapidly surged, along with the emergent smart city movement during the same period. Academics have become part of the smart city coalition, disseminating the concept and recommending policies and practices. Further, their publications have spilled over into the media and the community, and have influenced the government and business.

In 2019, the number of Chinese journal articles published on the smart city was more than twenty times that in 2010. This impressive increase shows not just the speed with which the subject emerged from obscurity to prominence in academic interest. It is also a benchmark of the formation and growth of a smart city coalition that has led and shaped the movement in China in the second decade of the twenty-first century. Academic research and publications provide

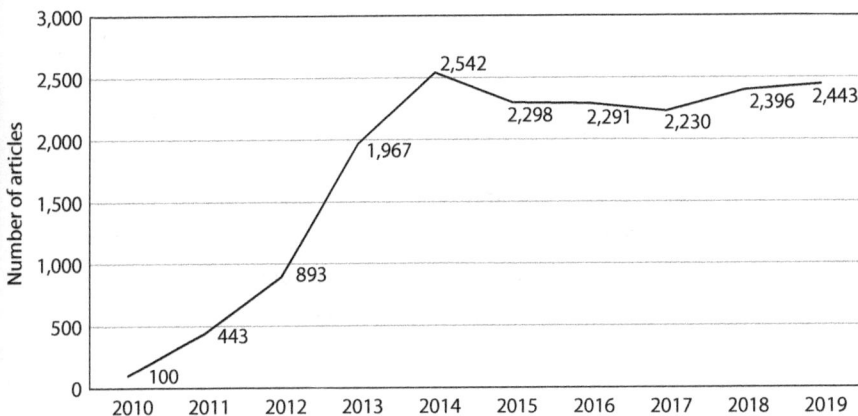

FIGURE 3.1 Chinese journal articles published about the smart city,
2010–2019

Source: Created by the author using data from https://www.cnki.net.

the intellectual base and steer the technical direction of the
smart city coalition; they also reflect the state and thematic
attributes of the smart city movement. Universities and institutes establish new programs on smart cities. Academics adjust
their research interests to respond to and incorporate smart
elements. Leading experts are invited to give public talks on
a smart future of Chinese cities or to interpret the political
will of building the smart city and the smart society. They
have collectively created the busyness and the buzziness of the
smart city in academia, and in the interface between academia
and the real world of policy and business.

Cities compete to be the smartest in the nation—and in
the world for some leading cities—or to be smarter than their
rival cities. Every year, consultancy firms and think tanks produce numerous reports to rank individual cities in terms of their
smart city readiness and performance to engage the government

and public and further to influence policy and discourse. Ultimately, these reports, despite their sometimes inconsistent and ambiguous definitions and indicators of smart cities, aim to win markets for their knowledge and create opportunities for smart services and products. Rather than informing a critical understanding of what makes a smart city and how to effectively build one, these reports, coupled with media debates and expert comments, have generated an anxiety among the policy makers and citizens of individual cities: your city needs to be "smartized," sooner rather than later; or your city—and you—will be left behind those smarter cities.

The smart city movement seems to be rushing forward, spurred by a smart city coalition comprising various interest groups. Smart city, an imported concept, has instantly become localized with Chinese characteristics, dominating the urban discourse and influencing urban practices.

TECHNOCENTRISM

The relationship between smart city and smart technology is not as clear as their terminology suggests. Smart technology, represented by the latest advances in information technology, has triggered all the imaginings, narratives, and practices of the smart city. On the other hand, the smart city discourse is often criticized for being technocentric. This presents a conceptual and ideological dilemma in approaching the smart city-technology relationship. The smart city is intrinsically technocentric. As an urban imaginary, it has been derived from technological progress, and every reimagining of the smart city has been driven by technological innovation milestones. But despite being technology-based, the smart city should not be just about technology—this notion is common sense and a consensus. But this notion has not always translated into policies, practices, and research about smart cities. In approaching the smart city-technology relationship, there seems to be a gap between a notional consensus and a practical deviation. This gap justifies the criticism of technocentrism about the smart city.

Smart cities are booming across the world. However, there is no shared understanding or commonly accepted definition of what it is. Smart city means different things in different contexts. The burgeoning literature, while trying to conceptually clarify and empirically test it, has simply added to the ambiguity and confusion about it. I have used a conceptual decoupling to tackle the ambiguity and confusion by differentiating between an "internal layer" of conceptual core and an "external layer" of conceptual articulation for the smart city.[13] The internal layer of the conceptual core is the smart technology that is the basis of the smart city. The external layer of the conceptual articulation connects the smart city with many contemporary urban challenges and aspirations: sustainability, innovation, competitiveness, climate change, pollution, traffic congestion, risk, disaster, governance, community participation, and inequality . . . everything we can think of in contemporary cities.

While theorists do not differ in accepting the internal layer of conceptual core of the smart city, they differ widely in approaching and interpreting its external layer of conceptual articulation. Their approaches to and interpretations of how the smart city is articulated with contemporary urban challenges and aspirations to create new urban imaginaries often differ, depending on the issues of concern, settings, and values. This external layer is where the conceptualization of the smart city is most entangled and debated.

So, how can one make sense of the problematic conceptualization of the smart city? To address this conundrum, I further argued that the smart city emerged as the latest representation of the neoliberal urbanism tradition that has dominated the global urban development and discourse since the 1970s.[14] The smart city carries with it a new urban vision, building on and extending its predecessor visions, such as the competitive city and the sustainable city. Each of these visions represents a paradigm of neoliberal urbanism. They interlink in that all are neoliberal urbanism paradigms; they differentiate in focusing on different aspects of contemporary urban development. While the imperatives of economic growth and competition have prioritized the pursuit of the competitive city, the challenges of environmental degradation and widening social inequality—often as a result of the prioritization of economic growth—have escalated a consciousness of the sustainable city, and the new technology has propelled an aspiration for the smart city.

These urban visions not only differ in terminology but also sometimes conflict in ideology and goals. They conflict in part because they have varying focuses and in part because none has a definite conceptualization—they are all evolutionary and dynamic, depending on the perspectives of the theoretical debates. What integrates them is the neoliberal urbanism—as a context and a framework—that articulates the smart city with other urban discourses. As discussed earlier, this articulation rests in the conceptual external layer of the smart city.

The Chinese conceptualization of smart city is highly technocentric. It largely builds on the latest advances in information technology—such as IoT, big data, 5G technology, artificial intelligence (AI), and cloud computing—to explore their application in urban data collection, analysis, and sharing to improve urban management and services, and to enhance productivity and efficiency. This technocentrism exactly conforms to the conceptual internal layer of the smart city discussed earlier. Technocentrism is a common feature, as well as a criticism, of the international smart city movement, and the Chinese smart city movement is no exception. The aforementioned Maslow's smart city model proposed by Huawei is representative of the technocentrism of the Chinese smart city. This model broadly divides the smart city into four layers of infrastructure, safety and support, industrial digitization, and smart brain, all of which concern urban management and operations, mostly in a technological sense.

The smart city movement is emerging when Chinese cities are pursuing transformative urban planning and development approaches (see chapter 1). It was immediately incorporated into the transformative urban discourse after it was imported from overseas. Further, the term captured the political will at the top and was endorsed as a national strategy, as stated earlier. However, the Chinese smart city does not necessarily translate into a new urban development paradigm. Rather, the smart city offers a new urban imaginary about a technological advantage in intercity and international competitions. In this sense, the smart city extends the competitive city along a neoliberal urbanism pathway that Chinese cities have followed in recent decades. The smart city is being neoliberalized, aiming to advance a new model of urban growth and competitiveness through exploiting new technology.

In September 2019, I visited the demonstration room of the Ping An Smart City Operations Command Centre in Shenzhen. This center is located in the basement of the Ping An Financial Centre, owned by the Ping An Group, which recently moved into the smart city market, as indicated earlier. The Ping An Finance Centre is the tallest tower in Shenzhen, at 599 meters.

The tower's completion in 2016 marked, architecturally and symbolically, the city's rise as an international metropolis and demonstrated the company's success.

The Ping An Smart City Operations Command Centre is open to the public, and it is the first stop leading to the lift for accessing the tower's top observation deck. This smart city center is a showroom for the Ping An Group's business expansion from finance into smart city, as well as for the group's understanding of the smart city. In the center of the room is a model of a cluster of high-rises, with the Ping An Finance Centre dominating in the center; the walls are screens showing videos and visualizations of data in areas like government services, transport conditions, public health, economy, and business (figure 3.2). The entire showroom is filled with flashing, dynamic, and fanciful representations of Shenzhen as a smart city, showing the Ping An Group's commitment to and capacity for operating and

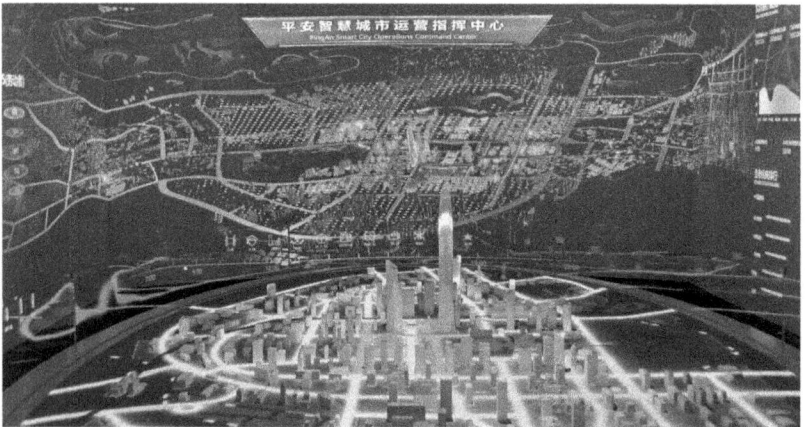

FIGURE 3.2 Ping An Smart City Operations Command Centre, Shenzhen

Source: The author.

commanding the smart city, in a technological sense, to advance future urban management and development.

The technology and services providers' perception of the smart city is not shaped just by their own understating of what a smart city is about. More importantly, it is shaped by what a smart city means for the government—the primary client of their technology and services. In July 2018, the Shenzhen government released the *Shenzhen Municipal New-Type Smart City Construction Master Scheme* to respond to the national strategy of building a smart society and strengthen the city's leadership in the national smart city movement. As the home city of such high-tech giants as Huawei and Tencent, and new-comers in the market like the Ping An Group, Shenzhen seems to be better positioned than any other Chinese city to develop itself into a smart city. Shenzhen is sometimes quoted as "the smartest Chinese city," while several other Chinese cities also claim the title. These claims seem more a branding campaign than a ranking of performance based on solid measurements and evidence.

Shenzhen's 2018 smart city scheme proposed a smart city structure, which echoed and expanded the technocentric under-standing of "smart city" by either Huawei or the Ping An Group. This structure contained two support systems—network and security support, and standard and regulation support—for a three-layer smart city structure. The three layers included a foundational layer of a sensory network system, a middle layer of big data operations and management, and an upper layer of smart city implementations in areas of public services, public security, urban governance, and smart industries.[15] Whether or not Shenzhen is the smartest Chinese city, its smart city struc-ture is typical of the "structural" understanding of the smart city adopted by the governments of many Chinese cities.

A technocentric approach is employed by both firms and the government to understand and inform policy making and technology-service provisions for smart cities in China, as illustrated in the case of Shenzhen. I further reveal this technocentrism in academia by dissecting the Chinese literature on the smart city. As stated earlier, the Chinese literature on the smart city surged in the second decade of the twenty-first century. As of May 2020, CNKI had collected 18,133 published journal articles on the subject smart city. A breakdown of these articles by keywords and disciplines further illustrates the focuses and attributes of this body of literature.

By keywords, the articles are predominantly concerned about the smart city and its associated technologies and technical concepts, like big data, IoT, and cloud computing (table 3.1). These keywords also extend to the application of the smart city concept in areas like construction, urban planning, tourism, and internet plus, but those were not the most commonly used keywords. "Internet plus" is a concept unique to China. It was proposed by then premier Li Keqiang in 2015 as a new pathway for transforming and upgrading the economy through applying the internet and other information technology in conventional industries, and he believed that "Internet Plus strategy has still untapped potential."[16] Internet plus and smart city have naturally fused to create new imaginings about how new technology could be utilized to innovate and transform the Chinese economy (to be further discussed in chapter 4).

This technology-economy fusion is even more evident in the breakdown of the journal articles by disciplines (table 3.2). The articles mostly fall into either the technology or economic disciplines; many come under both of these broad areas, as well as several related disciplines, such as planning, architecture, surveying, and engineering.

TABLE 3.1 KEYWORDS IN CHINESE JOURNAL
ARTICLES ON THE SMART CITY

Keywords	Frequency	Share (%)
Smart city	4,505	59.8
Big data	644	8.6
IoT	605	8
Cloud computing	287	3.8
Smart community	192	2.5
Informationalization	185	2.5
Construction	176	2.3
Application	152	2
Smart tourism platform	135	1.8
Urban planning	130	1.7
Internet plus	111	1.5
Top-level design	108	1.4
IoT technology	105	1.4
Digital city	98	1.3
Information technology	97	1.3
Total	7,530	100

Source: Created by the author using data from https://www.cnki.net.

The technocentric smart city is a reductionistic, simplified approach to the complexity of urban systems that involves the measurable and the unmeasurable, the predictable and the unpredictable, and the technological and nontechnological. Technology is a solution to many urban problems; technocentrism, however, may be the source of many problems that cannot be solved by technology itself. The smart technocentrism is not new or unique to the contemporary urban discourse. It is reminiscent of the heyday of the modernist "mechanization" of the city in the early and

TABLE 3.2 DISCIPLINES OF CHINESE JOURNAL
ARTICLES ON THE SMART CITY

Disciplines	Frequency	Share (%)
Telecommunication economy	6,876	29.7
Urban economy	6,846	29.6
Computer	1,620	7.0
Industrial economy	1,489	6.4
Urban-rural planning and civics	1,078	4.7
Telecommunication	826	3.6
Architectural science	721	3.1
Public administration	670	2.9
Surveying	646	2.8
News and media	517	2.2
National economy	489	2.1
Library intelligence and archival	385	1.7
Control engineering	349	1.5
Retail economy	333	1.4
Regional economy	306	1.3
Total	23,151	100

Note: Many articles fit into more than one discipline. As a result, the total of the frequencies of disciplines (23,151) is more than the total of journal articles (18,133).
Source: Created by the author using data from https://www.cnki.net.

mid-twentieth century and the subsequent "scientific urbanism" that occurred with the introduction of engineering and social sciences into the ways in which urban challenges were understood and tackled.[17] The smart city movement is, in a way, a continuation of this traditional mechanical, scientific urban thinking, which seems to be reemerging under a smart label. This smart technocentrism is being criticized in international scholarship. It is also being debated in policies and practices in developed societies, but not to the extent it should be.

In China, technocentrism is dominating the smart city movement in policy, practice, and research. The political and commercial powers and the influences of academia have together constrained critical debates about seeking smart alternatives. There has been some rhetorical transition from "tech-centered" to "human-centered" in the smart city discourse, but it will be a long time before this rhetoric comes true. Possible alternatives could be marginalized in an environment overwhelmed by buoyancy of the nation's emerging technological advances and aspirations for global leadership. This buoyancy is further mixed with pride and nationalism in the escalating China-U.S. confrontations in the high-tech sectors (see chapter 4). The development of smart cities and smart society is incorporated into the narratives of China's national rejuvenation and its technological race with the United States (and the West).

Politically and culturally, technocentrism is a hallmark of the Chinese smart city movement. It is hardly challenged, and is unlikely to be challenged, where smart technology is mingled with—and utilized by—a rising authoritarianism.

SMART AUTHORITARIANISM

The technocentrism of the Chinese smart city has been instantly linked with the rising authoritarianism, creating a technology-politics marriage with a Chinese characteristic, and with a Chinese worry at home and overseas. China has been an authoritarian state before and after the establishment of the PRC in 1949 and remained so after the reforms and opening-up in 1978. However, the decentralization of power and liberalization of control that had marked the reform era, in the 1980s and 1990s at least, triggered some expectation—mainly in the West—that China would transition from an autocracy to a (Western) democracy, under the assumption that "political freedom would follow the new economic freedoms."[18] As we enter the third decade of the twenty-first century, it has become clear that this expectation was largely a sort of wishful thinking. It is also clear that a dichotomy between autocracy and democracy is far from an accurate appreciation of Chinese culture and tradition, and of the rise of China and its disruption to the global system established after World War II.

Actually, a move to Western-style democracy was never part of Deng Xiaoping's reform and opening-up agenda. Deng was wary of Western democracy and strongly objected to it. His agenda aimed to legitimize the ruling of the CPC, to modernize the nation, and to pursue socialism with Chinese characteristics—a notion open to (mis)interpretations. The Dengist era remained one of authoritarianism, or authoritarianism with limited or controlled liberalization, but it was significantly different from the Maoist era of dictatorship.

A rising authoritarianism has been observed since Xi Jinping came into power in late 2012 and proclaimed a new era to differentiate it from the previous eras (see chapter 1). The smart city movement and a resurrected authoritarianism have emerged almost concurrently. Their marriage seems to have created a smart authoritarianism that characterizes not only the Chinese smart city but the sociopolitical transformation that the nation is experiencing in the new era.

Smart authoritarianism is coming at a high price, but that may or may not be a subject of concern, or even attention, for the government. In the smart city movement, technocentrism is preventing serious consideration for the importance of improving urban governance capacity and of engaging with and empowering the community in the construction of a smart city. Further, an overreliance on technology is negatively impacting governance capacity-building and community empowerment. These drawbacks are not easily recognized under an overwhelming technocentrism being endorsed and celebrated by a powerful urban coalition, but they could be immediately exposed in a crisis and generate grave outcomes.

SARS 2003 did not seem to teach a good lesson about improving urban governance and management. In the years after SARS, official reportage promised and boasted of the establishment of a nationwide public health emergency system to prevent and tackle the occurrence of a similar crisis. Such a system could be established in a technological sense. It was never established in a governance sense. COVID-19 first broke out in Wuhan, a city that actively participated in the smart city movement. The early response to COVID-19 in Wuhan nearly repeated a similar approach employed in the early response to SARS in Beijing. The local authorities tried to cover up the crisis and prevented the public from accessing and disseminating vital information. Despite the technological progress during the seventeen years between SARS and COVID-19, the path dependence of urban governance—top-down authoritarianism and a lack of transparency and community empowerment—in handling such a crisis persisted. There is no sign that such path dependence in urban governance will change in the future.

On December 22, 2020, almost at the one-year anniversary of the outbreak of COVID-19 in Wuhan, the city government released a plan for speeding up the construction of a new-type smart city.[19] This plan was an outline document, and it repeated the technocentric prototype of the Chinese smart city. Understandably, it listed public health as a focus area for building a new-type smart city through optimizing the public health emergency response and management system and through enhancing smart medical treatment and services. These are in no way "new-type"; they are repetitions of the old discourse. This smart city plan showed no genuine reflection on the city's early response to COVID-19, especially in terms of nontechnological approaches to a future public health crisis.

Smart authoritarianism took root before the emergence of the smart city movement in China in the second decade of the twenty-first century. The government decided to leverage information technology in the mid-1990s, when the internet was introduced into China. Ever since, both legal and technological architecture for digital censorship and surveillance has grown dramatically.[20] The well-known—indeed, notorious—Great Firewall was designed and deployed to prevent Chinese people from accessing overseas websites that the government deemed politically unacceptable. The smart technology that has enabled the booming smart cities has revolutionized the government's authoritarian use of it for censorship at will. It has also readily expanded the government's capacity for automating information collection and analysis for mass surveillance.[21]

There has been a clear surge of smart authoritarianism in the new era. Users of Chinese social media like WeChat or Weibo are not unfamiliar with censored posts on ordinary issues, like debates on the 2019 street movement in Hong Kong, personal memories of the harshness of the Cultural Revolution, or criticism of the government on hot issues, such as the lockdowns during COVID-19. The advance in smart technology seems to have simply boosted smart authoritarianism, charging the government with unprecedented capacity for censorship and surveillance. This smart authoritarianism is linked to the West's distrust of Chinese technology, like Huawei's products, although there is as yet no technopolitical evidence for this distrust that is geopolitically founded.

The early experience of COVID-19 in Wuhan is a public example of China's smart authoritarianism. Li Wenliang was one of the local doctors who first disclosed the existence and spread of the virus in private social media groups in December 2019. The information was immediately censored. The doctors were also immediately tracked down and summoned to police stations, and they were admonished for spreading "rumors." Dr Li contracted the virus himself from an infected patient when he was at work to combat the virus. He passed away on February 7, 2020.

Dr Li's death caused massive online mourning across the Chinese community, in China and overseas. People expressed sympathy and respect for his heroic role both as a doctor and a COVID-19 whistleblower; they also vented their anger for the way both Dr Li and the crisis had been treated by the local authorities. After the virus leading to his early alarm turned into a pandemic, Dr Li made the comment, "I think a healthy society should not have just one voice," when he was interviewed by the media.[22] This comment sounded like Dr Li's swansong, expressing his frustrations with smart authoritarianism.

COVID-19 has been much more severe than SARS in terms of its spreading area, duration, and damage. But certain patterns of China's responses to both crises are similar. The early problematic response at the local level was instantly replaced by an efficient response at the national level; both contrasting approaches are in the DNA of the authoritarian regime. The government's capacity for mobilizing nationwide resources and imposing draconian top-down enforcement, coupled with the cultural and historical traditions of collectivism and unity in combating crises and disasters, enabled China to be arguably the most successful major country in controlling the pandemic, at least in much of 2020–2021.

The use of smart technologies like AI, big data, and contact tracing—without the sort of controversy, hesitation, and resistance experienced in liberal societies—played a role in combating COVID-19 in China and other East Asian societies, which collectively performed better than elsewhere in tackling the pandemic in the early stage of its global spread. For this reason, the smart city discourse has been favorably received during the pandemic crisis. COVID-19 has tested some of China's smart city technologies and equipment. This has also encouraged promotion, donation, and export of some of them overseas, further boosting the smart city movement.[23]

In 2020–2021, compared with the situations in many other countries, China's draconian control of COVID-19 was generally effective—though numerous damages were also caused by such control—before the development and rollout of vaccination. Its economy also robustly recovered from the pandemic's disruption, ahead of other major economies. These were celebrated and boasted of as China's institutional superiority (*zhi du you yue xing*) by the government. The pandemic was politicized as a test of the performance of various forms of governance.

In 2022, while many countries were loosening their control over the pandemic—along with spreading vaccination—and were transitioning to a prepandemic normal, China still insisted on its "dynamic zero-COVID" policy, imposing strict restrictions on the more contagious but less harmful variants of the virus. These restrictions, while minimizing cases of illness and death, have caused related damages, disruption of social and economic activities, and widespread frustrations among residents. Both the scale and consequences of such social controls are unusual. The Chinese economy was impacted and was slowing down: its GDP grew by 3 percent in 2022, one of the lowest rates in recent decades. Many residents and households were struggling, psychologically and financially.

In much of 2022, there were mounting voices doubting the necessity, efficacy, and sustainability of China's dynamic zero-COVID policy and approach. At a meeting of the CPC Politburo on July 28, 2022, it was stated that a "political account" (*zheng zhi zhang*) needed to be calculated in preventing and controlling the pandemic, and that the relationship between pandemic control and socioeconomic development needed to be considered "from a comprehensive, systematic, long-term perspective, and especially from a political perspective."[24] In its political account of the dynamic zero-COVID policy, the government wanted to win a war against the pandemic; it also wanted to win a political war of controlling the pandemic more effectively than the West to demonstrate its institutional superiority. To win both wars seemed crucially important for Xi Jinping, who has indicated that he was directly leading the war against the pandemic and who counted the "tremendously encouraging achievements" in this war as a signature success in his new era.[25]

This politicization prevailed over alternative reasoning in imposing the dynamic zero-COVID policy, which had to be cancelled in December 2022, abruptly, due to its unsustainability and pressures from people's protests. It also sidelined any criticism of or reflection on the smart authoritarianism that had contributed to the problematic early response to the pandemic in Wuhan. Rather than providing an opportunity to revisit smart authoritarianism, COVID-19 seems to have strengthened its validity and legitimacy in China's (urban) governance.

HANGZHOU: SMARTIZING THE
BEAUTIFUL CITY

Hangzhou is the capital of coastal Zhejiang Province. As a municipality in the Chinese administrative system, it refers to Greater Hangzhou, containing both the urban area and its rural surrounds. Greater Hangzhou has a land area of 16,850 km² and had a population of 10.36 million at the end of 2019; the urban area occupies 49 percent of Greater Hangzhou's land (8,289 km²) but accommodates 88 percent of its population (9.119 million), at a population density of 1,100 people per km².[26] Whether considered in the national or international urban system, Hangzhou is a notable megacity. However, top cities like Beijing, Shanghai, Guangzhou, and Shenzhen have attracted most of the attention to Chinese cities and China's rapid urbanization and transformation, both at home and overseas. As a result, Hangzhou, despite its charm and interesting features, has not received the attention and recognition it deserves in urban research and general perception.

Hangzhou has all the features—geographical, economic, cultural, and historical—that would enable it to emerge and grow into a great city. Nestled in the Hangzhou Bay, the city has the Qiantang River running through it. Hangzhou is one of China's ancient cities: its administrative establishment can be traced back more than two thousand years, and it was the capital of the Wuyue Kingdom (907–978) and the Southern Song dynasty (1127–1279). Hangzhou's history as a capital city in ancient China is not as glorious as its counterparts in north China, like Xi'an, Luoyang, and Beijing, which were the capitals during the proudest golden ages of the Chinese empire.

Hangzhou does not occupy a central geographical position in China, and its location was regarded as distant and marginal in history. Thus, it was not an ideal city for serving as the capital, from the perspective of the regimes that traditionally had been based in north and central China. It became the capital of the Southern Song dynasty because the regime of its predecessor, the Northern Song dynasty (960–1127), was defeated by northern nomads. The Southern Song regime had to retreat to south China and selected Hangzhou as a temporary capital.

The rise of ancient Hangzhou witnessed the gravitational shifts of China's political, economic, and cultural weights from north to south. Compared with those capital cities in north China, Hangzhou has enviable qualities in history and today: it has a pleasant southern coastal climate; its hinterland region has been the richest and most prosperous in ancient and modern China; and it has a fine local culture long nurtured in the Yangtze River delta region.

Every Chinese person knows the saying, "Just as there is paradise in heaven, there are Suzhou and Hangzhou on earth" (*shang you tian tang, xia you su hang*). This saying was recorded as early as the Southern Song dynasty to describe the splendid beauty of the two cities and the prosperity of the Yangtze River delta region where they are located. Marco Polo, the Venetian explorer and writer who traveled along the Silk Road and in China between 1271 and 1295, is well known and respected in China, as he is perceived as the first Westerner to record observations and experiences about China and introduce them to Europeans. He visited Hangzhou and called it "the most noble city."[27] However, his descriptions of the wealth and prosperity of Hangzhou and many other Chinese places seem to have been a mixture of observation, imagination, and exaggeration. A statue of Marco Polo was erected beside the West Lake, the most famous scenic place of Hangzhou, in memory of his writing of the city's beauty and its glory in history.

Hangzhou's modern history has been closely associated with that of its giant neighboring city, Shanghai. If it were not for Shanghai, Hangzhou could have had a different development pathway in recent centuries. Shanghai was opened as a port city for international trade in 1843 under the Treaty of Nanking. This treaty resulted from the First Opium War in 1840–1842, in which the British army invaded China and defeated the army of the Qing dynasty (1644–1912). This humiliating start has made a great city and remade the urban structures of the Yangtze River delta region and of the nation. Within one century, Shanghai had surpassed other Chinese cities with much longer and more glorious histories and become China's prime gateway. By the 1920s–1930s, Shanghai had become a global financial center in the Far East and ranked with cities like New York, London, Paris, and Tokyo.

Since that time, Shanghai has been the "dragon's head" in the Yangtze River delta region. Its instant rise has left modern Hangzhou in its shadow in terms of size, importance, and recognition. Led by Shanghai, a dozen cities across the Yangtze delta constitute a global city region that is dominating in the nation and leading in the world, rivaling the U.S. northeast megalopolis centered on New York. The Yangtze delta is the nation's economic engine and a hotspot of the world's urbanization and economic growth. Being a major member of this global city region, Hangzhou, while benefiting from its agglomeration economy and spillover effects, suffers a loss of identity and prominence, mainly under the giantism of Shanghai.

Like many major cities in China, Hangzhou's economy has not only grown significantly in the twenty-first century but has also profoundly transformed its base. From 2000 to 2019, the city's total GDP increased eleven-fold; GDP per capita increased from RMB 90,862 in 2012 to RMB 152,465 in 2019.[28]

More importantly, the city's economic base transformed from an industrial to a postindustrial economy in the second decade of the twenty-first century.

This economic transformation is measured and manifested by indicators of both GDP and employment by industry sectors (see figure 3.3). Around 2010, the GDP share of the tertiary sectors (services and knowledge-intensive industries) surpassed not only the share of the secondary sectors (manufacturing, construction, civic facilities and provisions, etc.) but also 50 percent of the total GDP. In 2019, the GDP share of the tertiary sectors grew

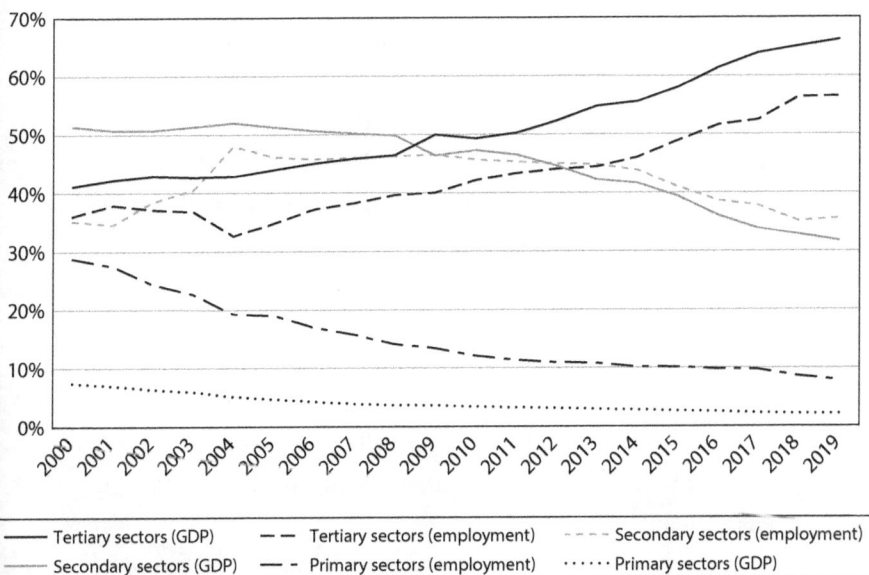

Legend		
—— Tertiary sectors (GDP)	— — Tertiary sectors (employment)	- - - Secondary sectors (employment)
—— Secondary sectors (GDP)	— - Primary sectors (employment)	·····Primary sectors (GDP)

FIGURE 3.3 GDP and employment composition by industry sectors in Hangzhou, 2000–2019

Source: Created by the author using data from Hangzhou Government, "Statistical Yearbooks" [in Chinese], accessed June 17, 2021, http://www.hangzhou.gov.cn/col/col805867/.

to 66 percent, doubling that of the secondary sectors. The employment share of the tertiary sectors surpassed that of the secondary sectors in 2014 and was more than 50 percent of the city's total employment in 2016. In 2019, the tertiary sectors accounted for 56 percent of Hangzhou's employed workforce, while the secondary sectors accounted for 36 percent and the primary sectors (e.g., agriculture), a modest 8 percent.

These indicators reveal the transformation of Hangzhou's economic base, which is increasingly postindustrial and knowledge-intensive. Technological advances alone cannot drive a city's pursuit of the smart city; a broader context must be the city's economic transformation toward a knowledge economy. Hangzhou's economic transformation, in the second decade of the twenty-first century especially, has underpinned its smart city imaginary and action.

Hangzhou has a distinctive identity: a scenic and livable city with great historical and cultural legacies. This identity is a source of pride that local residents cherish and an endowment that outsiders often envy. This identity and associated assets have long sustained tourism as one of the city's economic advantages.[29] While Hangzhou was endeavoring to seek new strategic development directions and identities—in great part to escape the shadow of Shanghai and differentiate itself from simply being a member city of the Yangtze River delta region—the smart city movement seemed to emerge at the right time for its strategic repositioning.

Hangzhou is home to two high-tech giants, NetEase and Alibaba, both founded by local talents. William Ding established NetEase and pioneered the rapid growth of the internet in China. Jack Ma created Alibaba, which has evolved into a global e-commerce giant. Both founders have been ranked as the richest Chinese individuals in various years; they are new ambassadors and symbols of Hangzhou's business environment. The leadership of their businesses in the new economy has injected new dynamics into Hangzhou's economic base and into the city's aspiration for a new smart city identity, in addition to it being a beautiful place. This new identity is based on Hangzhou's uniqueness and competitiveness, and it is not necessarily shared by Shanghai or other cities. Reportedly, a Shanghai leader once lamented that his city could not attract and retain Alibaba but had to lose it to Hangzhou. In certain aspects, this suggests Shanghai may be less competitive than Hangzhou in creating a business environment for the new economy. Cities like Hangzhou, with their beauty, amenity, and livability, could arguably be more attractive and friendly for the incubation and growth of the new economy than top cities like Shanghai.

The Hangzhou government has identified what it called "1 + 6" industrial clusters for the city's economy. The industrial cluster 1 refers to the digital economy, including subsectors like e-commerce, cloud computing and big data, IoT, digital content, software and information, electronic manufacturing, integrated circuits, and robots. The 6, representing industrial clusters, includes the cultural and creative economy, finance, tourism, health, fashion manufacturing, and high-end equipment manufacturing. These industrial clusters have mostly maintained two-digit growth rates in recent years. Both the digital economy and the cultural and creative economy are dominating the other industrial clusters; in 2019, both increased by more than 15 percent over 2018 in added value.[30]

Hangzhou's new identity as a smart city is built on its economic and technological bases; its traditional identity is rooted in its historical and natural landscapes. Hangzhou's economic transformation seems to have attracted due external recognition and confidence. In a 2021 report by the Intelligence Unit of *The Economist*, Hangzhou ranked first among Chinese cities in terms of growth potential, easing top-tier cities Shenzhen, Guangzhou, and Shanghai into the second, third, and fourth positions, respectively.[31]

Notions like digital urban management, intelligent city, or digital city emerged in Hangzhou in the second half of the 2000s. In November 2011, the Hangzhou government released a smart city master plan—a forerunner in producing such a plan among Chinese cities. The plan acknowledged the background for its creation: the emergence of the smart city and, more importantly, the production of similar smart city concepts and strategies by rival cities like Shenzhen, Nanjing, Nanchang, Shenyang, and Nanchang. Building a smart Hangzhou was a timely and necessary step in ensuring the city's competitiveness in the smart city movement. The plan, like many similar plans in other cities, was a technocentric document with a set of sweeping directions and broad goals, ticking the box for having a smart city plan in place.

In 2016, Hangzhou launched a "city brain" initiative—the first of its type in a Chinese city according to the city government—to speed up its smart city construction through shifting from a technical focus on issues like traffic management to a comprehensive governance approach. However, the city brain is still essentially a data-enabled urban platform that involves the co-production of private and public actors.[32] These are the groups that forge the smart city coalition discussed earlier. According to the *Hangzhou Daily*, a report called *Digital Governance Report of Chinese Cities 2020* ranked Hangzhou as the number one city for digital governance, and thus it is argued that Hangzhou is becoming "the smartest city."[33] Several cities have claimed to be the smartest city in China, using or citing various rankings, at home or overseas, to support their contention. Cities are competing, *smartly*, by joining in and riding on the smart city movement.

4

THE GREAT INNOVATION
LEAP FORWARD

Around 2000, I had a friend in Beijing. She worked for Hewlett-Packard and had a graduate degree in computer science from the University of Science and Technology of China (USTC), based in Hefei city. Both USTC and Hefei will be discussed at the end of this chapter to illustrate the role of a university in driving a city's innovative transformation. USTC is to China what MIT is to the United States. With USTC and Hewlett-Packard on her résumé, living and working in a dynamic city and nation at the dawn of a new century, she would have been the envy of many of her generation.

But she told me she could have joined Huawei when she graduated, her tone conveying slight regret for not having done so. I already knew about Huawei and its legendary founder, Ren Zhengfei, in those years, but they were not as well known as they are today. At that time, the business heroes in China were those engaged in real estate development, including Lenovo, Huawei's rival high-tech firm, which made a fortune from trade and property development. Twenty years later, as I write about China's great innovation leap forward, Huawei is a focal topic. I cannot help recalling this episode with my friend. In hindsight, she may have good reasons for lamenting her decision not to join Huawei when the opportunity was available.

On December 1, 2018, a breaking news item shocked the Chinese people and government. Meng Wanzhou, the chief financial officer of Huawei and daughter of Ren Zhengfei, was arrested at Vancouver International Airport by the Royal Canadian Mounted Police at the request of the United States. The issues involved in the arrest appeared to be too complicated and dubious to be instantly clarified and resolved. China's reaction to this news was analogous to the West's likely reaction to news that the daughter of Bill Gates had been arrested at a Moscow airport at the request of China.

The case of Meng Wanzhou went through long and complicated legal and geopolitical wrangling, maneuvering, and gaming—a nearly three-year process. It directly involved hostage diplomacy: in retaliation and for leverage, China arrested two Canadians soon after Meng's seizure. On September 24, 2021, the U.S. Justice Department and Meng Wanzhou reached a deal in which the U.S. extradition request was withdrawn in exchange for Meng's admission of wrongdoing in a fraud case. Meng and the two Canadians were freed on the same day. This reminded people of the swapping of hostages in the old days of the Cold War.

Even before Meng Wanzhou's arrest and to this day, Huawei has been debated, contested, and targeted in the West, especially by the so-called Five Eyes alliance of the United States, United Kingdom, Canada, Australia, and New Zealand. The attitudes and actions taken by individual Western countries, even by members of the Five Eyes, are not always concerted, and their approaches to Huawei often differ in rhetoric and tactics. Nevertheless, there is consensus in the West that Huawei is an issue that deserves strategic attention and reaction.

Huawei is a high-tech firm. In a business sense, it is no different from its rival technology and service providers like Ericsson or Nokia, nor is it different from other global high-tech firms like IBM, Cisco, or Qualcomm. Compared with the latter group, Huawei has a short and lackluster history. But it is now a global leader in 5G technology, offering competitive telecommunications equipment, often even at a more competitive cost than offered by its rivals, and for these reasons, it is aggressively spreading across the global market. What differentiates Huawei from its global rivals and other high-tech firms is that it is a Chinese firm, while the others are mostly Western companies. That is a major factor in the troubles it has encountered in the West.

Huawei presents an interesting case in the modern history of technology: a single high-tech firm targeted by the world's most powerful nation and restricted nearly by the entire West—a West whose own rise to world dominance in recent centuries has been in great part thanks to its technological advances and leadership. Huawei's rapid rise and international experiences are the most telling examples of China's great innovation leap forward and the geopolitics surrounding that leap. The Meng Wanzhou incident—and the Huawei experiences—served as a dividing line in the U.S.-China decoupling in high-tech sectors and their escalating innovation competition and confrontation (to be further discussed in the "inno-politics" section).

Innovation is not a new term or policy goal in the discourses of China's national development and urban development. It has been of strategic importance for governments at all levels since the launch of reform and opening up in 1978, but in the twenty-first century, it has come to the fore and occupied a central strategic position with new connotations and in new contexts. The frequent use—and sometimes overuse—of the term in official and unofficial discourses has rendered it nearly a cliché, and it has sometimes lost its original meaning.

On the other hand, the dominance of innovation in the policy rhetoric has also reflected the level of aspiration for it. Innovation is more than a buzzword, more than a policy goal; it is a paradigm shift that the nation is ardently pursuing to drive its economic transformation, urban development, and national modernization. When China opened its doors to the (Western) world in the late 1970s, its aim was not only to access investment and markets but also to learn advanced technology and knowhow—innovation. But in innovation, China does not want to be just a learner; it wants to be an innovator and an innovation leader.

Chinese cities—large and small, coastal and inland—have set innovation as a strategic development direction and policy goal, but the reasons for and expectations of innovation differ by local contexts. For the top-tier cities like Shanghai, Beijing, Shenzhen, and Guangzhou, which are well integrated into the global city system, innovation is the key to enhancing their global competitiveness. For the other cities that are major players in the national and regional urban systems, the focus of innovation is on transforming the local economic base from an industrial to a postindustrial economy, and on shifting the urban development paradigm from quantitative growth to qualitative upgrading (see chapter 1).

With top-down endorsement and support for building an innovative nation, pursuing an innovative city is not only urban policy rhetoric; it is also a form of political correctness for city leaders. Innovation-driven development is a growing factor in evaluating the performance of city leaders and thus determining the trajectory of their political careers. This innovation turn in the political landscape, coupled with the existing intercity competition for growth, has incentivized city leaders to explore all avenues for attracting and pursuing innovation opportunities. Innovation has become a new indicator and a new arena for intercity competition in China, injecting new dimension and dynamics into its urban transformation.

FROM "MADE IN CHINA" TO "INNOVATED IN CHINA"

The speed and scale of the industrialization of the Chinese economy since the early 1980s is unprecedented in history. However, the model itself—the development of an industrialized economy—is not unprecedented. Predecessors in Asia include Japan, followed by the "Four Little Dragons" of Taiwan, South Korea, Hong Kong, and Singapore, which all achieved rapid industrialization in the 1950s–1980s. In his book *The Four Little Dragons* (1991), Ezra F. Vogel studied the spread of industrialization in East Asia, which contributed to the restructuring of the world's economic geography in the post-World War II decades.[1] Several factors could explain the rise of these industrialized economies, such as the new international division of labor, which shifted manufacturing away from North America and Europe to the Asia-Pacific region, and the associated rapid growth of international trade. All these factors relate to economic globalization as we know it today.

In Vogel's view, Confucianism has played a unique and important role in the industrialization of these economies. Hard work, collectivism, discipline, family, conscientiousness, responsibility, and saving: all the cultural attributes of Confucianism are the sorts of qualities required for both the labor force and the organizations of rapid industrialization. The same cultural perspective on the industrialization of Japan and the Four Little Dragons could be extended to understand the industrialization of China, which is the most influential in restructuring the world economy and further political economy.

Confucianism is a cultural enabler not only for the rise of "made in China" but also for the strategic shift from "made in China" to "innovated in China" in the development paradigms of the nation and its cities. Emphasis on education and respect for scholars and scholarship—despite waves of politically-motivated anti-intellectualism in history—are rooted in Confucianism, which is the cultural DNA for pursuing innovation. This cultural DNA has prepared the workforce, managers, entrepreneurs, and policy makers for China's economic growth and economic transformation in recent decades.

Both president Xi Jinping and premier Li Keqiang—Li was in office in 2013–2023—obtained PhDs around 2000, before they came into the top positions. They belonged to the first generation of university students after the Cultural Revolution (1966–1976) and furthered their education during their political careers. Undertaking doctoral study when they were already in high-ranking political positions did not just reflect their personal academic interests. Pursuing further education and higher degrees was a trend at the time in the public and private sectors, reflecting broader societal demand and respect for knowledge.

Ancient Chinese officialdom had a tradition of recruiting officials by using exams to select the scholarly elites to serve the government. This tradition, as a culture and a practice, has lasted in various forms until today. While China is committed to modernizing through innovation, the cultural root of this future-oriented commitment is a very old and traditional one—Confucianism. Confucianism has shaped, consciously and unconsciously, China's innovation strategy and its evolution in the contexts of both national development and international engagement.

Mao Zedong lived in a time when China was transitioning from a premodern to a modern society. He could have been an old-style scholar of history and a prolific poet if he had not become a communist revolutionary and ultimately a dictator. Mao was an exception among modern Chinese leaders because, among other things, he employed extreme anti-intellectualism in power struggles to achieve his political goals. Mao's Great Leap Forward movement in 1958–1962 to grow the production of grain and steel and to rapidly modernize the economy was unrealistic and poorly implemented. It generated tremendous waste and resulted in a nationwide famine, which directly led to horrendous causalities. The number of deaths has never been disclosed, and it is still a taboo subject in official discourse. Unofficial estimates range from 15 million to 55 million deaths— a shocking record in both Chinese and human history. Mao's cruelty and his persecution of intellectuals and the educated hindered the progress of innovation except for those for military purposes, like nuclear weapons.

But the Maoist slogan of "four modernizations" (*si ge xian dai hua*)—which was proposed and developed in the 1950s and referred to the modernization of agriculture, industry, defense, and science and technology—was inherited by his successor, Deng Xiaoping. The four modernizations could be the earliest political narrative of innovation, even though it had not been substantiated or implemented in much of the Maoist era.

Innovation occupied a key position in Deng Xiaoping's agenda of reform and opening up, and an emphasis on innovation in national development policies has been consistently carried on and elevated by Deng's successors. In 1988, Deng posited that "science and technology are the primary productive force" (*ke xue ji shu shi di yi sheng chan li*), which was later incorporated into the so-called Deng Xiaoping Theory, which was enshrined as a development of Marxism and Mao Zedong Thought, the ideological orthodoxy of China, in the official discourse (see chapter 1). Indeed, Deng was clear and firm on developing science and technology, including the opening of China's doors to learning from the West, when not many of his conservative comrades would agree.

Deng's successor, Jiang Zemin, had a strong scholarly leaning. He could have become a professor at Shanghai Jiao Tong University, where he had graduated, after retiring from the position of Shanghai's party secretary had he not been selected by Deng Xiaoping to lead the nation after the Tiananmen Square Incident—the army's clampdown on a student-led anticorruption and prodemocracy movement—in June 1989. In 2008, five years after his retirement from the presidency, Jiang published two journal articles, one on China's energy resources strategy and the other on information technology development. These interests of Jiang and his publications on these topics could be seen as a broad reflection of the influence of Confucianism on the Chinese ruling elite.

In May 1995, during Jiang's reign, the central government formally adopted an initiative of "rejuvenating the nation through science and education" (*ke jiao xing guo*), which, together with sustainable development, was endorsed as the national development strategy in 1997 at the fifteenth CPC National Congress.

The innovation imperative and strategy have accelerated in the twenty-first century. In December 2003, more than one year after Hu Jintao had come into power, the central government held the first national conference on talent and proposed the strategy of building a strong nation through developing talent and enhancing human resources. In January 2006, the central government stipulated an initiative to grow China's indigenous innovation capacity and set a goal of building China into an innovative nation. Terms like talent, indigenous innovation, and innovative nation were not just bureaucratic rhetoric. They reflected a significant shift of the innovation discourse and strategy from the 1980s–1990s, when innovation was a general aspiration and more about learning from the West than developing home-grown capacity. From the second decade of the twenty-first century to today, it has become increasingly necessary for the Chinese economy to "move to a growth model that is more based on innovation and productivity increase than in the past" to respond to its increasing real manufacturing wages and shrinking workforce.[2]

At the eighteenth CPC National Congress in late 2012, when Xi Jinping and a new generation of leaders came into power, innovation was placed at the core of overall national development, formally ushering in an innovation-driven development paradigm. In May 2016, in the *Outline Plan for National Innovation-Driven Development*, the central government set out three steps for China to become an innovative nation: to join the ranks of innovative nations by 2020; to become one of the leading innovative nations by 2030; and to become a strong nation in science, technology, and innovation by 2050.[3] These ambitious goals were updated in the *14th Five-Year Plan* (2021–2025)—a national development plan produced every five years—which was released in March 2021 and set a vision for 2035. By then, China will have made significant breakthroughs in "key and core technologies" (*guan jian he xing ji shu*) and will join the "leading rank of innovative nations" (*chuang xin xing guo jia qian lie*).[4] This five-year plan came in the new context of COVID-19 and escalating geopolitics of innovation (to be further discussed).

In Xi Jinping's report to the twentieth CPC National Congress in October 2022, he described talent as the "primary resource" and innovation as the "primary driver of growth," in addition to Deng Xiaoping's notion of science and technology as the "primary productive force." He further stated that "innovation will remain at the heart of China's modernization drive."[5] These statements represent the latest and the most comprehensive Chinese discourse on innovation and national development.

A series of innovation visions and strategies has been translated into commitments and actions. China's innovation inputs have grown significantly, along with its economic growth. In the twenty-first century, the share of research and development (R&D) investment in GDP has increased consistently and robustly (figure 4.1). The speed and scale of growth in R&D investment are impressive compared with the country's historical growth rates and those of other countries.

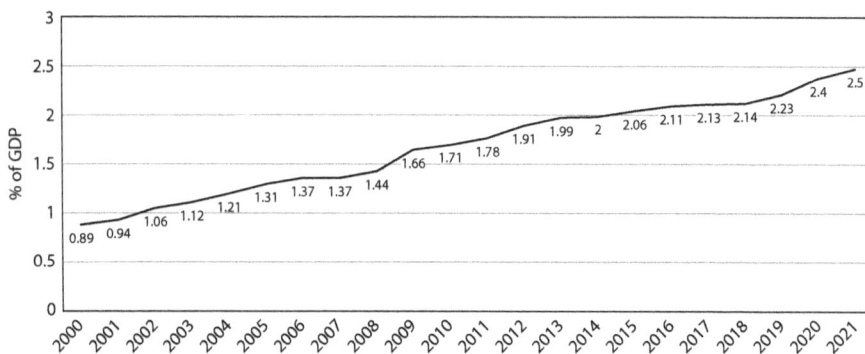

FIGURE 4.1 China's share of R&D investment in GDP, 2000–2021

Source: Created by the author using data for 2000–2019 from Dalian University of Technology, "Report on China's R&D Expenditure" [in Chinese] (Beijing: Zhi Shi Fen Zi, May 1, 2021), http://zhishifenzi.com/news/multiple/11239.html; for 2020, Chinese Government, "Bulletin on Statistics of National Investment in Research and Development in 2020" [in Chinese], September 22, 2021, http://www.gov.cn/xinwen/2021-09/22 /content_5638653.htm; and for 2021, "China Wants to Insulate Itself Against Western Sanctions," *Economist*, February 19, 2022, https://www.economist.com/business /2022/02/19/china-wants-to-insulate-itself-against-western-sanctions.

However, the figures for actual investment have been slightly lower than the targets set in the national five-year plans. For example, the *10th Five-Year Plan* (2001–2005) set the target of 1.5 percent of GDP in R&D investment for the year 2005 (in reality, 1.31 percent); the goal for 2010 in the *11th Five-Year Plan* (2006–2010) was 2 percent (1.71 percent was achieved); in the *12th Five-Year Plan* (2011–2015), 2.2 percent for 2015 versus the actual 2.06 percent; and in the *13th Five-Year Plan* (2016–2020), 2.5 percent for 2020 versus 2.4 percent.[6] These differences between the planned targets and actual figures should not be just seen as unfulfilled innovation commitments. They also reflect the government's strong aspiration for innovation and some sort of eagerness to achieve it.

Since 2013, China's R&D investment share in GDP has been more than 2 percent—a midlevel among the G7 countries. Now China's R&D investment, like its economy, is the second largest in the world, exceeded only by the United States, and China also has the largest number of R&D personnel.[7] But the investment gap between China and the United States remains considerable: data for 2021 show that China's combined public and private R&D spending reached a record RMB 2.8 trillion (US$440 billion), equivalent to 2.5 percent of its GDP. However, this R&D investment share in GDP is still considerably lower than the United States' 3 percent or so.[8]

This level of investment is restructuring the national and international innovation landscapes. In recent decades, numerous talent programs have mushroomed in China; they have been initiated and funded by different levels of government to grow, retain, and, most importantly, attract talent—especially expatriate Chinese talent—to work at Chinese universities or research institutes, or to join or start up innovation enterprises. Academics at international universities sometimes envy their peers at Chinese universities for their access to abundant research resources, which seem to be shrinking in some developed countries. The government has also funded young scholars and students to pursue education and develop research capacity in top international universities.

Years ago, one Chinese colleague from a university in Shanghai complained privately to me that the research resources available seemed excessive and were not always well used. These concerns contrast with an opposite impression from little more than a decade ago, and they are not just anecdotal; they reflect a drive to rapidly grow China's innovation capacity. Those efforts seem to be getting results: look at the rapid surge in rankings of Chinese universities in recent years.

PLANNED INNOVATION

Nearly every Chinese city has a sort of "development zone" (*kai fa qu*). Many of these zones have been planned and developed from scratch on urban fringes. Some are based on existing clusters of industries, R&D and education institutions, or anchor infrastructures (ports) to expand local economic bases and urban areas. Development zones have been a major component of China's rapid urbanization and have also played a critical role in its economic growth and transformation.

Development zones are not new, nor are they unique to China. They were learned from the success of the Four Little Dragons in Asia—especially those in Taiwan and Singapore, which seemed to have explored an East Asian way of integrating industrialization with urbanization in designated zones. The early developments of these zones in coastal cities were directly informed by those predecessors, a typical example of diffusion of international urbanism through geographical proximity and cultural affinity.

Shenzhen and the other three special economic zones (SEZs)—Zhuhai, Shantou, and Xiamen—were the earliest development zones, though they were labeled slightly differently from their overseas predecessors. Among the SEZs, the most successful and best known is Shenzhen, a city that is generally perceived as being "innovative, inclusive, young and high-tech."[9] The genesis of the SEZs had been informed and inspired by the proven success of such zones in the newly industrialized economies in East Asia. The locations for these SEZs were chosen for geographical proximity to Hong Kong, Macau, and Taiwan or for overseas connections.

Today, it is hard to calculate how many development zones have been proposed, planned, and developed in China. They have been approved and managed at different government levels, bear different names, and have had mixed outcomes of success and failure. Overall, these development zones of various types, especially in their early stages, have been the experimental labs of China's transition to a market economy, contributing to economic growth, attraction of foreign direct investment (FDI), and high-tech innovation.

Among other things, the central government has approved two major types of development zones: China National Economic and Technological Development Zone (CNETDZs) and China National High-Tech Industrial Development Zone (CNHIDZs). From 1984 to 1988, the first batch of fourteen CNETDZs were approved across twelve coastal cities; by 2021, there were 232 CNETDZs across China. The first CNHIDZ was approved for Zhongguancun Science Park in Beijing in 1988; by 2019, there were 169 CNHIDZs nationwide.[10] Here, my focus is not on the evolution of Chinese development zones; by referencing them, I wish to draw attention to the use of the terms "technological" and "high-tech" in the labels for these development zones, illustrating how early and widespread the influence of innovation has been on the planning and development of Chinese cities.

These two types of development zones have received favorable policy support and have differentiated development priorities. CNETDZs have aimed to attract investment, especially FDI, and international technologies; and then to generate export-oriented products to industrialize, transform, and grow the local economy. CNHIDZs have an exclusive aim of growing high-tech industries and innovation capacity to upgrade the local and further the national economies. The genesis of CNHIDZs was linked with the central government's Torch Plan (*Huo ju ji hua*), launched in 1988. This was a ten-year plan to advance the proportion of high-tech products and services in the Chinese economy, initiated at a time when the national economy was not yet even industrialized.

Of the many CNHIDZs in China, Zhongguancun Science Park in Beijing and Zhangjiang Science City in Shanghai are the top-tier performers and the best known. However, they have followed different trajectories, representing two major approaches of such high-tech development zones in China. They also represent two models of pursuing "place-based innovation," which is now a global phenomenon under the imperatives of both a globalized knowledge economy and a global innovation race.[11] Zhongguancun Science Park boasts of several "firsts" in China: the first CNHIDZ, first demonstration zone for indigenous innovation, and first national special zone for talent. These labels, despite their variations in terminology, have a common focus on innovation.

Zhongguancun sits in northwest Beijing. The area was already urban in the early 1980s, and it had the densest cluster of top universities and research institutes in China, including Beijing University, Tsinghua University, Renmin University, Chinese Academy of Sciences, and Chinese Academy of Engineering. Under China's market reform from the early 1980s, the value of this knowledge cluster has been recognized and utilized in a series of policy-making and planning efforts with national significance. The original notion of planning and building Zhongguancun Science Park, like numerous similar parks in the world, was inspired by Silicon Valley. It referred to itself as "China's Silicon Valley"—a branding as well as a development goal. The area has experienced massive urbanization and redevelopment thanks to Beijing's rapid urban expansion and a local innovation-driven development boom. Around 2000, I worked for a commercial high-rise project in the area, which was named "Cyber Tower" to capture the innovation-driven market demand.

After decades of transformative development, the area now has the highest concentration of innovation actors and factors in China, forging an innovation ecosystem that is different from Silicon Valley in both form and function. Today, Zhongguancun is not only a geographical name for the area but also an innovation brand for similar innovation districts across Beijing, and even elsewhere. A similar innovation district is being built in Tianjin; it bears the joint name of Tianjin and Zhongguancun, aiming to benefit from the latter's brand as well as its best practices of developing an innovation district.

Like Zhongguancun in Beijing, Zhangjiang is a citywide brand for all innovation districts in Shanghai. This brand originated from Zhangjiang, Pudong, which is now called Zhangjiang

Science City. Unlike Zhongguancun, which was originally an urban cluster of innovation, Zhangjiang was designated as a high-tech park in 1992 when the area was still a vast rural tract. Zhangjiang started as one of the four development zones in Pudong's early planning and development, which specialized in finance, free trade, industrial manufacturing, and high-tech, respectively.[12] The idea of building a high-tech park from scratch was, like the development of Pudong itself, ambitious and bold in the early 1990s. After three decades of geographical expansion and conceptual reorientation, it was named Zhangjiang Science City in early 2017. While it also branded itself as China's Silicon Valley or some sort of "valley," Zhangjiang Science City was directly informed and influenced by Tsukuba Science City in Tokyo, another East Asian example of planning and developing an innovation district close to (but distinctively separate from) a major metropolitan center.

Zhangjiang might have envied Zhongguancun for the innovation capacity the latter was endowed with through the existence of those universities and research institutes. Zhangjiang started with certain high-tech industries—like integrated circuits, software, information technology, and bio-pharmaceuticals—through attracting FDI. Incrementally, the area attracted branches of a small number of universities and research institutes, but they do not yet seem to have established the critical mass for an innovation cluster. The latest plan in 2017 delineated an area of 94 km² for Zhangjiang Science City, including a mix of urban, suburban, and periurban areas, and set an ambitious goal for Zhangjiang to become a world-class science city as part of Shanghai's strategy of becoming "the excellent global city."[13] Zhangjiang Science City is still growing and evolving.

UNPLANNED INNOVATION

Every Chinese student is educated about the "four great inventions" (*si da fa ming*) of ancient China—compass, gunpowder, papermaking, and printing—and pride in this history is often cherished throughout a student's life. Around 2017, Chinese netizens coined the term "four great new inventions" (*xin si da fa ming*) for high-speed rail, mobile payment, e-commerce, and bike-sharing. This new term has been used somewhat jokingly: none of those inventions originated in China, but they have been used and popularized there to a phenomenal degree in the second decade of the twenty-first century.

In the very short history of their emergence, these inventions have fared differently. China has the most advanced and connected high-speed rail system in the world, providing a foundational transport infrastructure across its vast land to sustain its development and growth goals. The other three inventions have directly benefited from the advances in digital technology. Mobile payment and e-commerce are revolutionizing the new economy and business models globally. But the scale and the pervasion of them in China are exceptional, innovating and disrupting its economy in ways whose influences are hard to gauge yet. Bike-sharing could become an innovative exploration of urban mobility in many Chinese cities. But as a business model, its overcapitalization has created bubbles and unsustainability. Unregulated (over)use of bike-sharing has presented problems for urban management. Along with other forms of the so-called sharing economy, including car-sharing, bike-sharing challenges many aspects of urban governance, regulation, and planning in response to the rise of disruptive urbanism.[14]

Premier Li Keqiang, who stepped down in March 2023, seemed to be keen to advocate an innovation-driven transformation of the Chinese economy, especially through utilizing the latest advances in digital technology. In 2015, the State Council released two nationwide initiatives—"mass entrepreneurship and innovation" (*da zhong chuang ye wan zhong chuang xin*) and "internet plus" (*hu lian wang jia*)—under Li's direct endorsement and promotion (see chapter 3). These terms had soon become popular policy slogans for their easy communication and trendy connotation. The combination of innovation and digital technology has been deemed an avenue of the new normal of the Chinese economy (see chapter 1). Li Keqiang did not coin the terms himself; he captured a trend that had already gained momentum and elevated it to become a policy focus at the central government level.

One prominent representation of this trend is e-commerce—online shopping and its underlying business model and value chain, as well as associated economic, social, and spatial disruption and reconstruction. E-commerce, as a technology or a business model, did not originate in China, but there it has found the perfect environment and the right timing to grow into a new consumerism with unparalleled speed and scale. In 2016, China accounted for 42.4 percent of the world's retail e-commerce transaction value, the United States' share was 24.1 percent, and for the rest of the world it was 33.5 percent.[15] Alibaba, a globally known Chinese business brand, is not the only leading e-commerce platform firm in China. Numerous firms—established and emerging, large and small—compete and collaborate, constructing an e-commerce ecosystem that is injecting new dynamics into the Chinese economy and its urbanization patterns.

Interpretations of e-commerce and its outcomes vary, however. The rise of e-commerce may have benefited from the government's policy and planning for growing and supporting innovation and innovation-driven economic transformation. While it has brought about remarkable growth and upgrading in certain sectors, many of its consequences could not have been readily anticipated, or necessarily expected or desired. These include the predominance of the digital economy at the cost of the traditional physical economy, and the hegemony of the platform economy and its capital in pursuit of maximum profits from the business model. These phenomena and their outcomes are still evolving, triggering debates and policy responses, which are further influencing the evolutionary ecosystem of e-commerce.

One aspect of the transformation associated with e-commerce is "e-urbanization": the urbanization of rural residents and areas through participation in the booming e-commerce sector. Contrary to the conventional urbanization of transferring rural population into cities, which has characterized China's rapid urbanization, e-urbanization seems to enable the rural population to be urbanized locally. This "despatialization" feature and the blurring urban-rural division associated with e-urbanization challenge the traditional understanding of and approach to urbanization.

Conceptually, e-urbanization sits squarely within the interface of Manuel Castells's (2000) notions of "space of places" and "space of flows" in the "network society."[16] On a practical level, it advances a new type of urbanization that is unanticipated and unplanned. The Chinese government has actively promoted the concept of new-type urbanization in the recent decade (see chapter 1), but it mainly focuses on advocating new planning thinking and approaches in cities without much recognition and incorporation of the emerging e-urbanization. E-urbanization is a new type of bottom-up urbanization that is based on spontaneous innovation and grassroots entrepreneurship. If the various types of development zones discussed earlier have been led by planned innovation, e-urbanization has been driven by unplanned innovation.

E-urbanization is a new spatial representation of the booming e-commerce sector and has multiple manifestations. Within the city, it generates new urban dynamics, reshaping urban spaces and intertwining social and spatial reorganization. More importantly, it urbanizes rural spaces, challenging and redefining conventional urbanization. Taobao is a dominating e-commerce platform owned by Alibaba. An associated e-urbanization phenomenon is so-called Taobao villages—the rural villages whose e-commerce on Taobao has reached a critical mass. AliResearch, a research branch of Alibaba, set the following criteria to define a Taobao village: the business venues are located in an administrative village in the rural area; annual e-commerce revenues of the village are more than RMB 10 million; and the village has more than one hundred active online shops, or such shops account for more than 10 percent of households in the village.[17] In 2020, there were 5,425 such Taobao villages in rural China, up from only twenty in 2013; together, they generated annual revenues of more than RMB 1,000 billion, contained 29,600 active online shops, and created 8.28 million jobs.[18] Geospatially, these Taobao villages are concentrated in coastal regions—especially in Zhejiang Province, where Alibaba is headquartered—and are spreading to inland regions.

Taobao villages, and similar e-commerce villages, are exploring new ways of localizing employment and urbanization despite the labels of "informality" and "unregulated development."[19] They are revolutionizing the circulation and transaction of agricultural products, pointing to a possible new direction for bridging the urban-rural gaps that have bifurcated Chinese society. Many of them are developing from isolated workshops in rural areas to small business clusters; some are even linked with global production and consumption systems. Without doubt, COVID-19 has boosted the growth and spread of e-commence and resultant e-urbanization. Neither e-commerce nor e-urbanization is innovative or new in China. However, they have experienced phenomenal growth in China, representing an innovation-driven transformation that is bottom-up and unplanned.[20]

INNO-POLITICS

Through much of the 1990s, "globalization" was a novel, exotic, and fashionable buzzword in China, one that was shaping its political-economic discourse and national development strategy. The nation was dedicated to economic growth, opening its doors, transitioning to a market economy, and embracing globalization. A good example was its relentless effort to join the General Agreement on Tariffs and Trade (GATT) and its successor, the World Trade Organization (WTO), to which China was ultimately admitted in 2001.

The fall of the Berlin Wall in 1989 and the dissolution of the Soviet Union in 1991 formally marked the end of the Cold War, which had dominated post-World War II geopolitics. China was reforming itself to engage with the West and integrate with the world. All signs seemed to suggest that the largest communist nation would be "normalized," along a pathway of democratization and liberalization, in a Western sense. At that time, this was a common understanding, a mixture of distant observation and wishful thinking in the West and among certain liberal Chinese circles (see chapter 3).

In the post-Cold War era, globalization was reinterpreted within China, in the new international and national contexts and, further, in an overwhelmingly globalized neoliberalism ethos. A new understanding, albeit generic and simplistic, was widely debated and communicated in the 1990s: the traditional geopolitical confrontation that had marked the Cold War would give way to economic competition; the new form of foreign invasion would be less about sending troops to occupy a nation's land and more about dominating its economy in an integrated, competitive global economy. The imperative of economic competitiveness was not unique to China; it was integral to the rise of a globalized neoliberalism discourse, as we have observed in the past decades. Innovation holds the key not only to economic growth but also to economic competitiveness in the new global context.

These "globalist" notions of the 1990s now sound naive, particularly in light of the U.S.-led invasion of Afghanistan and its subsequent withdrawal in 2001–2021 and the recent Russian invasion of Ukraine in 2022. But innovation and innovation-driven economic transformation provide new battlegrounds for international competition and confrontation.

As stated earlier, in the 1980s–1990s, China was a learner and importer of technology and innovation from the West, which was one major objective of opening its doors. Since the beginning of the twenty-first century, China has accelerated its drive to transform from a learner to a leader in the global innovation system. This drive is explicitly reflected in several terms that have reoriented China's innovation policy discourse, including indigenous innovation (*zi zhu chuang xin*) and self-reliance (*zi li geng sheng*). These somewhat nationalistic innovation policy goals have underpinned public debates, like "latecomer advantage" (see chapter 2), "overtake by alternative routes" (*bian dao*

chao che), and "overtake on the curve" (*wan dao chao che*).[21] These
debates are centered on the possibility that, thanks to contemporary waves of innovation, China could become a global leader
in industry and technology within a short time frame of several
decades, a process that took the West several hundreds of years.
Debates about how these aspirations could actually come to fruition lack rigorous reasoning and empirical evidence. However,
their appeal lies in their profoundly nationalistic imagining about
how China could possibly surpass the West in the new global
innovation race.

These aspirations and debates, and the nationalistic thinking
in the new context of the twenty-first century, are reminiscent of
the Maoist slogan of "catching up with the United Kingdom and
overtaking the United States" (*gan ying chao mei*) in industrial
production (especially steel production), which was proposed
during the Great Leap Forward movement in 1958–1962. Half a
century later, China's drive to win a competition with the West
has remained. Mao Zedong's Great Leap Forward movement
led to the gravest disaster for the nation and its people. Ironically, the targets set by Mao (for example, more steel production
than the United Kingdom and the United States) were achieved
in the post-Mao era of reform and opening up. This time, the
China-West competition is not in industrial production but in
innovation. In the United States, there is also a warning that
it can no longer take its leadership position in innovation for
granted given "a real threat" from China.[22]

Innovation, in history and at present, is never an equalizing
force; it is a dividing one, creating winners and losers. The new
wave of innovation is further complicating international affairs.
Innovation has become an issue of more than technological and
economic dimensions. It is being geopoliticized, creating the
"inno-politics"—innovation-centered geopolitical maneuvering

and confrontation—that characterizes contemporary global economic competition and geopolitical conflicts.[23] The ideological difference between the West and the East that had underlain the Cold War has not become extinct, as imagined and wished in the 1990s. It has reemerged in the new global innovation race, bifurcating the world according to ideology and mixing innovation with geopolitics. This inno-politics between China and the United States (and the West more broadly) has ostensibly escalated since the second half of the 2010s. There is no sign that this inno-politics is going to deescalate or ease soon.

The arrest of Meng Wanzhou, as discussed at the beginning of this chapter, was read in China as just one extreme representation of this inno-politics. Other representations, from China's perspective, include the widespread distrust and ban of Huawei in the West, the U.S. targeting of Huawei and other Chinese high-tech firms, and the U.S. ban on the export of microchips and U.S.-licensed high-tech products—the so-called chokehold technologies (*qia bo zi ji shu*), in which China has neither indigenous innovation nor self-reliance. This confrontation has played out in the innovation arena. But it has arisen in a broad geopolitical context, in which the globalization that has been accelerating from the end of the twentieth century seems to have reached a crossroads, facing a new circumstance of likely deglobalization or reglobalization.[24] The United States and China, the largest two economies and powers, seem to be on the verge of decoupling in trade, innovation, and geopolitics, exerting grave uncertainty on the prospects for themselves and the world.

The escalating inno-politics has exposed the competitive disadvantage of China's innovation capacity. *The Economist* made an assessment of China's progress in six critical technologies in the context of Western sanctions, concluding that "although there has been some self-strengthening, self-reliance is some way off."[25]

This disadvantage has bolstered the Chinese government's commitment to pursuing indigenous innovation and self-reliance and to achieving breakthroughs in those chokehold technologies. The Huawei crisis with the U.S. government has triggered a nationwide debate about the importance and imperative of supporting and undertaking basic research in the new context of inno-politics. There is general consensus that China has been active, and even leading, in certain applied R&D areas; it is lagging behind in basic, original research, which requires more strategic planning, action, and investment.

These understandings have been translated into innovation policy making. In the *14th Five-Year Plan* (2021–2025), the Chinese government vowed to increase investment in R&D by more than 7 percent annually; it further committed to strengthening basic research and set a goal of more than 8 percent of total R&D investment for it.[26] In 2020 alone, China's total investment in R&D reached RMB 2.44 billion, an increase of 10.2 percent from 2019; 6 percent was for basic research, 11.3 percent for applied research, and 82.7 percent for general R&D.[27] The *14th Five-Year Plan* set a rebalance of this investment structure to increase the share of basic research by at least 2 percentage points. These innovation strategies for investment growth and reorientation are sure to impact global inno-politics. According to the Aspen Institute, a Washington think tank, China will surpass the United States in R&D investment by 2025 if the current growth trajectory continues.[28]

Within the United States, confronting China's innovation rise and threat seemed to be stitching the bipartisan divisions. The CHIPS and Science Act became law in August 2022, authorizing $280 billion to boost research and production of advanced technologies like semiconductors. Debates and political negotiations concerning this act had preceded its passage for years.

One major concern was China's high-tech competition and its challenge to the U.S. leadership in innovation. The White House was explicit about the aims of the act: "lower costs, create jobs, strengthen supply chains, and counter China."[29] On October 7, 2022, the U.S. government announced a set of strict and sweeping export controls, restricting China's access to advanced technologies of U.S. origin, including chips for AI and software, and machinery for making them. This geopolitical decision would exact an economic price for both parties: the share prices of high-tech sectors in the United States and China fell after this announcement.[30]

Other countries are following in U.S. and Chinese footsteps in committing to innovation. These countries are jointly creating a "global boom" in innovation: in 2020, the world's spending on R&D exceeded $2.1 trillion; this was more than 2.5 percent of global GDP—a record.[31] But inno-politics is complicating the global innovation race. It is common wisdom that innovation calls for and benefits from both competition and collaboration. If inno-politics is driving the global innovation race toward a trajectory of technological and economical decoupling, the global boom measured by innovation inputs sounds questionable: will they also lead to a global boom measured by innovation outputs?

INNOVATION WITH ILLIBERALIZATION?

Qian Xuesen was a Chinese physical scientist. He is a household name in China for his ground-breaking contribution to the nation's nuclear, missile, and space programs. Like many Chinese scientists and intellectuals of his generation, Qian grew up and was educated during the period of the Republic of

THE GREAT INNOVATION LEAP FORWARD   C3 119

China (RoC, 1912–1949); these scholars then went to the United States or Europe for further education. Many of them returned after 1949, when the PRC was established, expecting to build their motherland and a new China. Their fates differed, and many of them suffered under the Maoist anti-intellectual persecutions. Qian returned from the United States in 1955, but his life and career fared better than those of many of his peers. He made remarkable achievements and received great support and recognition for his leadership in and contribution to scientific programs for military applications, which were on the government's priority agenda during the Cold War period.

On July 29, 2005, Chinese premier Wen Jiabao visited Qian, who was then ninety-four years old, following a sort of Confucian tradition of showing respect for scholars and knowledge. Qian shared this observation with Wen: "So many students have been educated in these years. None of them is comparable with those masters educated during the period of the RoC in terms of academic achievements. Why cannot our universities educate outstanding talent?"[32]

This is the famous Qian Xuesen's Question (*qian xue sen zhi wen*) in the Chinese discourse on innovation and education. Qian's observation was widely reported, echoed, and debated. He was not the first to raise the question and express the concern, but Qian's reputation and influence elevated the public attention paid to this widely accepted observation. China's progress in original innovation and education seems to have lagged behind its progress in economic growth and standard of living. A frequently cited indicator is the number of Chinese Nobel laureates: only three were recognized for their achievements in the PRC, including Liu Xiaobo, a political dissenter advocating human rights and democratization. The others were all foreign citizens: they either grew up and were educated during the RoC and then moved overseas, or they belonged to the Chinese diaspora.

Qian Xuesen's Question raises a fundamental issue: how can a communist regime be compatible with an innovation culture of freedoms, differences, diversity, inquiry, and criticality? These cultural attributes are neither encouraged nor tolerated in the current ideological orthodoxy. Debates and actions about reforming the tertiary education system have been escalating, along with the growing investment in education and R&D, but they cannot break through a bottom line—the authority of the CPC. Balancing a drive for achieving world-class education and innovation institutions with a commitment to strengthening the party's control has characterized and shaped the governance and operations of Chinese universities. This situation will continue in the foreseeable future.

The Southern University of Science and Technology (SUSTech) was established in Shenzhen in 2010. It had two major missions. First, SUSTech would be the second university in the city, after Shenzhen University (established in 1983), to enhance home-grown talent and innovation capacity. This was an important step toward implementation of Shenzhen's strategic aspiration to become an international innovation hub. A lack of top universities presented a barrier to achieving such an aspiration for Shenzhen, unlike other cities like Beijing, Shanghai, and Guangzhou, which are all home to leading universities. Second, a brand-new university like SUSTech could establish a new institution for Shenzhen but, more importantly, could possibly incubate a new culture to advance tertiary education and innovation in China.

In the years before and after the launch of SUSTech, it triggered debates and proposals about how it could explore a different—if not independent—trajectory of birth and growth. One of the topical issues was how its operations, unlike those of established universities, could benefit from "debureaucratization" (*qu xing zheng hua*)—a euphemism for the minimization of bureaucratic interference with academic activities and of the party's control of intellectual freedoms. Whether it should have a party secretary—who is of a higher rank than the president of a university—like any other Chinese university was raised in media debates in the early stage of its initiation.

SUSTech has grown rapidly, with a mix of progress, drawbacks, and controversies. It seems to be mimicking peers like Hong Kong University of Science and Technology and Stanford University in many aspects of the design of its organization and operations. SUSTech has built a beautiful campus, attracted global academics, and rapidly enhanced its reputation nationally and internationally. It was supposed to be the most innovative Chinese university in its original imagining. In certain respects, its design and organization as a new university are somewhat novel in a way not shared by many Chinese universities. But in governance and culture, it remains a typical Chinese university and is not living up to the expectation of debureaucratization.

Chinese universities and R&D institutions seem to have done what they could to advance innovation in a material sense—investment, equipment, infrastructure, building, and incentives. These inputs are continuing to grow and being translated into innovation outputs, measured by publications, citations, rankings of universities, patents, and commercialization. In 2016, China outnumbered the United States in scientific publications for the first time: 426,000 versus 409,000.[33] These inputs and outputs are important indicators of the nation's great innovation leap forward.

Meanwhile, however, there is a countertrend in China's pursuit of becoming an innovative nation—the increasing illiberalization in the recent decade. It is an enduring challenge for Chinese universities to cope with the contradiction between a growing innovation drive and a tightening of party control over academic affairs. The law of diminishing returns in economics applies to investment in innovation, too. China cannot become an innovative nation through increasing both investment and illiberalization at the same time. The nation's economic and social progress in the reform and opening-up period was a function not of illiberalization but of liberalization (albeit limited) through decentralization of power and loosened party control. This progress has been celebrated as a product of the party's leadership, leading to some complacency and misbelief around the compatibility of innovation and illiberalization; in fact, these are intrinsically incompatible.

HEFEI: SEEKING ALTERNATIVE GROWTH THROUGH INNOVATION

Not many people outside China have ever heard of Hefei. It is the capital of Anhui Province. Hefei has a land area of 11,445 km^2 and recorded a population of 9.37 million in 2020.[34] This is a megacity. However, it is not a star city within the Chinese urban system: as an inland city, it is not comparable to those coastal cities in many socioeconomic indicators, nor is it a leader among its peer inland cities. Even within Anhui Province, for a long period in the twentieth century, Hefei was in no sense an attractive place. It was designated as the provincial capital in 1952—a controversial decision at that time—largely for its location in the geographical center of the province, which has a north-south rhombus shape. In 1949, Hefei was just a "city" with a population of 50,000 and an urban area of 5 km^2.[35]

Several cities along the Yangtze River in south Anhui were better established and positioned to become the capital. Culturally and historically, residents in these southern cities cherished a sense of superiority over Hefei for a long period after Hefei became the provincial capital. Those southern cities include Anqing, along the Yangtze River, which was the capital of Anhui for much of the period from the late seventeenth to the early twentieth century. Today, none of those cities is comparable to Hefei in terms of size, economic power, and importance. Hefei's status and people's perceptions about it have fundamentally shifted in the twenty-first century. A political decision to make Hefei the provincial capital has restructured the development trajectories of Hefei and other cities within the province.

Why do I use Hefei as a case for this chapter's focus on innovation? The *14th Five-Year Plan* (2021–2025) set the goal of building four comprehensive national science centers—Huairou in Beijing, Zhangjiang in Shanghai, the Greater Bay Area, and Hefei in Anhui Province. It is an uncommon scenario in which Hefei ranks with Beijing, Shanghai, and the Greater Bay Area (which includes Shenzhen, Hong Kong, and Guangzhou). Hefei is selected as a case study here because of its innovation capacity: while it is not yet in a leading position internationally or even nationally, it is rapidly surging. More importantly, this innovation capacity has been married with the city's rapid urban growth to lead it along an innovation-driven urban development pathway.

Hefei does not have the same geographical and natural endowments as the coastal and riverside cities, which put them in an advantageous position for exploiting their comparative advantage. However, innovation seems to be providing an alternative pathway for this inland city to pursue a competitive advantage. In 2020, Hefei's GDP exceeded RMB 1 trillion for the first time, joining the so-called one trillion club of Chinese cities with a minimum yearly GDP of RMB 1 trillion, of which there were twenty-three that year.[36] Ranking twentieth among Chinese cities in terms of GDP in 2020, Hefei is still not a leading city in the country, but in 2005, it ranked only seventy-fifth.[37] From 2000 to 2020, Hefei increased its GDP by 1,274 percent, the fastest growth over the period among the one trillion club cities, while Shenzhen, considered the fastest-growing city in the world, increased its GDP by 904 percent during the same period.[38] How has Hefei achieved this growth?

Like many Chinese cities in the twenty-first century, Hefei experienced not only rapid economic growth but also economic restructuring (figure 4.2). Its economy seemed to be industry-based until the second half of the 2010s, when it started to shift

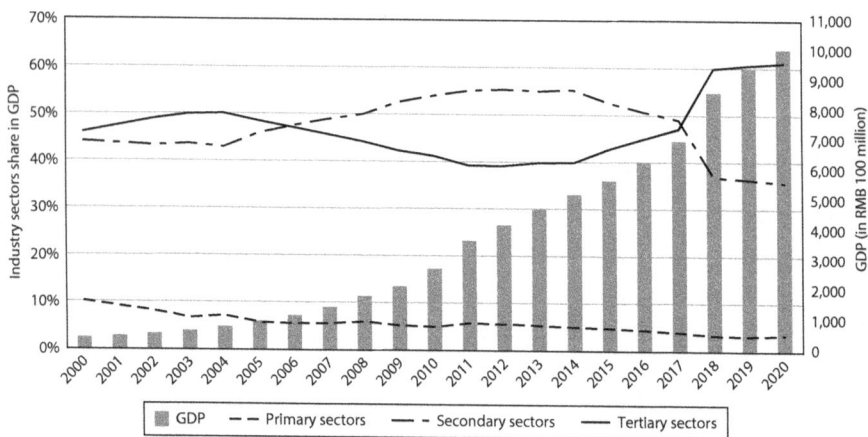

FIGURE 4.2 GDP growth and GDP share by industry sectors in Hefei, 2000–2020

Source: Created by the author using data from Wikipedia, s.v. "GDP in Hefei" [in Chinese], accessed January 31, 2023, https://zh.wikipedia.org/wiki /%E5%90%88%E8%82%A5%E5%B8%82%E5%9C%B0%E5%8C%BA %E7%94%9F%E4%BA%A7%E6%80%BB%E5%80%BC.

toward a postindustrial economy. From 2006 to 2017, the GDP share of the secondary sectors of manufacturing was higher than that of the tertiary sectors of services, and the former had a constant growth trend during most years of the decade. The robust growth of the secondary sectors in GDP composition in this period may have been an outcome of a new strategy of "industry-based city building" (*gong ye li shi*), which was put in place in 2005. The GDP share of the tertiary sectors reversed its downward trend in 2014 and started to grow; it surpassed the share of the secondary sectors in 2017 and seems to have dominated the city's economic base ever since. Presumably, the renewed growth of tertiary sectors has resulted from the city's reoriented strategy of developing so-called strategic emerging industries (*zhan lue xing xin xing chan ye*), which are mostly knowledge-intensive and innovation-driven. How has this economic transformation happened?

In much of the 1950s–1970s, China was engaged in geopolitical confrontations, first with the United States and later with the Soviet Union. Hefei seems to have benefited indirectly from these geopolitical circumstances during this period. At that time, many factories and institutions were relocated from coastal areas to inland cities out of concerns about possible foreign attack on or invasion of those areas. In the 1950s, fifty-six factories were relocated from Shanghai to Hefei, along with the personnel, technology, equipment, and capital associated with them, forging an industrial base comprising more than twenty industrial classifications that had not previously existed in Hefei, or even in Anhui Province.[39]

Similarly, Hefei received several key education and research institutions relocated from Beijing out of concerns about the national capital's geographical proximity to the Soviet Union in an escalating China-Soviet confrontation. In 1970, USTC was relocated to Hefei. In 1978, the Chinese Academy of Sciences established a branch in Hefei. After 1980, several electronics institutes were moved from Beijing to Hefei. These early education and R&D institutions laid the foundation for Hefei's innovation capacity and further attracted and incubated new institutes. By 2017, Hefei had become home to more than sixty universities and 564 research institutes.[40] These education and research capacities work together to qualify Hefei as one of China's four science centers identified in the *14th Five-Year Plan* (2021–2025). In the Nature Index 2020 Science Cities, which ranked cities by the outputs of their institutions published in high-quality journals, Hefei ranked twentieth globally.[41]

The genesis of Hefei's science center was not planned; it was accidental. Around 1970, when the whole nation was enmeshed in the Cultural Revolution and under the Maoist planned economy, receiving a university like USTC was deemed not as an asset, but as a burden, by local leaders and residents. Several candidate cities rejected USTC, including Anqing, the city beside the Yangtze River in south Anhui. The state offered Anqing the hosting of either USTC or a subordinate petrochemical refinery factory of the China Petroleum & Chemical Corporation. The latter was accepted for its obvious and instant economic return. Ever since its establishment in 1974, the factory has played a pivotal role in the local economy. However, in recent decades, it has also become a severe headache for the local residents for its pollution and the potential danger it presents to the public. The factory is now located right in the urban area—a result of poorly considered planning in the 1970s.

Despite apparent problems and escalating complaints from the community, to remove or relocate such a large factory lacks political will and economic incentives. In retrospect, people in Anqing sometimes regret the decision half a century ago to reject USTC and accept a petrochemical refinery factory. Hefei embraced USTC, accommodating and supporting it when the city—and the entire nation—was experiencing grave austerity. The settlement of USTC in Hefei was accidental but strategic—its contribution to the city's innovation and innovation-driven urban development would be realized decades later.

For much of the late twentieth century, the value of these education and research institutions had not immediately translated into economic growth and transformation for the city. Hefei's development was lagging behind not only the major coastal cities but also its peer inland capital cities. The city (and the province) was known for emigration and brain drain, mostly to neighboring cities in the Yangtze River delta region, like Nanjing and Shanghai.

Hefei's rapid growth, as indicated earlier, started in 2005 when the city employed a strategy of industry-based city building, initiated by a newly appointed Hefei party secretary, Sun Jinlong. Like many ambitious and entrepreneurial city leaders in China, Sun was determined to make a difference for the city as well as his political career. Sun prioritized several sectors, including automobile, electric appliance, and equipment manufacturing as the city's industrial base. The government established a department responsible for attracting investment, which sent more than 450 teams nationwide to visit enterprises and invite them to Hefei.[42] At the same time, Sun launched a "mega construction" (*da jian she*) program comprising neighborhood redevelopment, an expanded and elevated road system, a new rail system, and a new international airport, aiming at building a "modern lakeside metropolis" (Hefei boasts of several beautiful lakes). These efforts paid off for the city and for Sun himself. Hefei's GDP growth was the highest among the Chinese provincial capitals in subsequent years, and Sun was further promoted in 2011, finishing his tenure as the city's top leader.

Sun's legacies have been inherited and upgraded by his successors. The prioritization of traditional industries has been shifted to those strategic emerging industries aligned with national economic transformation policies. In this regard, the city government has demonstrated unusual entrepreneurship, boldness, and risk-taking; it has directly and aggressively participated in business decisions and activities, through the state-owned enterprises (SOEs) of investment and financing, to drive economic growth and restructure the economic base. For example, the city government invested in iFlytek, a USTC spin-off firm specializing in voice recognition; BOE Technology, the world's largest manufacturer of liquid crystal display (LCD), organic light-emitting diode (OLED), and flexible displays; and NIO, an emerging manufacturer of electric vehicles. In investing in these businesses, the city government acted in a sort of savior's role when they were in financial difficulty. Its investment rejuvenated and localized these businesses, boosting the local economy, and making profits for the city government. Its success in these investment activities in recent years has won the city government nicknames like "the best-performing venture capital agency" or "the best-performing investment bank" in China—the sort of titles seldom given to a government.

The Hefei government does not seem to take these nicknames as an irony but as recognition of its achievement. In a TV program called Dialogue Hefei broadcast in June 2021, the city's party secretary, Yu Aihua, an eloquent propogandist, boasted that the city's rapid growth has been driven by its unrelenting pursuit of innovation.[43] For him, the city government's investment success was a result of professionalism, not of luck, and of a combination of "capable government" (*you wei zheng fu*) and "effective market" (*you xiao shi chang*). He stressed the importance of risk-taking by the party cadres—especially by the leaders—in taking responsibility for these business investments. He insisted that it was not wrong to make money for the government and that certain amounts of these investment returns would be reinvested in building a value chain to further support business.

The state and SOEs have always played an important role in the Chinese economy. Much of the economic reform in the 1980s–1990s was centered on reducing the state's direct involvement in the economy and reforming the SOEs, which were generally considered inefficient, to develop a market economy. In the twenty-first century, there has been a gradual ascendency of SOEs and a resurgence of the state in the market.[44] The Hefei government's direct participation in the local economy and its self-claimed legitimacy reflects this broad transformation in the Chinese economy. While its achievements are celebrated and publicized to win recognition for the city and its leaders, the model also raises concerns about the reversal of market-oriented reforms and the hindering of fair competition between public and private market actors. Balancing the state and the market has been an enduring issue in any economy. But in the Chinese economy, despite decades of market reform, the state always has a tendency—and a legitimacy—to prevail over the market (see chapter 8).

In 1991, Hefei was among the first group of Chinese cities to establish a High-Tech Industrial Development Zone, but the city's innovation-driven development did not get into full swing until the second decade of the twenty-first century. In 2019, the city had more than one thousand enterprises, forging clusters in sectors of new displays and accessories, integrated circuits, and AI; all together, these sectors and other strategic emerging industries account for 52.6 percent of the city's industrial output.[45] In the nation's great innovation leap forward, innovation has become a new arena for intercity competition. Such competition has marked China's rapid economic growth and urbanization for more than forty years. Now, the cities are competing for and through innovation. Hefei, a latecomer to the previous intercity competitions, is seeking an alternative path to growth through innovation.

5

THE XIONG'AN EXPERIMENT

Xiong'an was a no-name place—really not a place at all—before April 1, 2017. On that day, the Chinese government announced the establishment of Xiong'an New Area, describing it with grand terms like a "millennium plan" (*qian nian da ji*) and a "national initiative" (*guo jia da shi*) to show its importance. Xiong'an is a coined term, combining the first characters of Xiong County and Anxin County; the new area sits across the intersection of the two as well as Rongcheng County. Literally and symbolically, the name Xiong'an sounds upbeat, grand, heroic, peaceful, and safe. Geographically, the three counties where the new area is designated are part of Baoding City in Hebei Province, 30 km from the city center. The new area is 105 km from both Beijing and Tianjin and 155 km from Shijiazhuang, the capital city of Hebei Province. It seems to be at a geometric center of major cities in the Beijing-Tianjin-Hebei region, one of the backbone city regions in China.

The announcement of Xiong'an's establishment was a surprise and a puzzle. The closest major city to the site is Baoding, an obscure city in the region under the dominance of Beijing and Tianjin. It lacks any locational or economic advantages for growing a new city: it has no access to infrastructure like ports or transport lines, nor is it in proximity to a major economic center. The area has a vast body of water called Baiyang Lake, including its surrounding water systems and wetlands. These are an unusual natural endowment in north China, which is normally short of water resources and water features. Baiyang Lake is probably the best-known local asset, naturally and culturally. Many Chinese know it from movies and literature that describe how the residents and communist guerrillas fought against Japanese enemies in the lake area during 1939–1943, sometimes using the water systems and thick reeds that grow in the lake as cover and protection. For this historical reason, Baiyang Lake embodies both scenic beauty and revolutionary romanticism. The area is mostly rural and undeveloped. At the time of announcement of the new area, the core area had a population of less than 100,000. These landscape and demographic features could make it easier to plan and develop a new city from scratch, according to the official reportage.[1]

The study and decision-making for Xiong'an had been kept confidential for two years. This was sensible: the secrecy was meant to prevent any prior construction on and occupation of land, and any market speculation in land and property, in anticipation of the area becoming a hotspot of urban development. Once the news was announced on April 1, Xiong'an instantly became a catchword and a sensation at home and abroad. Creative netizens made numerous comments, mostly through jokes, about what the news meant for people living in Xiong'an: they would become rich overnight. One common theme of the jokes was how these local residents would become popular for matchmaking. Here is one widely shared post about a matchmaking joke: "Male, 53-year-old, divorced, childless, rural household, owning 2-*mu* (around 1,333 m^2) farmland in Xiong'an; looking for a female under 25 years old, preferably a graduate from a university in the United Kingdom or the United States."

Jokes like this are not baseless. The massive urbanization and urban growth in China have generated numerous multimillionaires. These individuals have done nothing to amass wealth other than owning properties or occupying land that has been redeveloped or incorporated into urban areas, and thus they have received ample compensation from the government or developers. The news of Xiong'an New Area would, without doubt, increase the land value and change the lives of many residents.

The official reportage has emphasized that Xiong'an New Area was selected, decided, and planned by Xi Jinping himself. This is not merely praise that is typical of the official discourse about Xi; it is true. In a way, Xiong'an is Xi Jinping's personal project wrapped up in a national initiative. Xiong'an could be incorporated into a macro narrative of exploring a new vision of the Beijing-Tianjin-Hebei region and a new pathway for China's urbanization, as has been described in the official discourse. However, Xi Jinping's personal interest and political will played a crucial role in the idea of the project, which is bold and imaginative. Xi visited the site, set the vision, instructed on its planning, reviewed its plans, and appointed high-level officials to oversee the project. This top-down endorsement has provided Xiong'an with a level of opportunities and resources that no other urban development project in China, or elsewhere, could access. It has received unreserved and unlimited support from the state and state-owned enterprises (SOEs) and benefited from national and international planning and design expertise. Political will and state action have been part of Xiong'an's DNA from the very beginning.

It seems that Xi Jinping needs a city that bears his name to fulfill his political aspiration and ambition. It is commonly acknowledged that Deng Xiaoping orchestrated the building of Shenzhen and Pudong; the modern urban images of both mark Deng's great transformation of China for good. For a political leader with centralized and unchecked power, nothing is more symbolic and blood-stirring than building a new city. There is no such new city in the Beijing-Tianjin-Hebei region; Shenzhen sits in the Pearl River delta region and Pudong in the Yangtze River delta region. These three city regions form the backbone of China's urban structure and are its economic powerhouses.

Xi Jinping is interested in urban affairs and has given specific directives about urban development since he came into power in late 2012. But in Xiong'an, he seemed to want to build a city with his own imprint—to experiment with his urban vision and fulfill his political will. The timing of experimenting with an urban vision may be right, as China is exploring new directions and approaches for its urbanization. But the timing of building a new city from scratch, mainly through political will and state action, may not be right.

THE BEIJING SYNDROME

I lived in Beijing in the late 1990s and early 2000s, experiencing the city's great transformation. Since that time, I have closely followed and observed the changes in and debates about the city's development with great interest. In the first half-year I spent in the city, I suffered frequent colds and sometimes fevers before I gradually got used to its dry, cold weather and heavy pollution. I do not recall many days of blue sky except when there were strong winds. People sometimes complained and joked that in Beijing, the solution to pollution is wind. There I learned and lived the term "subhealth status" (*ya jian kang zhuang tai*)—a physical and mental status somewhere between health and ill-health resulting from the degraded urban environment and heavy pressure of living in a big city like Beijing. Indeed, while Beijing is a city of opportunities, attracting people from elsewhere in China and the world, it also suffers so-called big city syndrome (*da cheng shi bing*): pollution, pressure, traffic, overcrowding, unaffordability, and low quality of life. Major Chinese cities suffer this syndrome to various degrees. Beijing is probably among the worst and the most typical, and it is also the most debated.

Beijing's growth and expansion seem limitless, following a ring road structure that originates from and is centered on the ancient royal city. Construction of the ring roads has reflected the progress of the city's expansion. When I was there, the urban edge expanded to the fourth ring road; now it is expanding to the seventh. This ring road structure is said to be like that of Moscow and was influenced by Soviet planning. In the 1950s, when the communist parties of China and the former Soviet Union were in a honeymoon phase, many Soviet planners were sent to advise on and lead the planning and development of many Chinese cities. This Soviet tradition has heavily influenced Chinese urban planning of that time, including the planning of Beijing.[2]

Beijing's ring road structure has also been influenced by the traditional development patterns of the ancient inner city centered on the Forbidden City. Although called "ring roads," they have generally followed a square and symmetrical shape from the first to the fourth ring road; the outer ring roads are more circular. The expansive development from inner city to fringe in Beijing is metaphorically called "spreading a pancake" (*tan da bing*) by planners, residents, and observers. This urban expansion is generally regarded as one of the root causes of many urban problems the city is suffering.

As of 2019, Beijing, a provincial-level municipality in the Chinese administrative structure, had a permanent population of 21.536 million and a population density of 1,312 people per km².[3] This "moderate" population density—by the standards of Chinese cities—is averaged across the urban, suburban, periurban, and rural areas of the Greater Beijing region. It is much higher within the urban areas. The population density of several urban districts in 2019 illustrates this: Dongcheng District (18,968/km²) and Xicheng District (22,501/km²) within the inner city area; and Chaoyang District (7,632/km²) and Haidian District (7,515/km²) in the outer city area.[4] Beijing has the second-largest population (only after Shanghai) and is one of the most densely populated cities in China.

Controlling population growth of large cities has been a consistent goal of urban policies in China since the 1950s, although the contexts and rationale have differed by historical periods. The outcomes of urban population controls have tended to follow an opposite trajectory from planning, however. This is especially the case among those leading megacities. For Beijing, like other Chinese megacities, a series of master plans has set population limits, which have then been broken as reflected in actual population growth. For example, the *Beijing Municipal Master Plan (2004–2020)* stipulated that the city's total population would be controlled at around 18 million by 2020, but that civic infrastructure would be planned for a population of 20 million to buffer against floating population and other uncertainties.

In reality, radical population projection could turn out to be conservative: Beijing's population reached nearly 20 million in 2010,[5] a decade earlier than the time set by the more radical scenario of population growth in the 2004 master plan. The upward trend of Beijing's population, however, has started to reverse in recent years. From 2016, the city's population has been declining annually, albeit very slightly.[6] However, the latest China Census 2020 data showed that Beijing had a permanent population of 21,893,095,[7] representing an increase from 2019 and reversing the declining trend in the previous years.

Beijing's planning and infrastructure provision have lagged behind its rapid growth and development in recent decades. Consequently, Beijing, like many major Chinese cities, seems to have followed an approach of development-led planning and development-oriented infrastructure provision. This approach is especially prominent in public transport system planning and construction: urban development has expanded into certain locations, and then a subway system has had to be linked there to alleviate the escalating transport pressure. This development pattern sounds counterintuitive, and it can easily be attributed to poor planning. It is also arguable that the speed and scale of the city's growth, like many aspects of the nation's growth, are beyond the best knowledge and anticipation of local decision makers and planners.

The 2008 Olympics was a boost to the city's infrastructure funding and provision. This significantly increased the extent of its subway systems. The global event also triggered a new round of urban (re)development. The city's urban development and urban infrastructure have moved ahead fast, but in parallel: they have not been well coordinated, and the new infrastructure systems have not always been well connected with the old ones. Beijing has been growing bigger and bigger; the subway system has been extending farther and farther; traffic has been getting busier and busier; and the air has been getting grayer and grayer. Beijing is ill. Traffic congestion and air pollution are the city's new calling cards. The volume of traffic dilutes the difference between rush hours and nonrush hours (figure 5.1).

FIGURE 5.1 Traffic in Beijing

Note: This photo, taken on September 8, 2016, shows the "normal" traffic at the center of Beijing's central business district during non-rush hours.

Source: The author.

The city government has restricted private car ownership and use through setting strict quotas on issuing new plates and allocating the use of cars according to the odd or even numbers of their plates. These interventions, coupled with other policy and nonpolicy measures, have mitigated the problems in Beijing to only a limited degree. For example, studies show that more stringent driving restrictions, while having a positive impact on citywide traffic speed, have little or even negative impacts on air quality.[8] Piecemeal approaches do not seem to help solve the Beijing syndrome. The capital requires some fundamental reimagining of its future.

REIMAGINING THE CAPITAL

As the communist army was winning victories across the nation in the civil war with the nationalist army before the establishment of the PRC on October 1, 1949, the CPC leaders and political allies held discussions about which city should be chosen as the capital of the new regime. Options included Xi'an and Nanjing, which had both been historical capitals. Mao Zedong selected Beijing, restoring the name used in history—whose literal meaning is "capital in the north"—and changing it from the name Beiping, used in 1928–1949 under the nationalist regime of the RoC. Beijing is in north China and was close to the Soviet Union, with which the CPC and the new regime had great affinity at that time.

Geographically, politically, and symbolically, Beijing was an antithesis of Nanjing, which was the capital of the defeated nationalist regime and whose literal meaning is "capital in the south." During his youth, Mao Zedong was a librarian at Beijing University in 1918 and audited classes by elite intellectuals of that time. Three decades later, he returned to the city as the paramount leader. Mao later complained how he, then an obscure figure at Beijing University, was ignored and looked down on by those elite intellectuals, who mostly fled to Taiwan with the nationalist regime in 1949. It is not clear whether this youthful experience had influenced Mao's decision to select Beijing as the capital or whether it had further influenced his anti-intellectual attitude and action when he was in power in the 1950s–1970s.

Beijing is more than a capital city. It is a cultural center for its historical legacy and for the existence of its universities, research institutes, and other educational and cultural institutions. Further, it is an economic center. Beijing does not have any sort of geospatial advantage for becoming an economic center: it is not a port city or a trade center, like Shanghai, Tianjin, or

Nanjing, all of which have sea or river access. But its capital status has enabled it to access privileges and resources that other cities do not have. The political centripetal forces have attracted and concentrated economic, cultural, educational, social, and health resources and opportunities into the capital, along with the people who work for them and the people who need them.

The result has been the burgeoning of Beijing into a megacity in terms of population and built environment. From 1949 to 2020, Beijing's population increased ten-fold (figure 5.2). It increased especially quickly in two distinct periods: the 1950s and the 2000s. In the 1950s, the city experienced drastic socialist transformation and industrialization. Its population increased by 5.5 million from 1949 to 1964. The city's urban growth sped up again from the 1990s and went into full swing in the 2000s in the new context of globalization of the city and the nation.[9]

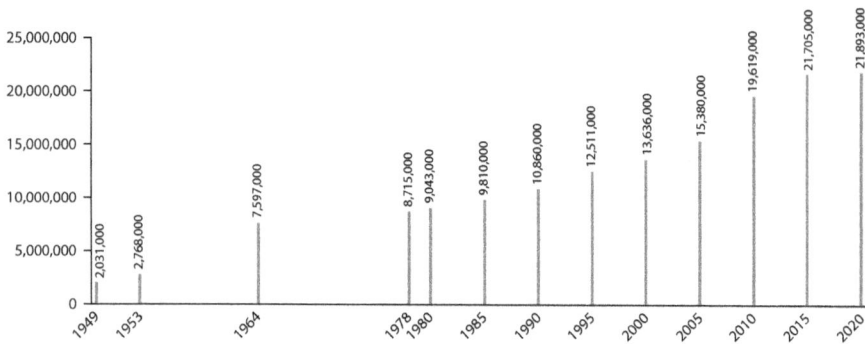

FIGURE 5.2 Beijing population, 1949–2020

Source: Created by the author using data from Beijing Bureau of Statistics, *Beijing Statistical Yearbook 2020* [in Chinese] (Beijing: Beijing Statistics Press, 2021), http://nj.tjj.beijing.gov.cn/nj/main/2020-tjnj/zk/indexch.htm; and "Beijing Bulletin on the 7th National Census (No. 1)" [in Chinese], May 19, 2021, http://tjj.beijing.gov.cn /tjsj_31433/tjgb_31445/rpgb_31449/202105/P020210519338453665400.pdf.

From 2000 to 2010, its population increased by nearly 6 million. The city's population surpassed 10 million around 1990 and 20 million around 2010, only 20 years apart. Spatially, this population growth led to massive urban expansion. From 1992 to 2010, Beijing's urban area increased from 1,627 km² to 2,666 km² at an average annual expansion rate of 57.7 km² per year.[10]

Concerns and debates about Beijing's population growth and associated urban densification and expansion have been intensifying since the late 1990s. Many of the ideas were considered in the context of the Beijing-Tianjin-Hebei region for seeking balanced, coordinated development of the constituent cities instead of the existing Beijing-dominated regional structure. One radical thought was even to relocate the capital elsewhere, considering the city's urban pressures and problems as well as constraints on land and water resources (see chapter 2).

The city's growth and drive for further growth seemed unstoppable. In 2000, the city launched its plan for building a global central business district (CBD) to advance its competitiveness against domestic rival cities like Shanghai, Shenzhen, and Guangzhou and to aspire to global city status. The Beijing CBD, with two decades of intensive development, has restructured the city's urban form and shifted its centrality.[11] It has also added to the city's density and urban problems.

By the second half of the 2000s, the consensus was that Beijing's growth had reached a bottleneck. Its air pollution and all-day traffic jams were not only complained about and derided by residents but also often became the subject of headlines in local and international media (see chapter 2). Beijing, despite its status as important and dynamic, was becoming a textbook case of an unsustainable and unlivable city. To change its growth trajectory required bold vision and strong political will.

Xi Jinping decided to make a difference in addressing the Beijing syndrome in the context of achieving coordinated development of the Beijing-Tianjin-Hebei region. Compared with the other two city regions in south China—the Pearl River delta region and the Yangtze River delta region—the northern one, where the capital lies, is the most unbalanced. While Beijing has been overdeveloped into a megacity with many contemporary urban problems, the other cities in the region have been disadvantaged in accessing opportunities and reaching their development potential. Tianjin, despite its proximity to Beijing and status as a provincial-level municipality as well, has been struggling in transformation from an industrial to a postindustrial city, and in intercity competition domestically and internationally. In 2020, Tianjin ranked eleventh in GDP among Chinese cities; Beijing (ranked second) was the only northern city among the top ten.[12]

In 2013–2014, soon after he came into power, Xi Jinping made remarks and gave directives on coordinating the development of the Beijing-Tianjin-Hebei region and alleviating Beijing's development pressure. He elevated the regional development to the level of a national strategy, one that would mark the new era that he was starting to claim for his political reign. On February 26, 2014, when Xi inspected Beijing and convened a meeting to discuss the development of the city and the region, he gave these instructions: "Good construction and management of the capital is an important part of the modernization of the national governance system and governance capacity. . . . Maintain and strengthen the core functions of the capital, adjust and reduce the functions that are incompatible with the capital, and relocate some functions to Hebei Province and Tianjin. This is the logic of Dayu's control of water (*da yu zhi shui*)."[13]

A series of instructions and directives like this led to the notion of planning and building a new city as a "centralized carrying place" (*ji zhong cheng zai di*) to relieve Beijing of its noncapital functions. This notion was formalized in the *Outline Plan for Coordinated Development of Beijing-Tianjin-Hebei*, which was released in June 2015. Before its release, the document had been discussed at meetings at the highest level, involving the Politburo Standing Committee, reflecting its strategic and political importance. This notion of a centralized carrying place for Beijing's noncapital functions was the origin of Xiong'an. It took another two years to survey sites and decide, in confidence, on Xiong'an before it was announced on April 1, 2017.

Xi Jinping's vision and will shifted the strategic development directions of Beijing, which were codified in the latest *Beijing Municipal Master Plan (2016–2035)* (further discussed in chapter 7). This master plan repositioned Beijing, stressing its role as the national political center, a cultural center, an international communication center, and a sci-tech innovation center—a so-called four-center vision.[14] A comparison with the 2004 master plan illustrates the strategic shift. The previous master plan set one strategic goal of building Beijing into a world city and enhancing its status and role in the world city system; this goal is totally absent from the latest master plan. In this strategic reorientation, a "global Beijing" is being replaced by a "capital Beijing."

Accordingly, alleviating the burden of the noncapital functions became a keynote of the new plan. For this purpose, the plan set a spatial structure of "one core two wings" (*yi he liang yi*), including as one core the central city, and as two wings a Beijing subcenter and Xiong'an. The two wings were designed to alleviate the urban pressures and crowding in the one core. The Beijing subcenter was designated in Tongzhou, a suburban district to the east of central Beijing (figure 5.3). The Beijing subcenter is

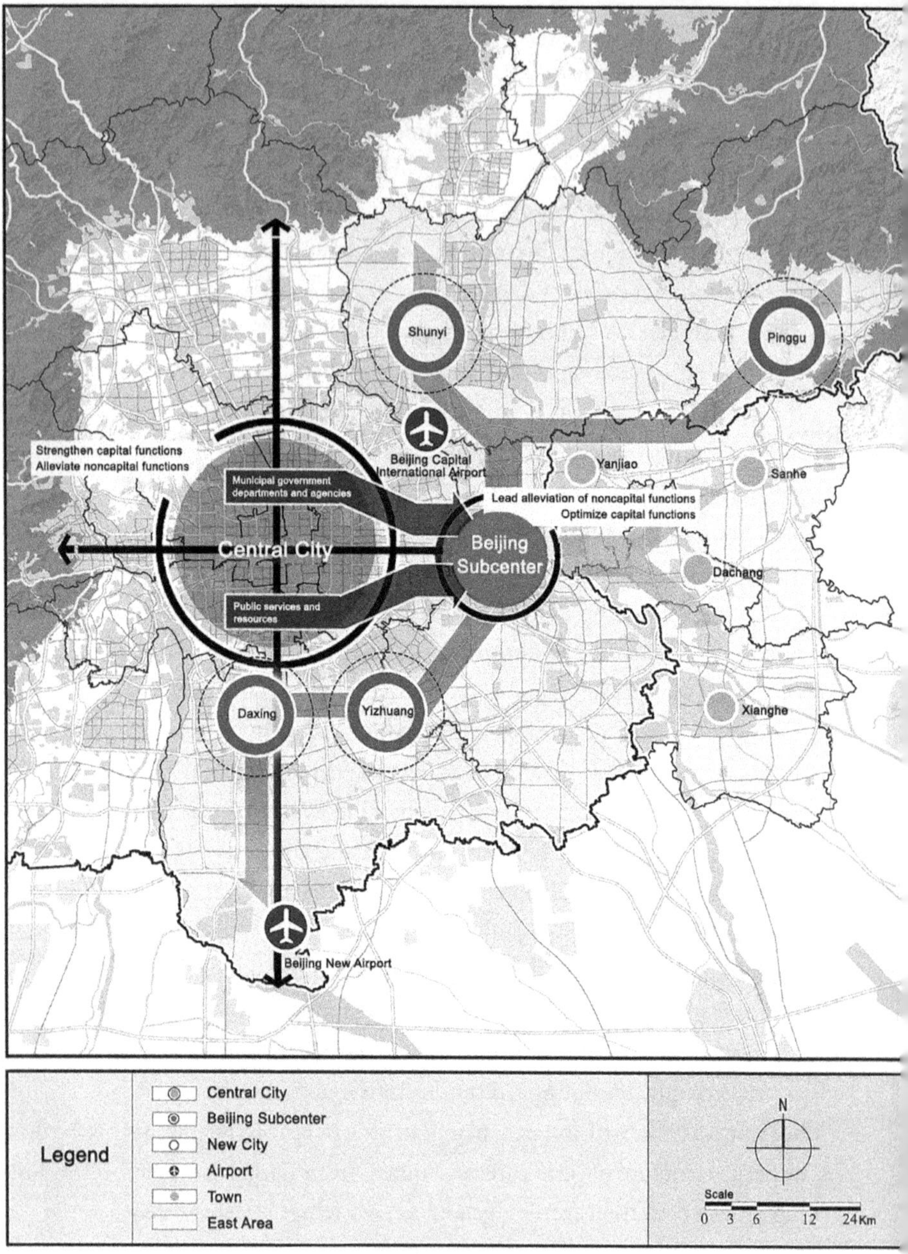

FIGURE 5.3 Beijing subcenter

Source: Beijing Municipal Commission of Planning and Natural Resources, *Beijing Municipal Master Plan (2016–2035)* [in Chinese] (Beijing: Beijing Municipal Commission of Planning and Natural Resources, January 19, 2018), http://ghzrzyw .beijing.gov.cn/zhengwuxinxi/zxzt/bjcsztgh20162035/202001/t20200102_1554613 .html, recreated by the author.

where the Beijing municipal government and its agencies have been relocated, a process completed by 2019; many other public services and resources will also be relocated there.

Xiong'an is where the noncapital functions—like universities and research institutes; health, finance, and advanced services; and high-tech and innovation sectors—are supposed to be relocated. So, the genesis of Xiong'an has derived from the reimagining of Beijing's role as the national capital.

ALL THE BUZZWORDS

Before Xiong'an was announced, Xi Jinping visited the site on February 23, 2017, and convened a meeting on its planning and development. Xi was intellectually prepared for this meeting. He expressed his aspiration for the new city to fulfill his new vision of urban development and the new normal of economic development (see chapter 1). He outlined the principles of "world vision, international standard, Chinese characteristics, and high positioning" (*shi jie yan guang, guo ji biao zhun, zhong guo te se, gao dian ding wei*) to guide the planning and development of Xiong'an to achieve a bundle of visions that contain terms like "ecology," "green," "people-centric," "livelihood," "traditional Chinese culture," "historical connection," "livable," "innovation," "coordination," and "opening"—all the buzzwords of the new Chinese city discourse.[15]

At the same meeting, Xi further gave a directive on seven key areas of planning and developing Xiong'an: (1) build a green, smart new city; (2) make a beautiful ecological environment; (3) develop high-end, high-tech industries; (4) provide quality public services; (5) construct convenient and fast transport systems; (6) reform governance systems and balance the roles of market and government; and (7) expand opening up.

It is not very common for a top leader to give such detailed directives on the planning of a city. Xiong'an is a "presidential signature initiative . . . part of a transformational leadership mode . . . illustrating the political leaders' will to engage in all-encompassing reforms."[16] There is a bit of exaggeration in this interpretation. However, it is a sensible judgment of the political ethos and drive behind the Xiong'an experiment. That aside, Xi seems, in a way, an urbanist. His visions and directives on urban affairs are specific for Xiong'an, Beijing, and elsewhere. In addition to his interest in and commitment to urban development, Xi's observations of and instructions on cities seem to be reasonably considered in a technical sense. Presumably, Xi has good advisers. A friend of mine is a planner in Beijing. He was involved in the planning of the Beijing subcenter and Xiong'an, both of which are part of Xi Jinping's plan for alleviating Beijing's urban development pressures and balancing the development of the Beijing-Tianjin-Hebei region. He observed, from a planner's perspective, that Xi's comments on cities are "professional, detailed, and to the point" compared with those of previous leaders, and that apparently Xi is well-advised.[17]

Xi's lead adviser for Xiong'an is Xu Kuangdi. In 2014, when he was in retirement, Xu was appointed to lead the advisory panel for the coordinated development of the Beijing-Tianjin-Hebei region and to take charge of selection of the Xiong'an site and its early planning. Xu was a professor at Shanghai University and later the mayor of Shanghai in 1995–2001, during which the Pudong New Area in Shanghai experienced fast growth. Probably Xu's academic background and his leadership of Pudong's planning and development made him the right person to advise Xi Jinping on Xiong'an.

After the announcement of Xiong'an in April 2017, it took nearly three years to intensively plan it. The year 2020 marked the transition from planning to development. On April 14, 2018, the *Outline Plan for Hebei Xiong'an New Area* was approved by the central government and released to the public. On the basis of this outline plan, the *Master Plan for Hebei Xiong'an New Area (2018–2035)* was developed. The official news reported that the master plan was approved by the State Council on December 25, 2018. The master plan is a statutory document, and thus the most important plan, in the Chinese planning system. For undisclosed reasons, this master plan of Xiong'an has been kept confidential and is not publicly available (as of March 2023). However, two development control plans, which are subordinate to the master plan, were released to the public in January 2020. They are, respectively, the development control plan for the "initial development zone" (*qi bu qu*)—the future central city area of 198 km²; and the detailed development control plan for the "launch development zone" (*qi dong qu*)—an inner core area of 38 km² within the future central city area. The outline plan and the two development control plans provide the basis for understanding the imagining of the Xiong'an experiment.

According to the outline plan, Xiong'an has an area of 1,770 km² for long-term planning; strategically, its development intensity will be controlled within 30 percent—that is, its total construction land will be around 530 km²; and the future population density there will be controlled at 10,000 persons/km².[18] From these planning indicators, it is inferred that the future Xiong'an will have a population of around five million, the size of a large city, benchmarked against cities with similar populations overseas and at home.

Spatially, Xiong'an has a structure comprising "one center, five subcenters, and multiple nodes" (*yi zhu, wu fu, duo jie dia*), mixing urban and natural spaces (figure 5.4). This spatial structure and imagery were informed and inspired by the Chinese

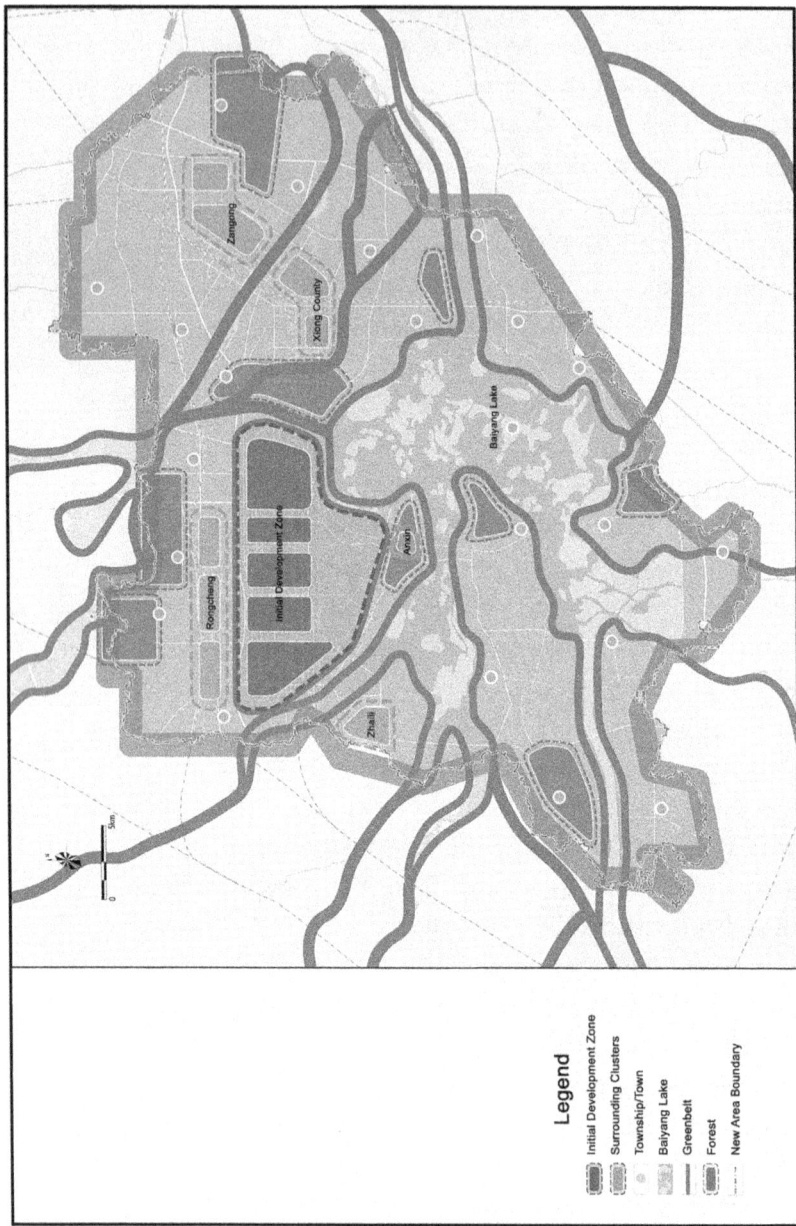

FIGURE 5.4 Spatial structure of Xiong'an

Source: Hebei Government, *Outline Plan for Hebei Xiong'an New Area* [in Chinese] (Xiong'an: Hebei Government, April 21, 2018),

Legend

- Initial Development Zone
- Surrounding Clusters
- Township/Town
- Baiyang Lake
- Greenbelt
- Forest
- New Area Boundary

Zhaoguang

Xiong County

Rongcheng

Initial Development Zone

Anxin

Zhaili

Baiyang Lake

traditional philosophy of the city and of living: the fusion of land and water, symmetry, and intimacy with nature. According to a public talk by Xu Kuangdi on June 6, 2017, the selection of the Xiong'an site was based on the Chinese traditional philosophy of positioning a city near mountains and rivers and along axial lines: Xiong'an sits on the far extension of Beijing's north-south axis and includes the Baiyang Lake water systems.[19]

The plans for Xiong'an, unsurprisingly, frequently refer to the several keywords that have characterized the new planning thinking and practice of the Chinese city (table 5.1). These keywords underpin planning visions and targets and also development controls. The outline plan even specified major planning indicators, or goals, to be achieved by 2035 in the three broad categories of innovation and intelligence, green and ecology, and happiness and livability. For example, for innovation and intelligence, the plan indicated 6 percent of GDP for R&D expenses and 100 patents per 10,000 persons; for green and ecology, it

TABLE 5.1 FREQUENCIES OF KEYWORDS IN THE PLANS FOR XIONG'AN

Plans	Green	Smart	Innovation
Outline Plan for Hebei Xiong'an New Area	213	107	72
Development Control Plan for "Initial Development Zone"	625	328	300
Detailed Development Control Plan for "Launch Development Zone"	247	221	181

Note: The numbers are sums of frequencies of the keywords and words that are conceptually related to them: "green" includes "ecology," "environment," "livability," "environmental protection," and "low-carbon"; "smart" includes "intelligence" and "technology"; "innovation" includes "high-tech."

Source: The author, counted from the three plan documents.

indicated 100 percent of green buildings for new residential buildings; and for happiness and livability, it indicated 100 percent of fifteen-minute living.[20] These indicators are mixtures of targets, aspirations, and some utopian thinking. There is no indication of their feasibility and implementation. The specificity of the measures also betrays the prescriptive nature and top-down approach in their imagining and planning.

A NATIONAL INITIATIVE

Xiong'an, without doubt, is a national initiative, as it has been envisioned and branded from the beginning. As stated earlier, no contemporary city project seems to have ever received the same level of support as Xiong'an, in China or overseas. It has received nationwide support in terms of leadership, planning expertise, resources, funding, and, most importantly, political endorsement. It is a conscious but unstated understanding that this is Xi Jinping's project. Supporting the project, rhetorically and substantially, represents a sort of political stance, which has been emphasized in the political atmosphere of the new era. Some political and professional honor is attached to being involved in the making of Xiong'an in whatever capacity.

The leadership of the Management Commission of Xiong'an New Area has been selected from a nationwide pool of cadres who have proven track records elsewhere. Some of them were assigned to the leadership team from Beijing, Shenzhen, Shanghai, and central government departments. Chen Gang, the inaugural director of the management commission from June 2017 to October 2020, had impressive administrative leadership experiences in Beijing in 2000–2013. Those experiences included his involvement in the rapid development of Beijing CBD. He later worked in Guiyang, a less developed capital city of Guizhou Province, and reimagined the city into a big data center (see chapter 3).

Chen Gang's successor on the management commission, Zhang Guohua, took up the director role in December 2020. Zhang has a no less impressive track record of leading the development of cities in Jiangsu Province, a coastal province that is more developed than inland provinces. Zhang was the mayor and later party secretary of Kunshan, a small city in Jiangsu Province to the west of Shanghai, from 2002 to 2011. The city's rapid growth has led to discussions about a so-called Kunshan model for inviting foreign direct investment (FDI) and developing the local economy under the leadership of capable and entrepreneurial officials.[21] Kunshan's GDP has been the highest among the Chinese county-level cities—small low-level cities in the Chinese administrative system—for many years in the twenty-first century; its GDP was even higher than that of some inland provincial capital cities.

The appointment of these leaders to the management commission has a clear purpose: to transplant their successful experiences, leadership, and entrepreneurship to Xiong'an. Since Xiong'an was launched, numerous groups of leaders and cadres from the central government departments or SOEs have visited Xiong'an, following in the steps of Xi Jinping, to express commitment to supporting the project as well as show political loyalty to Xi.

After Xiong'an was announced in April 2017, a planning workshop was convened, comprising member teams of the China Planning Institute, Beijing Planning Institute, Tianjin Planning Institute, and Shenzhen Planning Institute (all semigovernmental entities), in addition to Tsinghua University, Tongji University, and Southeast University (the Chinese universities known for architecture and planning education, research, and practice). This team represents the nation's best planning expertise. In addition, around one hundred planners were seconded from nationwide planning institutes and universities that have reputations in planning and urban design. A friend of mine, who worked for the planning of Pudong, Shanghai, was seconded to Xiong'an to join other planners brought in from across the nation to collectively work on the planning of Xiong'an. For these planners, Xiong'an presented an unusual opportunity to both satisfy their professional interests and boost their career development. The Shenzhen Planning Institute even established a branch in Xiong'an. On the basis of these initial, tentative nationwide planning supports, a local Xiong'an Planning Institute was established.

These Chinese planners were responsible for the master plan of Xiong'an New Area, as well as the development control plans of the initial development zone and the launch development zone, which are all statutory plan documents. The exclusive use of Chinese planning expertise was meant to create a "Chinese model of new urban development," according to one participating planner.[22] A so-called responsible planning institute (*ze ren gui hua shi dan wei*) system—one planning institute is charged with the planning of a single precinct and the coordination of its management and implementation—was applied to ensure quality and consistency in the whole process from planning, to development, and to completion. However, the more creative part of urban design and architecture was open to international expertise.

In July 2018, the Management Commission of Xiong'an New Area undertook an international urban design competition for the initial development zone to underpin the creation of the

detailed development control plan for the zone. The competition received ninety-six submissions, from which twelve teams—
both Chinese and international teams, including well-known
names like Foster + Partners, AECOM, Arup, and Cox—were
shortlisted to further develop their schemes. These teams were
also involved in a series of urban design workshops organized by
the management commission from February to May 2019. In the
end, the commission selected the urban design scheme proposed
by Skidmore, Owings & Merrill LLP (SOM) and Tom Leader
Studio (TLS).

Based on the evaluation of a jury of experts, this winning
scheme was selected for "its global vision, world-class standards,
sensitivity to Chinese heritage and culture, and innovative
approach to urban design"—the sort of language for imagining
the new Chinese city in Xiong'an and elsewhere: "[The scheme]
prioritized ecology and the human experience through several
urban design principles: respect the natural environment, create
holistic sustainable systems, and introduce green infrastructure;
establish an appropriate urban scale; integrate advanced technologies and a multi-modal public transit system; honor local
culture and lifestyle by infusing the urban space and landscape
with regional characteristics."[23]

A primary and critical question about building a city like
Xiong'an—from scratch and in the middle of nowhere—is,
"Where is the money coming from?" To address people's curios-
ity and concern at the outset, the official reportage confirmed
that the funding for Xiong'an would not rely on "land financing"
(*tu di cai zheng*) and real estate development, an approach that
has been employed by many city governments to source funding
for urban development through selling land for property development. This financing approach has characterized the rapid

urbanization of many Chinese cities but has also proven problematic, in that this singular financing source for urban development has contributed to the surge in property prices, housing unaffordability, and market bubbles.

In acquiring land for residential development, Xiong'an seems to be experimenting with a "new urbanization dividend distribution mechanism."[24] According to this mechanism, first, farmers are not to be compensated wholly for the lands acquired; instead, through their land contribution, they become shareholders of the urban development—together with the government and developers—and in the long run will receive benefits annually. Second, the newly built housing will be shared property between the government and the buyers; the government will buy the housing back if the buyers decide to sell their own portions of the housing ownership.

Xiong'an's new mechanism seems to be preventing market forces and private developers from actively participating in its development, at least in the early stages. However, it is not clear yet how Xiong'an will follow a "new" mechanism that would sustain the long duration and the large scale of its development. As of March 2023, the website of the Management Commission of Xiong'an New Area outlined a financing approach that includes fiscal support, innovative tax policies, multichannel financing, and clustering of financial resources. But the wording is generic and sweeping; it awaits substantiation and, more importantly, needs to be tested by practice and time.

As this chapter was written in mid-2021, it had been more than four years since Xiong'an was announced. The details about how it has been funded and how it is going to funded in the future have remained opaque; maybe all will never be disclosed. However, sporadic public information and media reportage show that so far it has been funded by the state through fiscal allocation, state bank loans, investment by SOEs, and intercity partnerships. The National Development and Reform Commission (NDRC), the agency in charge of nationwide planning and development, allocated RMB 3.5 billion from the central government's budget for Xiong'an in 2020; in June 2021, the NDRC allocated RMB 1.7 billion to Xiong'an.[25] However, the fiscal allocations, at both central and provincial government levels, are far from meeting the funding required for Xiong'an.

On April 27, 2017, the China Development Bank (CDB), a development finance agency under the State Council, signed a memorandum of understanding with the Hebei government agreeing to provide RMB 130 billion to fund infrastructure and environmental upgrading in Xiong'an and the planning and construction of the initial development zone.[26] According to its board director at the time, Hu Huaibang, the CDB further established its own leadership group to provide services for Xiong'an and was also planning to establish a subsidiary branch in Xiong'an. These commitments sounded more like Hu's declaration of political loyalty to Xi Jinping than a business decision on development investment. Ironically, Hu was arrested for corruption in 2019, after he retired from his position, and was sentenced to life imprisonment in January 2021.

Xiong'an was imagined and initiated to tackle the Beijing syndrome. It seems natural, therefore, that Beijing has some sort of obligation to support Xiong'an. The Beijing government has supported the construction of three schools (one kindergarten, one primary school, and one middle school) and one hospital, which were among the first group of projects built in Xiong'an. This support is more than merely the construction of the buildings, which commenced in September 2019; their operation is going to be supported by corresponding schools and hospital in

Beijing, which all have good reputations. The Beijing government has invested in these institutions, presumably expecting that these facilities will help attract Beijing residents to relocate to Xiong'an. The Beijing-Xiong'an partnership is representative of the model through which Xiong'an has been supported by other government agencies in multiple ways.

Xiong'an Civic Center is the first major project completed on the site, providing a glimpse of the city's development approach and funding model. Occupying a precinct of 24.24 hectares, this center is a mixed-use development of around 100,000 m², comprising spaces for civic, public, residential, and commercial uses. The different functions are organized in different blocks on the precinct, designed by several celebrity Chinese architects; together, they make up a business park with an architectural flavor that mixes the traditional and the modern. The project's funding and management are described as having followed a model of so-called special purpose vehicle, comprising the China Xiong'an Group—an SOE dedicated to Xiong'an development—and several development, design, and investment companies subordinate to the China State Construction Engineering Group. All are SOEs and have names starting with "China," according to public information available on the website of the China Xiong'an Group as of March 2023.

Xiong'an Civic Center is a state project; all the major infrastructure projects are also state projects. In December 2020, the Xiong'an Railway Station came into use, its high-speed trains taking twenty minutes to the new Beijing International Airport and fifty minutes to West Beijing Railway Station. By mid-2021, three major expressways linking Xiong'an with its surrounds had been completed and were in operation. Years after its announcement, Xiong'an seemed to be marching forward at an accelerated speed, propelled by a state development engine.

SHENZHEN, PUDONG, AND . . . XIONG'AN?

When Xiong'an was announced, it was compared, in the media and public perception, with Shenzhen and Pudong in terms of the making of new cities. The official discourse further proposed that Shenzhen represented China's urbanization in the 1980s, Pudong in the 1990s, and Xiong'an in the twenty-first century, implying that Xiong'an would surpass both predecessor cities in terms of urban vision, approach, and outcome.

The year 2020 marked the fortieth anniversary of Shenzhen and the thirtieth of Pudong. Xi Jinping attended the ceremonies for both anniversaries and made speeches on the significance of each of them in China's urbanization and reform and opening up, paying tribute to Deng Xiaoping, to whom the making of both cities was attributed. Presumably, when he celebrated the success of Shenzhen and Pudong, Xi Jinping might have been interested in knowing how future generations would appraise his city of Xiong'an.

Will Xiong'an replicate the success of Shenzhen and Pudong and even outperform them? Or is Xiong'an comparable to them at all?

My books *The Shenzhen Phenomenon* (2020) and *Global Shanghai Remade* (2019, coauthored with Weijie Chen) examine the decision-making, planning, and development of Shenzhen and Pudong. The settings and triggering factors for these cities were fundamentally different from those for Xiong'an. Deng Xiaoping did not select the site of Shenzhen by "drawing a circle beside the South China Sea," as described in the popular song "The Story of Spring" (*Chun tian de gu shi*), which is dedicated to the praise of Deng Xiaoping (see chapter 8). The genesis of Shenzhen came out of the ingenuity and boldness of local residents and local cadres, but Deng Xiaoping played the most important role in endorsing and supporting its growth in the 1980s and early 1990s. In 1979, when the idea of building a special economic zone (SEZ) near Hong Kong was first proposed to Deng by Xi Zhongxun, Xi Jinping's father and then party secretary of Guangdong Province, Deng indicated that the central government had no money but could offer some favorable policies. Deng encouraged Guangdong leaders to "slash a bloody way out" (*sha chu yi tiao xue lu*), to explore and experiment with a new, bold way to grow the local economy and improve livelihoods. This is the earliest episode in the Shenzhen story of building an international metropolis within forty years.

Pudong is the "new" Shanghai, to the east of the "old" Shanghai across the Huangpu River. Developing Pudong had been discussed through much of the late 1980s at the city level, but it lacked strong political vision and will to make it happen. Deng Xiaoping initiated the development of Pudong in 1990 as an "ace card" (*wang pai*) to relaunch his reform and opening-up agenda and to rebuild international confidence in it, both of which were stalled after the Tiananmen Square Incident in June 1989. As with the development of Shenzhen, the central government had no money to invest in Pudong, and nor did the city government. But Pudong was granted even more favorable policies than SEZs like Shenzhen in attracting FDI and growing the local economy. For this reason, and to differentiate itself from Shenzhen as an SEZ, Pudong was called a "new area," a designation that was meant to be "more special than special [economic zone]" (*bi te hai te*)—in the words of then Shanghai mayor Zhu Rongji—in terms of receiving favorable policies.[27] The compelling urban image of Pudong is now symbolic not only of a new Shanghai but also of a new China, one that has been transformed through rapid urbanization and economic growth.

Xiong'an is not envisioned to be another Shenzhen or Pudong per se: it is not going to be a new economic center, as they are. Xiong'an is a derivative city of Beijing, aiming to relieve the latter of functions not essential to its role as the national capital. Both Shenzhen and Pudong have relied heavily on FDI and learning about international planning and development. They were both pioneers of China's market reform, and thus market forces have played a crucial role in their growth. Contrary to the international aspirations of Shenzhen and Pudong, Xiong'an is set to advance a Chinese model of new-type urbanization in thinking and approach. Xiong'an is not going to replicate the urban morphology of Shenzhen and Pudong, which is manifestly international or Western. Instead, Xiong'an draws inspiration from the ancient Chinese philosophy of living and urban settlement; it fuses both the traditional and the modern into a new urban utopia with local authenticity. So far, the funding of Xiong'an has been from the state; it is not clear yet whether and how international investment and market forces may play a role in its future development. In all these senses, Xiong'an is not comparable to Shenzhen or Pudong.

However, what has linked Shenzhen, Pudong, and Xiong'an and made them comparable is the political will and power that has enabled, in all three cases, the imagining and making of a new Chinese city from scratch.

6

REORIENTING HONG KONG

On the morning of September 23, 2019, I was on a ferry from Shenzhen to Macau, a trip of forty minutes. When the ferry was in the middle of the Pearl River estuary, I looked around in awe: in front of me was a megastructure, a 55-km bridge that links Hong Kong on the left with Macau and Zhuhai on the right; behind me was a chain of cities including Shenzhen, Dongguan, Zhongshan, and Guangzhou, as well as other cities in Guangdong Province. This Pearl River delta region, commonly known as the Greater Bay Area (*Da wan qu*), is one of the three city regions—the other two are the Yangtze River delta region and the Beijing-Tianjin-Hebei region (see chapter 5)—that together constitute the backbone structure of China's urban system. They are the economic engines of the second-largest economy in the world; they are also the country's social and political power centers.

Geospatially, these cities in the Greater Bay Area are nestled around the area's greatest natural endowment: a bay, as its name suggests. They are interlinked by a multitude of transport modes, including bridges, tunnels, rails, and expressways, forming a one-hour commuting circle. Indeed, the Greater Bay Area has many features that are envied by its counterpart city regions in China and overseas. However, its uniqueness is not only geospatial but also historical, cultural, and political.

The Greater Bay Area has a unique "one country, two systems" (*yi guo liang zhi*) governance structure that separates Hong Kong and Macau from the other mainland cities. When I traveled between Shenzhen and Macau, I had to clear customs at both ends, in the same way as when I fly between Shanghai and Sydney. This governance structure has a historical backdrop. The area has witnessed several milestone moments in late Chinese history. In 1840, the British army invaded it, which resulted in the colonization of Hong Kong and ushered in more invasions of the area and into China by Western powers, including the colonization of Macau by the Portuguese.

Every Chinese student knows what the year 1840 means from their history textbooks. That year did not just mark the start of foreign invasions and a humiliating period in the long history of a great civilization; it also marked the beginning of the collapse of an ancient empire as well as the beginning of unrelenting efforts by the coming generations to rebuild one. One of the most impressive efforts was Deng Xiaoping's reform and opening up—a modernization and nation-building agenda, the first experiment of which occurred in the Greater Bay Area. The experiment was made, ironically, through capitalizing on the area's colonial legacies. In 1980, Shenzhen and Zhuhai were designated as special economic zones (SEZs)—together with Shantou and Xiamen in Fujian Province—to spearhead China's open-door policies, simply because of their proximity to Hong Kong and Macau. Deng was successful: he transformed the Greater Bay Area, invented one country, two systems, and, most importantly, remade China.

While my ferry was traveling across the estuary smoothly and peacefully, and I was lost in awe of a contemporary regional development miracle, I knew Hong Kong, not far away, was in a state of chaos and disorder. The city was experiencing the most disruptive, divisive, and controversial street movement since its return to China in 1997. That movement was ignited by a bill proposed by the Hong Kong government that would allow the extradition of criminal suspects to the mainland, Taiwan, and Macau. The extradition bill was later suspended and ultimately withdrawn in the same year under the pressure of protests and unrest. But the street movement did not cease; it kept escalating in scale, violence, and extremity.

In its later stages, the movement went far beyond concerns of a controversial extradition bill and involved social and political divisions within the city, the shifting Hong Kong-mainland relationship, and complex geopolitics. Readings of and responses to this street movement have been complicated; they depend on politics, ideologies, values, beliefs, and stances, often confusing fact with fiction and mixing information, misinformation, and disinformation.

Within the Greater Bay Area, what was happening in Hong Kong presented a contrast to other cities. In Macau, life was as usual: busy, vibrant, and full of visitors, many of whom were from the mainland, mostly on day trips. Shenzhen was in an upbeat mood: energetic, optimistic, and confident. In September 2019, when I was in the city, the streets were filled with numerous national flags, banners, and flowers, in readiness to celebrate the seventieth birthday of the PRC on October 1 (see chapter 3). The cityscape looked orderly, grand, and organized—the features of a young, rapidly growing city. Despite Hong Kong's proximity, its status did not stir as much interest or concern in Shenzhen as in the outside world. This "calmness" seemed to be based on mixed feelings of familiarity, indifference, and a bit of cynicism, as well as a sense of assurance and confidence that things in Hong Kong would be "solved" in the end.

One month earlier, in August, the central government announced its endorsement for building Shenzhen into a "pilot demonstration zone" of socialism with Chinese characteristics. This endorsement was an acknowledgment of the city's progress, as well as an expression of expectations for its future, at a time when the city was approaching its fortieth birthday in 2020. This endorsement had been planned for several years, but the timing of its announcement—when Hong Kong was experiencing an unprecedented crisis—triggered different interpretations. One was that the central government would build up Shenzhen to rival Hong Kong, or even to leave Hong Kong well behind, given the troublesome status of the latter. This, surely, was a misinterpretation, but it reflected a sort of uncertainty and anxiety about Hong Kong's future at the time.

From the severity of the 2019 street movement, people could foresee its likely aftermath and the changes that would happen to Hong Kong. As is now widely known, the central government imposed a national security law in 2020 and changed Hong Kong's electoral system in 2021, fundamentally restructuring the city's governance and institution. These changes happened at the midpoint of the fifty-year tenure of the one country, two systems policy for Hong Kong. Indeed, they are the turning point of the policy; they are also the turning point of the city's trajectory, reorienting Hong Kong in the regional, national, and international contexts.

PEARL OF THE ORIENT

Lo Ta-yu, a Taiwanese singer and songwriter, is one of the best-known and most respected cultural icons in Greater China and the Chinese diaspora. He moved to Hong Kong to restart his music career there in 1986. Prior to that time, he had escaped Taiwan and its political pressure on his songwriting freedom. He stayed in New York for a year. While artistic cross-fertilization between the East and the West enriched his musical creativity, he was disenchanted with life there—Lo relinquished his U.S. citizenship in 2004—and suffered cultural rootlessness.

Hong Kong seemed to be the right place for him and his music, for its political and artistic freedoms, its booming entertainment industry, and, most of all, its cultural affinity. In the same year that he arrived in Hong Kong, Lo wrote the music for a song called "Pearl of the Orient" (*Dong fang zhi zhu*), Hong Kong's nickname, to express his emotion and love for the city. Lo fused Eastern and Western music expressions into the song, acknowledging the very nature of the city as a connection of the East and the West. Its lyrics have two versions, in Cantonese and Mandarin. The Mandarin version, written by Lo himself, was formally released in 1991. It became an instant hit and is now a classic Chinese pop song. These are the translated lyrics.

> A winding river flows to the south
> Flows to Hong Kong to take a look
> Pearl of the Orient, my lover
> Is your elegance romantic as ever
>
> Crescent moon harbor
> The night is dark, the lights are bright
> Pearl of the Orient, stay up all night
> Keep the promise despite the vicissitudes of life
>
> Let the sea breeze blow for 5,000 years
> As if every teardrop speaks to your dignity
> Let the waves accompany me to protect you
> Please never forget my unwavering yellow face

A boat meanders into the harbor
Turn around, look at the vast and hazy sea
The Pearl of the Orient is embracing me
Let me warm up your cold chest[1]

The late 1980s and early 1990s were a golden age of Hong Kong's pop culture and entertainment industry. It was also an age of uncertainty and anxiety, socially and politically. The city was in a countdown to its return to China in 1997. The coming reunification with the motherland was accompanied by complicated emotions and perceptions about the mainland. At that time, Hong Kong was already an international metropolis and a developed economy, bearing most of the hallmarks depicted and imagined for a Western society: dynamism, freedoms, and prosperity. The Western stereotype of the mainland, in contrast, was one of backwardness, poverty, and repression. The prospect of national unification did not generate hope and excitement; rather, it created fear and lack of confidence in the city's future. It even created a short wave of emigration and flight of capital, which were later reversed along with the soothing of the shock and the growing opportunities brought to Hong Kong by the mainland's economic boom. Cultural kinship and ideological alienation contradicted each other in many Hong Kongers' perceptions about, and (un)acceptance of, the mainland and motherland.

Lo's song captured a mentality in Hong Kong at a time when the city was transitioning from a colonial past to an uncertain postcolonial future. Lo was a newcomer: his reading of Hong Kong was neither parochial nor Western; it was cultural and historical—a prominent theme in Lo's music. His song sympathized with the city's colonial suffering and humiliation; it took great pride in its historical origins and cultural roots. The song's popularity cannot be explained just by Lo's artistic expression; it has stricken a deep chord with many Chinese in light of the nation's history since it was first invaded by the British army in 1840 and Hong Kong was ceded. The song situated the story of Hong Kong against a longer historical experience and a wider cultural scenario: Hong Kong is more than a city delimited by its geography and size; it is integral to a nation's past and future, substantially and emotionally. In large part for this reason, Lo's song was included by the Chinese government in a list of patriotic songs when it celebrated the one hundredth birthday of the CPC in 2021, even though patriotism may not have been part of Lo's artistic inspiration or intention.

A revisiting of Lo's song—a product of three decades ago—reminds us of a cultural and historical perspective on Hong Kong. This perspective is often prevailed over or sidelined in the recent debates and controversies about the city, which are dominated by politics and geopolitics. Hong Kong, the place where the East and the West converged for so long in a cultural sense during much of the colonial period, has become a place where the East and the West increasingly diverge in a (geo)political sense in the postcolonial period. The Pearl of the Orient was made by the East-West fusion. It is being remade by the East-West confrontation, within the city and outside it.

A CITY GOES ASTRAY

For much of the second half of 2019, the escalation of the street movement in Hong Kong, and the extremity of its actions and outcomes, concerned people with connections to this city—personally, culturally, or emotionally. During this period, I had meetings with several colleagues who were originally from Hong Kong, and our conversations would always end with some discussions about what was happening in their hometown.

Several common themes emerged from these conversations, although they were, of course, personal and anecdotal. First, street movements have not been uncommon in Hong Kong, but the movement this time seemed different in nature, scale, and destruction. For these colleagues, Hong Kongers are not generally political animals, and there could be complex factors—internal and external—behind the scenes. Second, they expressed grave concern and disappointment that the city has provided its ordinary residents—young people especially—with very limited, or nearly no, opportunities for surviving and prospering in this most "capitalist" city. The long-existing and worsening social stratification and economic difficulty in the city has underlain many of its problems and increasing political unrest. Third, they were critical of the Hong Kong government for its incompetence in solving the city's problems and listening to the people's voices. In comparison, they were less critical of the central government—to my surprise—but still pointed out that the distant central government failed to know and engage with the "real" Hong Kong.

What is the real Hong Kong, one that not many outsiders (in the mainland and the world) would fully comprehend? I decided to see it for myself, and my colleagues asked a local friend to show me around. On September 24, 2019, when Hong Kong was in an uncertain state and it was inadvisable to visit, I arrived there from Shenzhen—a fourteen-minute commute by the high-speed rail system that links Hong Kong with the mainland. The local friend did an excellent job of showing me around the real Hong Kong. She took me to the Central, the glamourous financial center that has (mis)represented the image and reading of Hong Kong: international, dynamic, prosperous, and wealthy. She also took me to Sham Shui Po, a community in contrast to the Central in cityscape and social structure (figure 6.1).

FIGURE 6.1 A city in duality: Central and Sham Shui Po in Hong Kong

Source: The author.

We explored several local communities where not many visitors would go, but they told more about Hong Kong than the Central.

I had visited Hong Kong before. Like many visitors, my engagement with the city during those visits had been no more than the most advanced international airport, a five-star hotel, the Central, and the harbor—all the iconic and breath-taking elements that have constructed the imagery of Hong Kong as a leading international metropolis. There is another Hong Kong that has been largely missing in the perception and understanding of the city, for outsiders and probably in terms of the government's policy focus. Hong Kong is a city in duality.

I visited Hong Kong on a weekday; my local guide said the protests would normally happen on weekends. Nevertheless, I could still observe and feel that the city was not in a normal state. The damage and graffiti in public spaces were fresh and agitating, betraying what had happened just days ago. On every public exhibit board in a local community or school that we passed by, there were plenty of posts that contained slogans or text venting

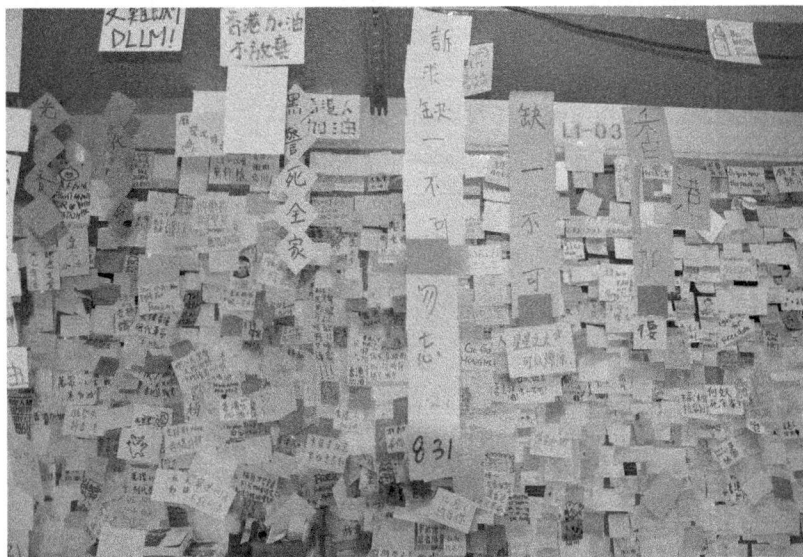

FIGURE 6.2 Public posts in opposition to the government and
police in Hong Kong

Source: The author.

anger at the government or the police, including curses and
personal attacks (figure 6.2). These posts seemed to be written
mostly by young people or students, judging from their tone and
handwriting. We did see several middle school students standing in front of one such board, reading those posts in detail and
adding several themselves before they left. In fact, many of the
protesters were indeed young people, including college and even
middle school students. Every sign seemed to suggest that the
city was experiencing frustration, disappointment, and anger.
In 2019, the controversial extradition bill simply detonated an
explosion that had been in the making in the decades after the
city's return to China.

Hong Kong's internal problems have been situated in a rapidly changing outside environment. Since Hong Kong's return to China in 1997, its position in relation to the Greater Bay Area and the national urban system has been shifting rapidly. The macro backdrop to this shift is the rapid rise of the mainland and the relative decline of Hong Kong.

This shifting relationality is the most salient in an economic sense. Hong Kong had, in the past, arguably played the most important role in the urbanization and industrialization of the Greater Bay Area, and even of the mainland. But this role has become history. In 1997, Hong Kong's share of China's GDP was 18.4 percent; the historical peak for its GDP share was 27 percent in 1993, and it had fallen to 2.7 percent by 2018.[2] An even starker contrast can be seen between the economic trajectories of Hong Kong and Shenzhen: in 2017, Shenzhen's GDP surpassed Hong Kong's for the first time. This was unimaginable in 1980, when Shenzhen was first designated as an SEZ and when it remained largely a rural area, often referred to as a fishing village. Within the Chinese urban system, three cities—Shanghai, Beijing, and Shenzhen—have now surpassed Hong Kong in GDP value. Further, they are challenging, if not replacing, Hong Kong's role as China's gateway city and as a strategic urban node of the global economy.[3]

A comparison with Singapore presents an international perspective on how Hong Kong's economy has fared in recent decades. As of 2020, Hong Kong had a population of 7.5 million and a land area of 1,110 km^2; Singapore had a population 5.7 million and a land area of 719 km^2.[4] Both cities belong to the Four Little Dragons, which rapidly industrialized their economies in the post–World War II decades,[5] and both have become leading global cities and financial centers across the century. Their rise signified, in a way, the start of the shifting of the world economic center to the Asia-Pacific region and the coming of an Asian century. Their success has greatly inspired and informed the development of Chinese and other Asian cities. They have shared cultural and historical backgrounds connecting the East and the West and followed similar development approaches in the late twentieth century.

However, in the twenty-first century, the development trajectories of the two cities have been bifurcating, as measured by their economic performance. Hong Kong's GDP, for a long period, had been consistently higher than Singapore's (figure 6.3). But this gap started to narrow from the mid-1990s until 2010, when Singapore's GDP surpassed Hong Kong's for the first time; Singapore's lead has been mostly constant ever since. In terms of GDP per capita, the two cities had similar figures and

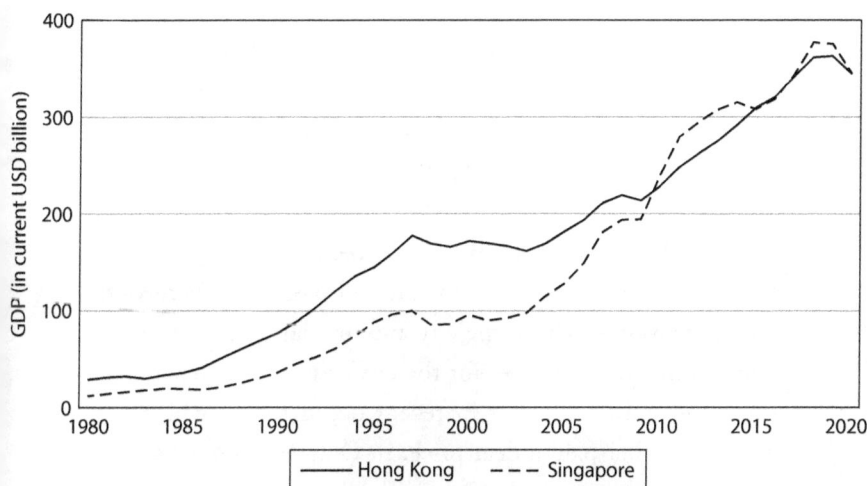

FIGURE 6.3 GDP of Hong Kong and Singapore, 1980–2020

Source: Created by the author using data from World Bank, "GDP (Current USs)," accessed January 19, 2023, https://data.worldbank.org/indicator/NY.GDP.PCAP.CD.

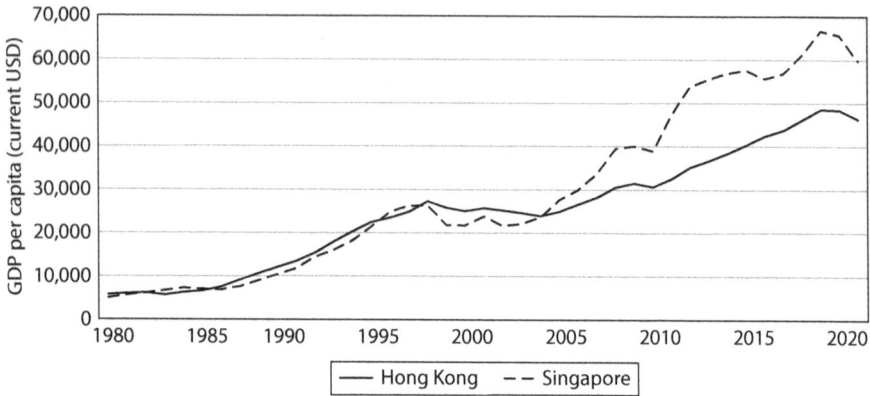

FIGURE 6.4 GDP per capital of Hong Kong and Singapore, 1980–2020

Source: Created by the author using data from World Bank, "GDP per Capita (Current USs)," accessed January 20, 2023, https://data.worldbank.org/indicator /NY.GDP.PCAP.CD.

followed similar growth patterns until 2004, when Singapore surpassed Hong Kong; this gap has been growing ever since (figure 6.4). As of 2020, Hong Kong's GDP was nearly the same as Singapore's, but its GDP per capita was 81 percent of Singapore's.

Hong Kong's competitiveness is being challenged by its counterpart cities in the mainland and overseas. There were economic roots—within the city and in relation to the rise of China and globalization—for the city's escalating social divisions and political unrest in recent decades,[6] for which the city has further paid a dear price. In October 2019, when the street movement turned increasingly violent, a cartoon—said to be published in a Singapore newspaper—was posted in a Hong Kong news discussion website.[7] In this cartoon, a group of protesters are digging bricks from the foundation of a building imprinted with name "Hong Kong" and throwing the bricks at the police. The comments on the post—assumed to be made by Hong Kongers—were critical of the radicalization of the protesters and the damages they were doing to their home city, expressing anger and satire that Hong Kong was being laughed at by people elsewhere who would not really care about the city. This cartoon was instantly transmitted in the mainland's social media, which echoed similar ethos and concerns. Hong Kong was being split internally, and so was the reading of it externally.

"A BEAUTIFUL SIGHT" IN CONTEST

Chinese audiences observed the George Floyd protests and the Black Lives Matter movement in U.S. cities with great interest through much of 2020; this interest reached its climax during the Capitol attack on January 6, 2021. They observed the evolution of these events into violence, how they were responded to by the government and police, and how they were covered by the media and commented on by pundits. The street movement in Hong Kong only months before was still a fresh memory; what happened in the United States were ready analogies.

In Chinese social media, the term "a beautiful sight" (*yi dao mei li de feng jing xian*) was often quoted in mockery of the turmoil of the U.S. events. The term was said to be used by Nancy Pelosi, then speaker of the House of Representatives, to describe the street movement (and, by implication, its violence) in Hong Kong. This was a misrepresentation. Pelosi used the term to refer to a related occurrence, but in a different context, in Hong Kong.

On June 4, 2019, she delivered testimony at the Congressional Executive Commission on China and the Tom Lantos Human Rights Commission hearing:

> I just want to point out to you, as you were speaking right now, someone gave me a picture of a candlelight vigil in Victoria Square in Hong Kong, where tens of thousands of people are doing a candlelight vigil in honor of those who lost their lives in Tiananmen Square and other uprisings around China. So, this is happening as we speak. . . . Well, let me just thank you for showing that picture of what is happening in Hong Kong because that is the only place in China where people are able to speak out. It is *a beautiful sight* [italics added] to behold and I commend the courage of the people there for speaking out in light of China's actions in Hong Kong these days.[8]

Here, "a beautiful sight" by Pelosi referred to the picture of a candlelight vigil commemorating the thirtieth anniversary of the Tiananmen Square Incident, which involved the killing of students and civilians by the army. That incident has been a taboo topic in mainland China. Hong Kong was the only Chinese territory in which it could be publicly debated and commemorated. However, the candlelight vigil in 2019 was probably its finale in Hong Kong. For three years after, the Hong Kong police banned such vigils, citing COVID-19 social distancing restrictions. In September 2021, the organizing body of the vigils declared it would disband under pressure of the new national security law.

The term used by Nancy Pelosi, and how it has been misrepresented, reflect a profound difference between China and the United States (and the West in a broader sense) in Hong Kong affairs. Ideology bifurcates the reading of them, and geopolitics complicates the evolution of and responses to them. In the

West, Hong Kong was readily and easily placed in a discourse of democracy, human rights, and freedoms; for China, these terms were just instrumentalized to cover up the double standards, hypocrisy, and interference behind the scenes. This bifurcation has caused misreading and misrepresentation of the complexity of things in the city; this complexity is far more than what either set of these stereotyped discourses can tell. Hong Kong, previously the connector between the East and the West, is being repositioned as a new battlefield between them in areas not only of ideological difference and geopolitical confrontation but also of discourse power (*hu yu quan*), which, for China, remains one of Western hegemony.

Regina Ip, a legislator and member of the Executive Council in Hong Kong, published an op-ed in *The New York Times* on October 1, 2020. Entitled "Hong Kong Is China, Like It or Not," the opinion piece appeared nearly a year after the 2019 street movement. During that interval, the central government had imposed a national security law, and China and the West had mutually criticized, accused, and sanctioned each other with regard to Hong Kong affairs. Ip's piece served as a reminder, through a mainstream Western newspaper, of several fundamental elements of Hong Kong's reality.

No amount of outcry, condemnation or sanctions over the Chinese government's purported encroachment in Hong Kong's affairs will alter the fact that Hong Kong is part of China and that its destiny is intertwined with the mainland's. . . . Hong Kongers who wanted the city promptly to return to peace thought the authorities' handling of the situation, which dragged on for months and grew more and more violent, was incompetent. For other locals, many outsiders and apparently much of the global media, a people's legitimate quest for more democracy was being suppressed. . . . Something had to be done, and the Chinese authorities did it. . . . The West tends to glorify these people as defenders of Hong Kong's freedoms, but they have done great harm to the city by going against its constitutional order and stirring up chaos and disaffection toward our motherland.

Like it or not, Hong Kong is part of China. And given the two's vast disparity in size and Hong Kong's growing economic dependence on the mainland, the city's progressive integration with China is unavoidable. . . . *A realistic goal for Hong Kong ought to be remaining the freest and most international city in China and retaining its unique international status* [italics added], thanks to the city's many bilateral agreements with foreign countries and its membership in numerous international organizations.[9]

THE "ONE COUNTRY, TWO SYSTEMS" MYTH

Deng Xiaoping invented one country, two systems for Hong Kong, Macau, and Taiwan, which were separated from mainland China for various reasons: Hong Kong and Macau were colonized as a result of foreign invasions; Taiwan was a legacy of the 1946–1949 civil war between the communists and the nationalists, in which the latter were defeated and fled to Taiwan. This policy was first applied to Hong Kong and has attracted the most debates concerning the city's relationship with its motherland.

As an umbrella principle, one country, two systems was a great invention, combining boldness, imagination, compromise, and pragmatism. However, its interpretations and implementations have been shaped by various forces and circumstances, all of which are evolving and changing. Readings of the policy and its effects are often colored by stances, interests, ideologies, and geopolitics, as we have observed in recent decades. One common (mis)reading is that one country, two systems is a policy assuring Hong Kong's freedoms, autonomy, and democracy—in a Western sense—while it is unified with China constitutionally within one sovereign state. Even though Hong Kong was neither a democracy nor autonomous before its handover, a selective reading of one country, two systems created such an imagining. Pursuing this imagining has been a frustrating process, since it has been built on wishful thinking rather than reality, deviating from the original basis and rationale for the policy as designed and expressed by Deng Xiaoping.

For Deng, one country, two systems was not about Hong Kong's democracy and autonomy: strategically, it was about national unification; tactically, it was about his modernization agenda of reform and opening up, in which Hong Kong played an indispensable role when the policy was designed in the 1980s. Deng was a far-seeing strategist; he was also a shrewd politician. He had a sharp comprehension of the historical, political, and social complexity in Hong Kong, which was rooted in the city's colonial DNA and associated with communist China's ideological difference from and geopolitical conflict with the West.

On several key occasions when discussing Hong Kong's future, Deng warned of possible instability, which could be caused by "destructive forces" inside and outside the city and might happen both before and after its handover. For Deng, Hong Kong's "prosperity" (*fan rong*) and "stability" (*wen ding*) mattered much more than its democracy and autonomy. Deng was an ardent believer in the limitations of Western democracy: he considered the Western political system a challenge to the prosperity and stability of Hong Kong. He also justified the necessity of the central government's intervention into Hong

Kong affairs in certain uncontrollable circumstances. He stressed these points repeatedly, as the quotes below demonstrate.

In October 1984, when meeting with a Hong Kong delegation to Beijing, Deng said,

> Do not just worry about interventions generally. Certain interventions are necessary. We need to see if the interventions are conducive or harmful to the interests of Hong Kongers and Hong Kong's prosperity and stability. . . . Don't assume that there are no destructive forces. . . . Once turmoil happens [in Hong Kong], the central government should intervene. . . . There will be some factors of turmoil, troublemaking, and instability. Honestly, these factors won't come from Beijing; they may exist within Hong Kong or come from certain international forces.[10]

In April 1987, when meeting with the committee for drafting the Hong Kong Special Administrative Region (SAR) Basic Law (a bespoke miniconstitution for Hong Kong after its handover), Deng articulated his views on one country, two systems most comprehensively. He emphasized,

> Hong Kong's [political] system should not be completely Westernized, should not just transplant the Western way. . . . If we just completely transplant, for example, the separation of powers and the British or American parliamentary systems, and judge whether it is a democracy according to this, I'm afraid it is inappropriate. . . . For Hong Kong, is universal suffrage definitely advantageous? I don't believe it. . . . The people who govern Hong Kong affairs must be those Hong Kongers who are patriots of the motherland and Hong Kong. Will universal suffrage definitely elect the right people? . . . Don't assume that Hong Kong affairs will be the responsibility of Hong Kongers only, and the central

government won't care at all, and then everything will be ok. This is impossible, and this thought is unrealistic. The central government won't intervene into the daily business of the SAR; it is unnecessary. But will there be events in the SAR that will damage the fundamental national interests? Won't they happen? . . . Think about it soberly: will Hong Kong sometimes have problems that cannot be solved without Beijing's involvement? . . . What if Hong Kong is turned into an antimainland base under the pretext of "democracy"? Then we must intervene.[11]

In June 1988, Deng said,

Hong Kong needs stability. It needs to be stable during the transition period; it also needs to be stable after China resumes sovereignty and Hong Kongers are responsible for governing. This is the key. Hong Kong's stability, apart from economic development, requires a stable political system. . . . Hong Kong's political system today is neither the British system nor the American system, and it should not transplant the Western way in the future.[12]

Deng Xiaoping made these statements and warnings more than thirty years ago. They seemed to anticipate many political episodes happening in the city before and after its handover in 1997.

In 1994–1995, the last colonial governor, Chris Patten, introduced an electoral reform to broaden the democratic base of elections, which created the first—as well as the only—fully elected legislature in Hong Kong's history. This reform was highly controversial, causing a political storm in the city and between the Chinese and British governments in those years. Although the reform was reversed and the legislature was dissolved on the handover, they significantly impacted the city's political landscape for a long time afterward. There could be well-grounded justification and legitimacy for this reform of democratization in Hong Kong, but the timing of introducing it in the last several years of the colonial rule that spanned one and a half centuries betrayed its multiple intentions. For Beijing, this reform was "troublemaking" by "destructive forces" under the pretext of "democracy"—all the words said by Deng Xiaoping in the 1980s.

Since the handover, various episodes of political unrest, mixed with the city's economic fluctuations and social problems, have challenged and transformed the perception and practice of one country, two systems. But the fundamentals of the policy were clearly defined and delineated by its inventor, Deng Xiaoping: Hong Kong would not be democratized in a Western sense; it would not be autonomous in a complete sense; patriotic Hong Kongers would govern the city; the central government would intervene should Hong Kong turn into a pocket of turmoil or an antimainland base. These fundamentals have been at the heart of the construction and reconstruction of one country, two systems in different contexts.

In June 2014, the central government released a white paper on one country, two systems in Hong Kong—the first paper of its type—clarifying and affirming its "comprehensive jurisdiction" (*quan mian guan zhi quan*) over the Hong Kong SAR as a level of local administrative region:

> As a unitary state, China's central government has comprehensive jurisdiction over all local administrative regions, including the [Hong Kong] SAR. The high degree of autonomy of Hong Kong SAR is not an inherent power, but one that comes solely from the authorization by the central leadership. The high degree of autonomy of the Hong Kong SAR is not full autonomy, nor a

decentralized power. It is the power to run local affairs as authorized by the central leadership. The high degree of autonomy of
Hong Kong SAR is subject to the level of the central leadership's
authorization. There is no such thing called "residual power."[13]

This central-local administrative hierarchy and the central government's comprehensive jurisdiction, while being established on
the fundamentals of one country, two systems, disappointed many
who imagined Hong Kong's democratization and wished for its
alternative political relationship with Beijing.[14]

A "CHINESE" CITY IN REBIRTH?

Is Hong Kong a Chinese city? Yes it is, constitutionally and
jurisdictionally. However, when answering this question, many
people may pause for thought about what that means culturally
and emotionally. The city's colonial history and unique governance structure of one country, two systems differentiate it from
other Chinese cities. Demographically and culturally, Hong
Kong is a cosmopolitan city: while the Chinese are the predominant ethnic group, many Hong Kongers are from non-Chinese
backgrounds. The perception of Hong Kongers as merely Chinese compatriots is inaccurate and incorrect. These factors qualify Hong Kong as the most "un-Chinese" Chinese city.

Economically, Hong Kong's integration with the Greater
Bay Area and the mainland, a process that already had some
momentum before its return, has been accelerating along with
the rapid growth of the Chinese economy.[15] But cultural and
social integration has followed a different trajectory. The unification of Hong Kong and the mainland has not brought the
two social groups closer; instead, they have been further divided

by a series of social and political events in Hong Kong. Around 2010, there was a conspicuous antimainland sentiment in Hong Kong; and in the mainland, there was an explicit sense of disillusionment with Hong Kong.[16] Within Hong Kong, a city-state mentality, localism, and even populism have been on the rise in recent decades, in great part driven by the escalating political unrest and frustrations in pursuing the city's democratization and freedoms, as many Hong Kongers had wished for under one country, two systems. Since its return, the city has experienced a series of political movements, transforming its political landscape and governance trajectory (table 6.1).

Unsurprisingly, the 2019 street movement and its backlashes are reorienting Hong Kong, speeding up its identification as, and transformation into, a Chinese city. The central government changed the high-level officials in charge of Hong Kong affairs in early 2020: Luo Huining was appointed as director of the Liaison Office of the Central People's Government in Hong Kong on January 4; Xia Baolong was appointed as director of the Hong Kong and Macau Affairs Office on February 13. Both appointees are veteran provincial party secretaries. They resumed their political careers in a sort of alien area, probably reflecting the central government's hope of bringing some fresh thinking and new approaches to Hong Kong affairs through these appointees' political experience and leadership.

One common observation and criticism in the mainland was that the leadership of Hong Kong affairs at both the central government and SAR government levels needed to be revamped, drawing on the lessons of the city's poor governance since its return. At the central government level, the leadership of Hong Kong affairs had been traditionally taken by cadres with career backgrounds in diplomacy and international relations. They lack the political vision and skills to tackle the

TABLE 6.1 MAJOR POLITICAL MOVEMENTS IN HONG KONG

Movements	Time	Causes	Aftermaths
Anti–Article 23 protest	July 1, 2003	The Hong Kong government introduced an antisubversion bill according to Article 23 of the Basic Law.	The Hong Kong government withdrew the bill.
National education protests	July–September 2012	The Hong Kong government attempted to introduce a national educational curriculum covering Chinese history, culture, and national identity.	The Hong Kong government gave up the attempt.
Umbrella Movement/ Occupy Central	September–December 2014	In June 2014, the central government released a white paper to affirm its "comprehensive jurisdiction" over Hong Kong. On August 31, 2014, the National People's Congress made a decision on limited universal suffrage for the 2017 chief executive's election.	The seventy-nine-day occupation of Central ceased and was cleared by police. The decision of the National People's Congress was rejected by Hong Kong's Legislative Council in June 2015.
Rally for Hong Kong's independence	August 2016	The electoral commission banned six proindependence candidates from running in elections for the Legislative Council.	The Hong Kong government declared the proindependence Hong Kong National Party illegal in 2018.
Antiextradition movement	March–December 2019	The Hong Kong government attempted to introduce a bill that would allow extradition to the mainland.	The Hong Kong government withdrew the extradition bill in September 2019. The central government imposed a national security law in June 2020. The central government changed the electoral system for the chief executive and the Legislative Council in March 2021.

complexity of Hong Kong and have failed to engage with the people and real issues within the city. Meanwhile, the long British rule of Hong Kong and the short history of its return have created a situation in which the top administrators within the SAR government have been mostly elevated from a public service background. They are not homegrown political leaders who are expected to have the sort of political vision, wisdom, capacity, responsibility, and experience needed for governing the city in adversity.

The appointment of veteran party secretaries to take charge of Hong Kong affairs came as a surprise to people who had been pondering, during and after 2019, what Hong Kong's future might hold. Even more of a surprise were the measures taken by the central government after these appointments. On June 30, 2020, the National People's Congress (NPC), China's legislative body and nominally the highest organ of state power, passed the Law of the People's Republic of China on Safeguarding National Security in the Hong Kong Special Administrative Region; on March 11, 2021, the NPC further enacted the Decision on Improving the Electoral System of the Hong Kong Special Administrative Region.

The 2020 national security law and the 2021 electoral system change indeed constitute the most fundamental transformation of Hong Kong's governance, responding to many issues and tensions that have been accumulating since its return and culminated in 2019. The scale and extremity of the 2019 movement exposed many of the structural problems—economic polarization, social division, and political distrust—within Hong Kong and between Hong Kong and the mainland, which further involved geopolitical complexities. The 2019 movement ultimately wore out the central government's patience—especially in light of its concerns about national unification and security—as well as its confidence in the capacity of Hong Kong's self-governance.

A similar national security law was supposed to be enacted in and by Hong Kong SAR under Article 23 of the Basic Law. However, for twenty-three years after the city's return to China, this law could not get through because of strong opposition based on concerns over its potential impacts on human rights and freedoms of expression and assembly. The central government always had the legitimacy to enforce such a law. It did not do so, with unusual patience, tolerance, and probably goodwill. In theory, Hong Kong remained somewhat undefended for twenty-three years—which global city operates without having some type of national security law in place? But now that this law has been in effect, the timing and manner of its enaction, and its draconian and sweeping provisions—an intentional policy design—are raising justifiable concerns over its potential (mis) use to clamp down on dissent in the name of national security.

The electoral system change adheres to the principle of "patriots governing Hong Kong" set by Deng Xiaoping for one country, two systems, changing the election methods and processes for the chief executive and Legislative Council (LegCo). For the chief executive, the new system increased the membership of the Election Committee—the electoral college—from 1,200 to 1,500: 967 elected seats (reduced from the previous 1,034), 156 nominated seats (increased from the previous 60), and 377 ex-officio seats (increased from the previous 106). The new system increased the number of seats in the LegCo from 70 to 90: 20 being directly elected seats (reduced from the previous 35), 30 seats indirectly elected by trade-based functional constituencies (professional or special interest groups), and 40 seats elected by the new 1,500-member Election Committee. These measures aim to ensure that the "right" people—right for the central government—will be "elected" to work in and with the Hong Kong SAR government, which has been previously impacted and even paralyzed by the political divisions and confrontations in the LegCo.

This change systematically prevents antigovernment or broadly prodemocracy candidates, and possibly those who might be foreign-influenced, from entering the governance system. Most of all, it puts an end to any imagining or wishful thinking that someday Hong Kong would be democratized in a Western sense.

On December 19, 2021, the seventh LegCo election was held under the new electoral system. The central government achieved what it wanted: nearly all seats were taken by proestablishment "patriots," with only one nonestablishment member elected. But Hong Kongers also cast their ballots in alternative ways: the turnout rate was 30.2 percent, the lowest in the history of LegCo elections, in sharp contrast to the local council elections in November 2019, which had a turnout rate of 71 percent and in which prodemocracy candidates won 90 percent of seats.[17]

One day after the seventh LegCo election, the central government released a second white paper on "democratic progress" in Hong Kong—following the first one released in June 2014—and affirmed the central government's comprehensive jurisdiction over Hong Kong. In this white paper, the central government expressed its definition of "democracy" in Hong Kong and confirmed an executive-led governance arrangement to ensure the city's governance capacity and efficacy:

> There is no single set of criteria for democracy and no single model of democracy that is universally acceptable. . . . The political system of the Hong Kong SAR applies locally. . . . The system of democracy in Hong Kong should not be a replica of some other model. . . . The central authorities have the final say in

determining the system of democracy in the Hong Kong SAR, which is a matter of national sovereignty and security, a reflection of the nature of the relationship between the central authorities and the Hong Kong SAR.

In developing democracy in Hong Kong, it is imperative to implement the executive-led system and consolidate the Chief Executive's core position and authority in the region's governance. There should be strong and steady support for the Chief Executive and the Hong Kong SAR government in the LegCo to end the long-standing conflict between the legislature and the executive and resolve the internal strife within the LegCo. This will enable Hong Kong and its government to focus on economic development, improve people's lives, and boost Hong Kong's strengths in the face of fierce international competition.[18]

On January 5, 2022, Xia Baolong met with around twenty newly elected LegCo members in Shenzhen. Xia reiterated the views expressed in the foregoing quotation, stressing that Hong Kong's governance model was executive-led and the legislative branch's role was to check and balance the executive branch while cooperating with it.[19] Xia urged them to support the SAR government and, as patriots, to safeguard national sovereignty, security, and development. He further highlighted that developing the economy and improving livelihoods should be the city's priority. Xia reaffirmed the central government's interest and sincerity in developing democracy in Hong Kong. But, he stated, the democracy should be aligned to the city's actual situation and to one country, two systems, and it should not be a Western-style democracy.

On May 8, 2022, in the election of the sixth term of Chief Executive John Lee, the only candidate and a firm "patriot," won it unanimously.

Hong Kong is being reoriented by the central government's forceful interventions in critical situations within and outside the city. These interventions, and situations that have ultimately led to them, would instantly remind people in (mainland) China of Deng Xiaoping's prophecies and warnings made in the 1980s. Deng's notions for one country, two systems have bolstered the central government's commitment to top-down interventions. In principle, none of these interventions is a deviation: they are a return to the fundamentals set by Deng Xiaoping. At an operational level, these interventions responded to the changing circumstances confronting Hong Kong and its governance structure.

There is a current discourse—within the mainland at least—that one country, two systems is shifting from a passive to an active mode and that Hong Kong is being returned for the second time. The central government's interventions were triggered by the 2019 street movement. Strategically, they have in large part drawn on some critical reflections on Hong Kong's bumpy road after its return and on the governance and policy failures at both the central government and SAR government levels under one country, two systems—itself an experimental policy design. There are also concerns and criticism that these interventions have gone too far and that Hong Kong is being "mainlandized," which is not in the original design of one country, two systems, however.

What will the future of Hong Kong look like?

What happened in 2019 may not happen again. Hong Kong's prosperity and stability, as highlighted by the Chinese government before the city's handover, will continue to be the key words and primary policy goals of one country, two systems in rhetoric and practice. The central government, on several strategic occasions, has committed to strengthening Hong Kong's governance capacity, rejuvenating its economy, and enhancing the livelihood of its residents. The *14th Five-Year Plan* (2021–2025) reaffirmed the central government's support for growing Hong Kong's competitive advantages in finance, high-end business services, and innovation, and for its integration with national development.[20] On August 23, 2021, at a public event promoting the *14th Five-Year Plan* organized by the Hong Kong SAR government, Luo Huining, the central government's top representative in Hong Kong, stated that the city was transitioning from chaos to order and was facing a new round of historic opportunities from integrating into national development; he urged Hong Kong to grasp these opportunities firmly.[21]

Several recent activities and remarks by Luo Huining seemed to suggest some gestures toward new policy approaches. In 2021, on the eve of China's National Day, October 1, in Hong Kong, Luo visited tenants of the "cage home" (*long wu*)—an extremely crowded living arrangement with wire-mesh hutches stacked on top of each other—and other community residents to listen to people at the grassroots level. Luo expressed, on behalf of the central government, concerns about their livelihoods and promised "people-centric" development measures like housing provision.[22] Luo had made similar visits to the underprivileged social groups before the National Day in 2020 and the Chinese Spring Festival in 2021.

Government leaders visiting ordinary or poor residents and households is a routine practice in the mainland, which normally happens before festivals, as a token to show that the government cares for people. It was an alien practice in Hong Kong: before 2019, officials in Hong Kong assigned by the central government shunned direct engagement with local communities in light of the principles of one country, two systems. Luo Huining changed this nonparticipation or noninterference approach. Transferring a community engagement practice from the mainland to Hong Kong, Luo was explicit about the central government's stance on direct connection with Hong Kong's people as well as direct intervention in the governance and well-being of the local communities. Following in the steps of Luo, Hong Kong's then chief executive, Carrie Lam, visited residents living in transitory housing—a type of social housing converted from nonhousing or underutilized space uses—on October 10, 2021, pledging the SAR government's commitment to housing provision and affordability.

These visits by Luo and Lam seemed to be a lesson learned from the 2019 street movement—a way to avoid the dangers of disengagement between the government and the people. These visits looked so "un-Hong Kong": they were more than a political gesture; they marked a substantial shift in governance thinking and approach. It is reported that Luo Huining's team in the liaison office conducted an outreach campaign, which was said to become a regular act in the future, to listen to ordinary Hong Kongers and gauge public sentiment; following this engagement, they prepared a to-do list of five hundred items for the SAR government to address.[23] Certainly, since Luo's appointment as director, the liaison office has been outspoken in commenting on Hong Kong affairs, including justification of the central government's new intervention measures there and criticism of the local prodemocracy bodies and Western responses.

Interpretations of the liaison office's actions differ: are they representative of the central government's strengthened engagement with the people and of its support for the SAR government? Or are they simply top-down interference in Hong Kong's autonomy through deploying a second, shadow government in the city? Answers to these questions depend on perspectives and stances. But in any case, the changed behavior of the liaison office likely signifies the changes to come, and probably also the central government's lack of confidence—if not distrust—in Hong Kong's self-governance capacity and its path dependence from the colonial period.

It is anticipated that the central government will support the SAR government, with delegated policy tools and state resources, to address the political divisions and resultant governance ineffectiveness in Hong Kong, and the city's enlarging economic inequality and enduring social problems. Some of the structural problems have been present in Hong Kong for a long time. But they have not been given sufficient policy attention in a city that has inherited a "capitalist" tradition of small government and a free market; or solutions to the problems have been constrained by the weak governance capacity. These problems, however, are the root causes of the series of street movements in the twenty-first century—this is a view in the mainland.

Hong Kong will be further integrated in the regional development of the Greater Bay Area and the national development system, a process that had begun before 2019 and is being accelerated. At the same time, the city, having been under British rule and part of the Western world for so long, is being decolonized and degeopoliticized—a process that has begun, swiftly and explicitly, since 2019. These processes are being boosted and legitimized by a surging nationalism and a pride in the China model, which is intentionally differentiated from the Western model in the new narrative of Xi Jinping's new era and Chinese dream (see chapter 1). Hong Kong, traditionally a place where the East and the West converged to make it the Pearl of the Orient, is being reoriented jurisdictionally, institutionally, and economically. But socially, culturally, and emotionally, the way ahead is long and uncertain. The central government may have the will, legitimacy, and resources to reorient the city; the ultimate test is whether it can win the people's hearts.

NEW DEVELOPMENT BLUEPRINT

High density and (over)crowding are the stereotyped images of Hong Kong's built environment for visitors and other outsiders. The city has an urban form that is tense, vertical, and volumetric.[24] Scarcity of land and space is always a characteristic—as well as a resultant effect—of global cities like Hong Kong. Geospatially, the development of Hong Kong is south-north unbalanced: the images that we have of the city are concentrated in the southern part across Victoria Harbour; the vast area in the northern part, especially along the border with Shenzhen, is underdeveloped or undeveloped. Along the winding Shenzhen River, which separates the two cities, the images of the two sides are in stark contrast: the Shenzhen side is a modern international metropolis; the Hong Kong side remains farmlands and forests.

This urban-rural separation and contrast is an outcome of different development trajectories, approaches, and mindsets of the two cities. Collaboration and integration with Hong Kong are in the DNA of Shenzhen's planning and development. For Hong Kong, engagement with Shenzhen and the broader mainland has experienced a gradual shift from disinterest to interest since its return to China in 1997. This change has been driven by a complicated social and political ethos within Hong Kong and by the shifting Hong Kong-mainland relationality in terms of reciprocal perceptions and economic powers.[25] In recent years, Hong Kong-Shenzhen integration has been more emphasized in regional strategies for the Greater Bay Area and in national plans—both of which have been directly developed and endorsed by the central government.

On October 6, 2021, Hong Kong's chief executive, Carrie Lam, presented her policy address, "Building a Bright Future

Together," the last such address of her term (2017–2022) but the first one after the national security law and new electoral system were put in place. Among many initiatives offered in the address that were explicitly aligned to national development strategies and integration with neighboring city Shenzhen and the Greater Bay Area, the most prominent one was the Northern Metropolis. On the same day, the *Northern Metropolis Development Strategy* report was released. The Northern Metropolis is a twenty-year initiative: it covers an area of 300 km² in north Hong Kong along the border with Shenzhen (figure 6.5) and is planned to house some 2.5 million people and offer 650,000 jobs.[26] The future of the Northern Metropolis will be as an innovation and technology hub, complementing the Harbour Metropolis in the southern part of Hong Kong, which is an established leading international financial hub, defining Hong Kong as a global city as we know it today.

This is a bold, ambitious blueprint, aiming to reorient Hong Kong's development through boosting Hong Kong-Shenzhen integration and in large part capitalizing on the spillover from Shenzhen, a city that is already an innovation center of global leadership. Although linking and interacting with regional development in the Greater Bay Area has been an integral component in Hong Kong's planning strategies since its return,[27] this is the first plan of its type initiated by the Hong Kong side to advance spatial and strategic integration of the two cities across the border between them. Closer intercity collaboration has long been pursued by the Shenzhen side, as both a local plan and a national strategy. The latest (draft) strategy of *Shenzhen 2035* (further discussed in chapter 7) echoes a similar ethos, prioritizing collaboration with Hong Kong in areas of technology, innovation, and finance, committing to supporting Hong Kong's (and Macau's) integration with overall national development.[28]

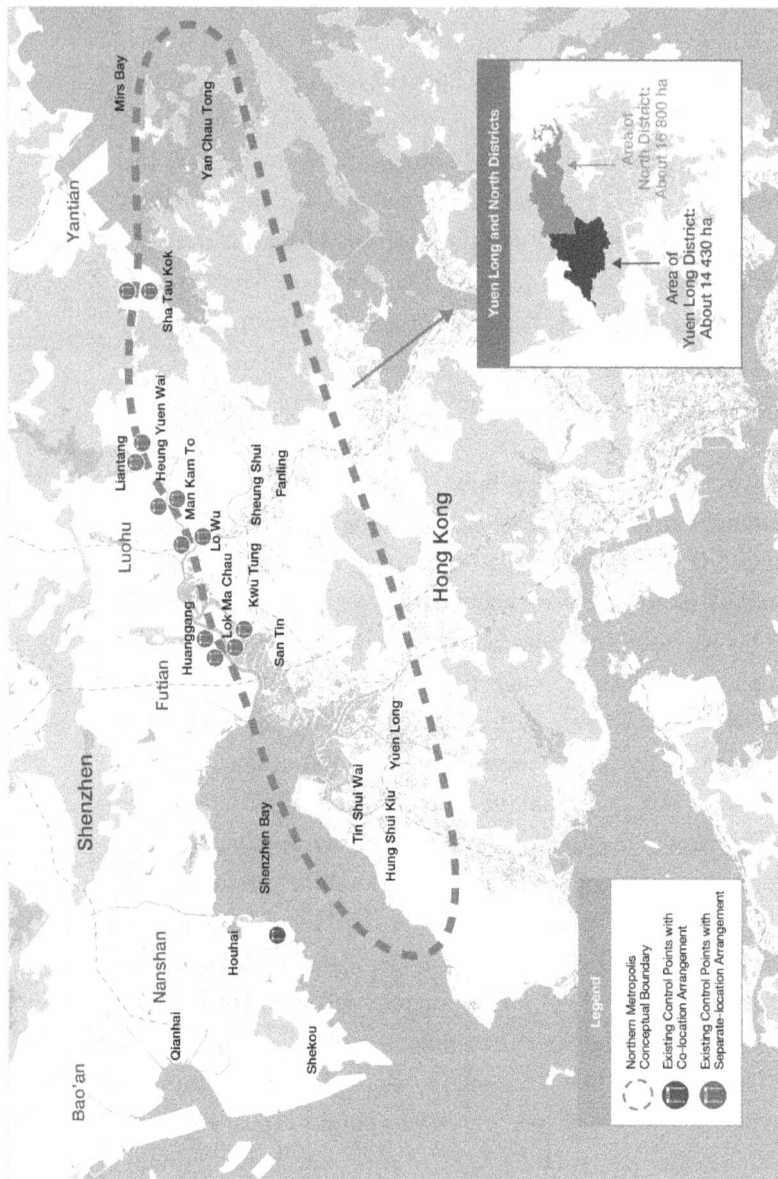

FIGURE 6.5 Conceptual boundary of Northern Metropolis, Hong Kong

Source: Hong Kong Special Administrative Region Government, *Northern Metropolis Development Strategy* (Hong Kong: Hong Kong Special Administrative Region Government, October 6, 2021), 12,

In 1979–1980, the area of Shenzhen was a vast expanse of farmlands. A new city—an SEZ then—was imagined there simply because of its proximity to Hong Kong. More than forty years later, a new city—called the Northern Metropolis—is being imagined on the Hong Kong side simply because of the area's proximity to Shenzhen. Will history repeat itself?

7

IMAGING 2035 AND BEYOND

The year 2035 has now become a critical benchmark in the Chinese discourse on strategy and policy, including for urban planning and development. This year instantly became important on October 18, 2017, when Xi Jinping outlined a three-step roadmap for China's modernization in his report delivered at the nineteenth CPC National Congress: first, to "finish building a moderately prosperous society in all respects" by 2020; second, to see that "socialist modernization is basically realized" by 2035; and third, to develop China into "a great modern socialist country" by the mid-twenty-first century.[1]

These three steps of national development focus on achieving so-called two centenary goals. "A moderately prosperous society" (*xiao kang she hui*) is the first goal, to be achieved within the centenary the CPC established in 1921; and "a great modern socialist country" is the second goal, to be achieved within the centenary of the PRC, established in 1949. Clearly, achieving these goals aims to celebrate the centenaries of the party and the regime and, more importantly, justify and bolster their legitimacy.

This modernization roadmap is not new. It is an updated version of a modernization roadmap first outlined by Deng Xiaoping in 1987, but this one is more ambitious and radical in terms of goals and timelines. For example, in Deng's roadmap, China would achieve modernization "basically" by around 2050; Xi moved up the time of achieving this goal by fifteen years. Chinese people are not unfamiliar with such modernization plans or similar rhetoric. The most famous one was the Maoist four modernizations, which were supposed to be achieved by 2000 (see also chapter 4). Even though Mao did not modernize China, the modernization drive and imagining of long-term modernization roadmaps have been passed on to his successors. For a nation with a long premodern history and that has had complicated experiences of encountering "modern" forces, nothing is more appealing to its people than a grand vision of modernization. This drive for modernization has captivated both pre- and post-1949 China, regardless of regime changes or political power shifts.

On July 1, 2021, when celebrating the centenary of the CPC, Xi Jinping announced the successful achievement of the first centenary goal and the eradication of "absolute poverty" in China. It is arguable whether such socioeconomic development progress should be measured in one specific year. It is also arguable whether the criterion of absolute poverty and the top-down approach to eradicating it by a predesignated year are plausible and sustainable. But it is important that this goal must be achieved to mark the centenary of the CPC. This "historic" progress has been incorporated into the narrative of the achievements in the new era. Achieving the second centenary goal involves the implementation of the remaining two steps by 2035 and 2050, respectively. Now, the immediate task is to modernize the nation, basically, by 2035.

Thus, the vision of socialist modernization that will be basically realized by 2035 is the focal target of political imaginings, development strategies, and action guidelines at all government levels. The terms "socialist modernization" and "basically realized" lack clear conceptualization and specificity. The vision comprises a set of aspirations in broad areas of economy, innovation, governance, rule of law, culture, well-being, equality, and environment, all of which will be more advanced in 2035 than today. The scope and measurement of these aspirations will surely evolve and are open to new interpretations and conceptualizations, pending the trajectory of China's future development and policy making.

From the mid-1980s, when the notion of basic modernization was proposed by Deng Xiaoping, it has generally referred to the level of moderately developed countries, a transitory stage between developing and developed countries. In October 2020, at a plenary session of the CPC Central Committee, a set of long-range objectives—broad and generic—were outlined about the basic modernization by 2035, but one economic indicator was specified: to reach the level of moderately developed countries by GDP per capita.[2] This means China's GDP per capita will reach around $20,000 in 2035, doubling its 2019 level.

The 2035 vision of national development has set a new discourse, new contexts, and new directions for urban planning at all levels. Starting in 2014, the Shanghai government commenced the process of preparing a new master plan to guide the city's future development. As a strategic plan, it set a long-term vision up to 2040; thus, the plan was titled *Shanghai 2040* during its creation. The process took several years. In 2016–2017, the draft *Shanghai 2040* plan was nearly complete and was already exhibited for public consultation. However, the new 2035 national vision announced in October 2017 injected new contexts and factors into the making of *Shanghai 2040*. The Shanghai plan's vision and timeline had to be reimagined and adjusted to align with those of the national strategy. As a result, the plan's name was changed to *Shanghai 2035* before it was officially released in early 2018.

The 2035 national vision has influenced the plan making for major cities ever since. These new plans have all aligned the timeline of city visions with that of the national vision and set 2035 as a benchmark year for achieving their visions. These cities include Beijing and Shenzhen, which will be compared with Shanghai later in this chapter in terms of their 2035 visions. But the 2035 national vision is not the only factor influencing urban planning. The Chinese planning system is also being revamped to fit the new era discourse of urban governance and planning.

NEW PLANNING SYSTEM

Reforming the Chinese planning system has been an enduring topic in policy debates and proposals since the early 1980s, when urban planning was resurrected as a discipline and a profession to meet the demand of the nation's emerging urbanization. The imperative for planning reform has rapidly escalated in the twenty-first century, along with the growing scale and speed of massive urbanization and its associated problems—some of them rooted in the planning system—and along with growing professional advocacy and political will for such a reform. One major problem in the planning system has been the fragmentation between different government departments responsible for planning affairs and, as a result, the lack of coordination between different plan types. This fragmentation has created both overlaps and gaps between government departments and in plan making and implementation.

This problem has affected the efficiency and effectiveness of planning management and practice for decades. For example, a city's master plan was the most important plan and had statutory status in the Chinese spatial planning system, but it was separate from the land use plan in terms of administration and plan making: the master plan and the land use plan were the responsibility of two different departments. This separation often created a disconnection between the two important plans for a city's development: a master plan's development goals and parameters for a precinct would be futile if they were not compatible with or supported by land provision in a land use plan.

"Integrating multiple plans into one" (*duo gui he yi*) is a central concept in the discourse around reforming the Chinese planning system. The concept is essentially about integrating the multiple plans (such as the economic and social development plan, urban-rural plan, land use plan, ecological and environmental protection plan, and water resources plan) into a single plan structure at one administrative level (e.g., city or county). The reform aims to streamline the management and making of these multiple plans, which have historically belonged to separate planning subsystems and government departments and, as a result, have often lacked articulation and followed different or even contradictory approaches. The goal is to achieve one blueprint for the comprehensive development of a city or county to ensure effective long-term implementation. Some incremental reforms have been undertaken, for example, through the merging of the departments of land use planning and urban-rural planning and through the integration of the master plan and the land use plan into one plan. These were first implemented experimentally in Pudong New Area, Shanghai, in 2011.[3] A series of trial programs was piloted in 2014–2016 to draw experiences and lessons for planning system reform.

In the official discourse, planning system reform is part of the modernization of the Chinese governance system and governance capacity, an integral component of the modernization agenda for the new era. The most recent and most comprehensive planning system reform came in early 2018, when the Chinese government established a new Ministry of Natural Resources to take charge of the repackaged "territorial spatial planning" (*guo tu kong jian gui hua*). This is an all-in-one spatial planning system integrating multiple planning types, including main function zone planning (the planning of the development or protection of zones whose main function is industrial products or services, agriculture, or ecology), land use planning, urban-rural planning, and other types of spatial planning. These formerly belonged to separate planning systems and were the responsibility of different government agencies.

The new term territorial spatial planning is essentially about spatial planning; but—conceptually, administratively, and geographically—the former is broader than the latter because of the integration and repackaging of the multiple spatial planning responsibilities under one umbrella planning term and agency. Debates on the new territorial spatial planning and its advances from the traditional spatial planning are still ongoing. There is some confusion between the two very similar terms, and certain conceptual gray areas are yet to be clarified. The new term's conceptualization and its implications for planning practices are evolving and open to interpretation and experimentation.

China also has a development planning system of economic and social development, for which a new plan is made every five years. This is the so-called five-year plan that the Chinese government has made since 1953—a legacy from the influence of Soviet planning—until today (except for 1963–1965, the years after the Great Leap Forward movement, which no five-year plan covered). With the recent reform, the new planning system contains two subsystems: a development planning system and a territorial spatial planning system. The different plan types

Plan Types　　　　　　　　　　　**Plan Levels**

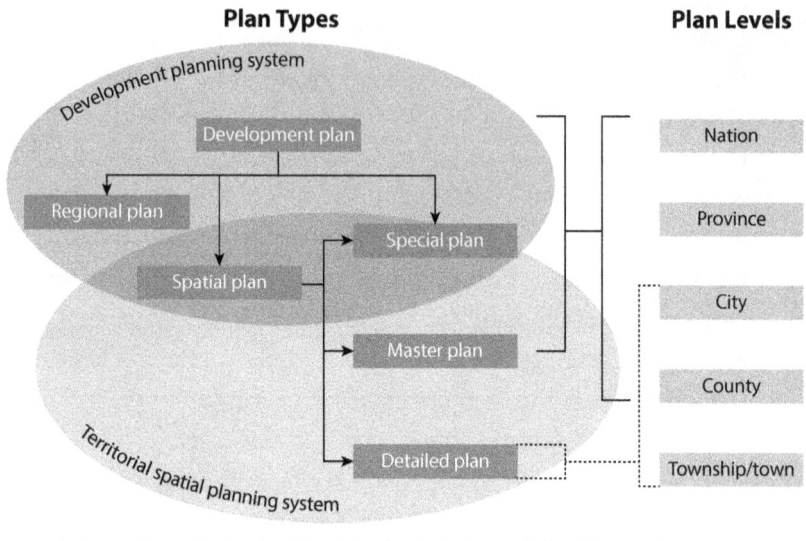

FIGURE 7.1　New Chinese planning system

Source: The author.

within them apply to different administrative levels (figure 7.1). These two planning systems articulate with each other in a broad sense. The former sets the strategic planning goals and approaches, addressing "what to do and how to do it." The latter sets the spatial arrangements for achieving them, addressing "where to do it." The primary responsibilities of the two belong to different government departments. At the national level, the National Development and Reform Commission (NDRC, called the National Planning Commission in 1954–1998) oversees development planning, mainly through making the five-year plans; the newly established Ministry of Natural Resources takes the lead in managing territorial spatial planning.

　　Development planning applies to national, provincial, and city/county levels. Within this system, the development plan (the five-year plan) is the lead, the spatial plan is the base, and the regional plan and the special plan provide support at the national level:

- Development plan: five-year national development strategy; goals of economic and social development; priority areas of government policies and actions; guidelines for market actors; interdepartmental and intersector macro policies; interregional megaprojects; strategic spatial structures; and strategic zones for development or protection.

- Spatial plan: spatial governance and optimalization of spatial structures; spatial provision for implementing the national development strategy and achieving its goals; delineation of urban, agricultural, and ecological zones—the so-called three zones (*san qu*); enforcement of the ecological conservation red line, permanent prime farmland protection line, and urban development boundary line—the so-called three lines (*san xian*); guidelines on infrastructure, urban development, energy and resources, and ecological protection.

- Special plan: planning in special fields where the market fails and government intervention is necessary.

- Regional plan: planning of strategic regions of close economic and social connectivity across administrative areas or planning of strategic regional issues to achieve regional coordination.[4]

Similar interplan relationships and classifications apply to development planning at subnational—provincial and city/county—levels, which should respond to the national plans as well as be based on local situations.

Territorial spatial planning works with development planning through materializing the spatial plan part of the latter (figure 7.1). It contains three major plan types that apply to five administrative levels, creating a so-called five-level, three-type (*wu ji, san lei*) structure:

- Master plan: master plans have different focuses by administrative levels. At the national level: strategic national territorial spatial arrangement, and national policy and guidelines of spatial preservation, development, utilization, and restoration. At the provincial level: coordinated implementation of the national master plan within the province and guidelines for plan making at lower city/county levels. At the city/county level: detailed implementation of planning requirements from higher administrative levels, and detailed arrangements for and implementation of spatial development and protection within the administrative areas. Territorial spatial plans can also be made at township/town levels, but they are not called a master plan.
- Detailed plan: arrangement and specification of land uses and development intensity of land lots. This plan is the statutory basis for spatial development and preservation, space use control, development control, and issuance of construction permits.
- Special plan: in the territorial spatial planning system, special plans overlap those in the development planning system, but they have a spatial focus. A special plan concerns planning for special zones like coastal zones and natural reserves, spatial planning for cross-administrative areas or river basins, or spatial planning for special sectors, like transport, energy, water, agriculture, information, civic infrastructure, public service infrastructure, military facilities, ecological and environmental protection, cultural heritage, forests, and grasslands.[5]

This territorial spatial planning system was formally in place for implementation starting in May 2019, replacing the old system and its plan types—including the main function zone plan, land use plan, urban system plan, and municipal master plan—to achieve the goal of integrating multiple plans into one, or a "one-plan" system. It was expected that by 2020, the new planning system would be basically established nationwide, encompassing four subsystems of a plan-making and approval system, an implementation and supervision system, a legal and policy system, and a technical standards system. Further, the new territorial spatial master plans would be basically completed at the city/county level and above. This planning reform explains the discrepancies between several master plans released by major cities in the years before and after 2019–2020 (to be further discussed later).

NEW URBANIZATION STRUCTURE

In March 2021, the Chinese government released the *14th Five-Year Plan* (2021–2025). This is the first five-year plan after the 2035 national vision was mapped out in 2017. The plan's full title is "The People's Republic of China's 14th Five-Year Plan for National Economic and Social Development & Outline Objectives of the 2035 Vision." This title reflects the 2035 national vision's influence on the making of this national development plan, which is at the highest level and of the utmost importance in the Chinese planning system. Within the new planning system (figure 7.1), this five-year plan belongs to the type of development plan and is thus the lead in the whole planning system, as explained earlier. The development strategies, goals, and actions set in this five-year plan are the guidelines or the "constitution" for making other types of plans at all administrative levels for at least the period 2021–2025.

The *14th Five-Year Plan* set a target urbanization rate of 65 percent (measured by permanent population living in cities/towns, not by registered urban population with *hukou*) for China by 2025. This target figure was based on China's urbanization rate of 60.6 percent recorded in 2020.[6] However, the seventh national census in 2020 indicated an urbanization rate of 63.89 percent, an increase of 14.21 percentage points over the 2010 rate.[7] Based on the latest and supposedly more accurate census data and following the historical urban growth trajectory, China's urbanization rate is likely to reach nearly 70 percent in 2025. By any measure, China is becoming a highly urbanized society. This is transforming the nation's social structure as well as its spatial structure.

Under the umbrella discourse of pursuing human-centered new-type urbanization, the *14th Five-Year Plan* outlined a national urbanization structure underpinned by the concepts of "city cluster" (*cheng shi qun*) and "metropolitan circle" (*du shi quan*)—two spatial representations of China's urbanization that are raising new issues and challenges in regional development and planning.

In the previous *13th Five-Year Plan* (2016–2020), a total of nineteen city clusters were identified across the nation. The *14th Five-Year Plan* highlighted the "development and strengthening" of these city clusters, which forge a spatial structure of "two horizontals and three verticals" (*liang heng san zong*) for China's strategic urbanization (figure 7.2). These nineteen city clusters, essentially mega urban agglomerations, are of different scales and at different developmental stages. Several of them are China's economic engines. They are internationally competitive and leading in terms of economic power and outreach—like the Beijing-Tianjin-Hebei region, Yangtze River delta region, and Pearl River delta region (Greater Bay Area). There are also

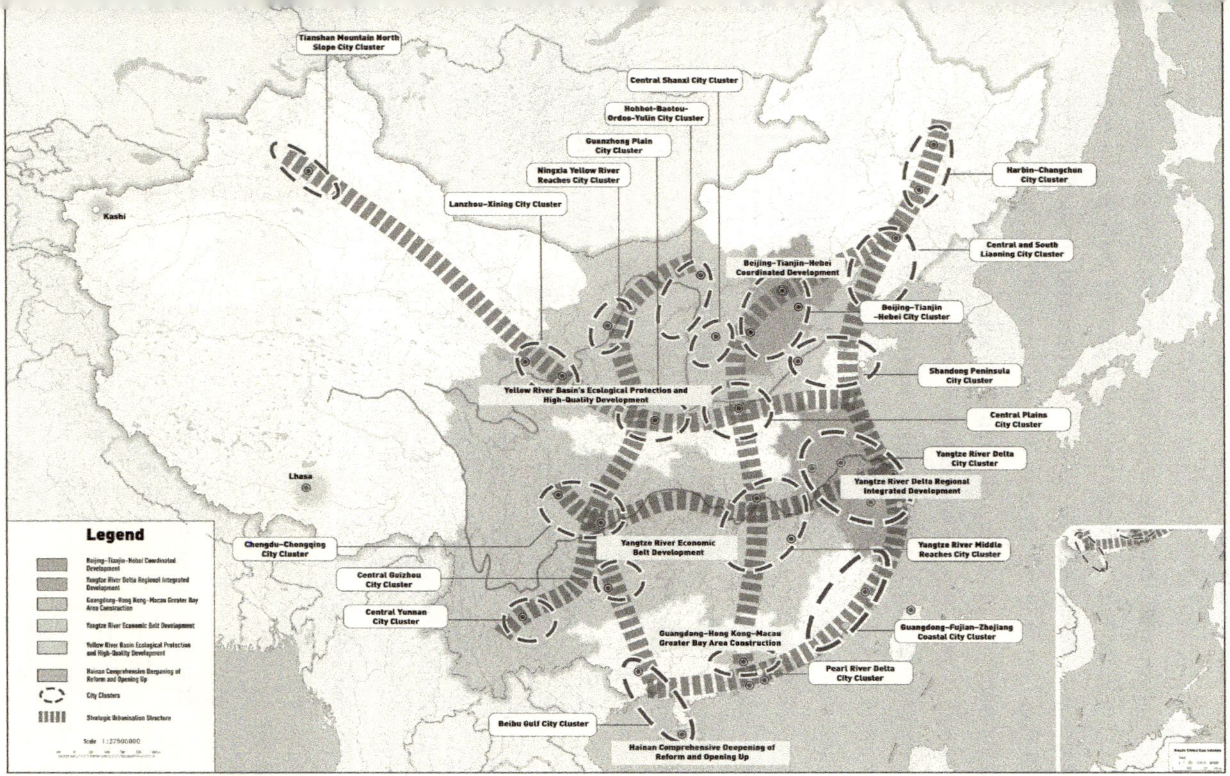

FIGURE 7.2 China's urbanization structure

Source: Chinese Government, *The People's Republic of China's 14th Five-Year Plan for National Economic and Social Development & Outline Objectives of the 2035 Vision* [in Chinese] (Beijing: Chinese Government, March 13, 2021), 66, http://www.gov.cn/xinwen/2021-03/13/content_5592681.htm, recreated by the author.

smaller, obscure city clusters in inland and western areas, which are emerging and growing. They are not comparable with those in eastern coastal areas in size, influence, or economic power.

The differences between these city clusters truly reflect the regional disparity of China's urbanization and socioeconomic development. The central tenet of planning these city clusters is to achieve integrated and coordinated development of each in terms of establishing regional coordination systems, sharing of development costs and benefits, holistic infrastructure planning and construction, collaborative industrial development and division of labor, sharing of public services, and coprotection and cogovernance of ecological environments.[8] These are the key issues that are confronting regional development in China.

The other regional spatial concept, metropolitan circle, refers to the congregated and closely connected urban area within a one-hour commute of a central city—mostly a powerful provincial capital city. This central city has a strong regional outreach that goes beyond its own administrative border. Thus, a metropolitan circle generally comprises one large central city and several smaller cities (in terms of population size, economic power, and administrative level) in its surrounds. In terms of urban functions and connectivity, these cities constitute one metropolitan circle entity, despite the administrative divisions between them. Definitions of a metropolitan circle—including the terminology of the concept—differ in the international literature, depending on the contexts and issues of concern. It is also called metropolitan region or metropolitan area. Within China, how to delineate the territorial extent of a metropolitan circle is being debated.

One common definition of a metropolitan circle is based on the coverage of the one-hour commuting time isochrone from the central city. The commute can involve various means of transportation, including public rail transit, automobile, and bus. This is how a metropolitan circle is defined in policy documents like the *14th Five-Year Plan* and the *Guiding Opinions on Cultivating and Developing Modern Metropolitan Circles*. The latter document was released by the NDRC in February 2019 specifically to guide the planning and development of metropolitan circles in light of their emerging importance in shaping the spatial structure of China's urbanization. However, the one-hour commute is a mechanical criterion for delineating metropolitan circles among numerous Chinese cities that have diverse local circumstances. For example, the one-hour commute involves significantly different scenarios in Beijing, Hangzhou, and Hefei in terms of commuting distance, as well as of associated urban functions and connectivity. The one-hour commute criterion is hardly applicable in planning for metropolitan circles, as I will show in the case of Chengdu metropolitan circle.

A report by Tsinghua University suggested two criteria for delineating the territorial scope of a metropolitan circle in China based on the one-hour commuting definition: (1) it has an urban population of more than 5 million and a population density of more than 1,500 inhabitants per km², and (2) its peripheral urban districts and counties have on average more than 1.5 percent of their populations conducting daily two-way commuting with the central city. Using these criteria, the report identified thirty-four metropolitan circles in mainland China. Altogether, they accounted for 24 percent of the national land area, 59 percent of its population, and 77.8 percent of its GDP.[9]

The definitions and criteria for city cluster or metropolitan circle could differ in a technical sense. But the ascendance of these concepts in Chinese planning discourse suggests that regionalization is the new spatial form of China's urbanization. Geospatially, a city cluster contains metropolitan circles; they are both regional spatial concepts of different scales. The central tenet of planning a metropolitan circle is to achieve "one-city development" (*tong cheng hua fa zhan*) among the several cities within the circle through intercity collaborations like connected transport systems; coordinated public policies and services in social security, the *hukou* household system, and educational and medical resources; and collaborative industrial parks and R&D platforms, according to the *14th Five-Year Plan*. The plan further suggested the establishment of a metropolitan regional planning commission to coordinate regionwide plan making and implementation, and to coordinate land and demographic management, across one metropolitan circle.[10]

Regionalization is a spatial manifestation of China's ever-growing urbanization that is breaking through the administrative boundaries of local jurisdictions, posing new issues and challenges for regional governance and planning. Interjurisdictional fragmentation and lack of coordination are the most common and prominent problems in regional development in China and elsewhere. It is presumed that China's unitary governance structure and top-down approach could possibly enable a comparatively smooth process for setting agendas for regional development, but similar challenges in interjurisdictional collaboration exist at an operational level.

The two concepts of city cluster and metropolitan circle concern regional planning. The development of several backbone city clusters—the Beijing-Tianjin-Hebei region, the Yangtze River delta region, and the Pearl River delta region—has been elevated to national strategies in the recent decade. The key notions in these regional development plans are integration, coordination, and collaboration, denoting the lack of them in practice and the need to enhance them in the development of these city clusters. Likewise, several development plans for metropolitan circles have been formulated and were approved by the NDRC—the lead agency of the development planning system—in recent years. These regional development plans for city clusters or metropolitan circles belong to the type of regional plan in the new planning system (figure 7.1).

The NDRC's *Guiding Opinions on Cultivating and Developing Modern Metropolitan Circles* (2019) has played an important role in guiding recent plan making for metropolitan circles. This is the first guideline of its type on the regional development of metropolitan circles issued by the national-level agency. The document identified these key areas of governing and planning metropolitan circles: integrating infrastructure and facilities, enhancing intercity industrial division of labor and cooperation, accelerating the development of a unified open market, facilitating joint provision of and shared access to public services, strengthening coprotection and cogovernance of ecosystems, advancing urban-rural integration, and establishing an integrated development mechanism.

The document further highlighted the importance of improving the planning coordination mechanism for metropolitan circles. To do so, the document proposed exploring approaches to formulating development plans and special plans in key areas, with a central objective of enhancing the development quality and modernization level of metropolitan circles; and strengthening the articulation between metropolitan circle plans, city cluster plans, and municipal master plans to ensure coordination between them.[11]

Since the introduction of this document, plan making for metropolitan circles has surged. Some metropolitan circles have taken the lead in producing development plans or special plans in key sector areas. As of March 2023, the NDRC has approved development plans for seven metropolitan circles:

Nanjing, Fuzhou, Chengdu, Changsha-Zhuzhou-Xiangtan, Xi'an, Chongqing, and Wuhan. It is anticipated that more such plans will be submitted to the NDRC for approval and released in the near future. Next, I use the *Chengdu Metropolitan Circle Development Plan*, which was approved by the national agency on November 18, 2021, to illustrate major features of these new development plans for metropolitan circles.

The Chengdu metropolitan circle's plan was organized by the Sichuan Provincial Development and Reform Commission with the participation of agencies in Chengdu, Deyang, Meishan, and Ziyang—the member cities in the metropolitan circle. The Chengdu metropolitan circle is centered geographically and functionally on Chengdu and contains its surrounding urban areas. It covers an area of 26,400 km^2 and had a permanent population of 27.61 million at the end of 2020. However, the planning area in the plan extended to the entire administrative areas of the four cities, which cover a total area of 33,100 km^2 and had a permanent population of 29.66 million at the end of 2020.[12] Either area defies the aforementioned one-hour commuting criterion for defining a metropolitan circle. In the international context, this is a mega city region. But in the Chinese context, it is just one regional end of the Chengdu-Chongqing city cluster (Chongqing anchors a metropolitan circle in its own right), one of the nineteen such city clusters across China (figure 7.2).

This plan for the Chengdu metropolitan circle set development objectives up to 2025 and a long-term outlook toward 2035, aligned to the national vision timeline discussed earlier. This plan serves as the lead for making a territorial spatial plan for the metropolitan circle; for making special plans in sectors like transport, public services, and ecological and environmental protection; and for formulating relevant policies on technology and innovation, talent support, financing, and industrial cooperation. According to the plan, by 2025, the urbanization rate of permanent population in the Chengdu metropolitan circle will reach 75 percent; the region's total GDP will exceed RMB 3.3 trillion (it was RMB 2.15 trillion in 2019); and urban and rural residents' disposable income will get close to the level of eastern developed regions.[13] Within the Chinese urban and regional development context, the Chengdu metropolitan circle lags behind its counterparts like the Hangzhou and Nanjing metropolitan circles.

The plan identified major areas for implementation and action, which are broadly aligned with the major areas of a metropolitan circle's development identified in the NDRC's *Guiding Opinions on Cultivating and Developing Modern Metropolitan Circles*. Spatially, the plan mapped a structure comprising two development axes that break through the administrative borders between cities and three industrial development belts that concentrate the prioritized economic activities.

Prior to the new *Chengdu Metropolitan Circle Development Plan*, a series of regional plans had been produced to promote intercity collaboration and integrated development. In 2020, the Sichuan government established a leading group for one-city development in the metropolitan circle. This is a voluntary planning and coordinating agency headed by high-profile provincial leaders, with membership consisting of executive deputy mayors of constituent cities. There is certainly no lack of plans or institutions for the Chengdu metropolitan circle. How well the new development plan integrates with the multiple existing plans and how it will be implemented through the agency and mechanism in place remains an unanswered question.

Regional planning stands out in China at the intersection of its rapid urbanization and recent pursuit of high-quality, coordinated, sustainable development. These transformative processes call for new thinking and practice for planning and managing urban regions. While some analogies can be drawn with international experiences, the scale and speed of the transformation in China's urbanization, coupled with its different political and socioeconomic contexts and environmental challenges, make its regional planning more complex and contingent than that in other countries.

Among other things, two prominent issues remain uncertain and would impact the implementation and outcomes of Chinese regional planning. One is the interjurisdictional collaboration required and the incentives for the local governments to engage in it. The other is the articulation between these regional development plans and the territorial spatial plans—the former do not have the statutory status of the latter in the new planning system (see figure 7.1). The voluntary and partnership-based governance arrangement for regional planning impacts the local city governments' incentives for and commitment to promoting intercity collaboration rather than competition. The lack of statutory status and legal strength further impacts the effectiveness of regional planning governance, organization, and implementation. These factors also have an impact on the authority of the agencies responsible for regional planning and implementation. Chinese regional planning is in a nascent stage, with progress mixed with uncertainties and challenges.

NEW URBAN IMAGINARY

Beijing, Shanghai, and Shenzhen are the top three cities in mainland China, as measured by economic power, political significance, and prestige. They are also gaining increasing leadership in the global urban system thanks to the growth of the Chinese economy and the roles they play in the Chinese and the global economies. They are the prime cases and prisms for capturing the urban transformation in China. Their futures are being reimagined in the new national development strategy and new planning system. Each has set a new master plan in recent years, establishing development visions, goals, and strategies up through 2035 and long-term visions until 2050. These plans are hereafter called *Beijing 2035*, *Shanghai 2035*, and *Shenzhen 2035*, respectively. The aforementioned 2035 national vision and planning system reform have influenced the making of these plans to various degrees. The differences in the contexts of their creation vividly reflect the recent changes in Chinese planning discourse and practice.

Beijing 2035 covers a planning time frame of 2016–2035. This plan was formalized before the 2035 national vision came out in late 2017. As a result, the latter was not explicitly incorporated into the plan's development vision and goals for Beijing. The bookend year 2035 in the plan's time frame could be simply a coincidence due to a master plan's lifespan of twenty years—in this case, from 2016 to 2035; and/or planners in Beijing presumably could have been advised of the benchmarks of 2035 and, further, 2050 in the forthcoming national vision, given their proximity to and connections with planners of the central government—just a guess! *Beijing 2035* was the latest and probably the last master plan of a major city that was produced before the 2035 national vision and the planning system reform that were unveiled in 2017–2019.

Shanghai 2035 covers a planning time frame of 2017–2035. As noted earlier, its title and time frame were adapted toward the end of the process of its crafting, changing from the original *Shanghai 2040* to respond to the newly born 2035 national vision. This plan was endorsed by the State Council in December 2017 and officially released in January 2018, ahead of the planning system reform that began in March 2018. Consequently, *Shanghai*

2035 was probably the first master plan of a major city that was closely and explicitly aligned to the new national 2035 vision. But it was made and released as a municipal master plan under the old planning system rather than a territorial spatial master plan in the new system.

Discussions about and preparation of a new master plan for Shenzhen started in the same period as those of the other two major cities. But progress was put on hold during those years of changes in the planning system until 2021, when a draft territorial spatial master plan—*Shenzhen 2035*—was released for public consultation. This draft plan covers a time frame of 2020–2035. The public consultation process has already concluded. As of March 2023, the final version of the plan had not yet been released, but presumably that will happen soon. The final version will reflect revisions based on public feedback and will have been formally endorsed, normally by the State Council. It can also be assumed that the vision and major development goals in the final version will not be significantly different from those in the version for public consultation. *Shenzhen 2035* is probably the first master plan of a major city that fully captures the 2035 national vision set out in 2017 and the new planning system set in place in 2019. These are both reflected in the plan's full title, "Shenzhen 2035: Territorial Spatial Master Plan of Shenzhen."

The master plan is the most important strategic and spatial planning document of a Chinese city, in both the old and the new planning systems. The recent master plans of Beijing, Shanghai, and Shenzhen had different contexts for their making within a period of several years when both the national planning discourse and system changed. They are the newest manifestos of urban planning and development in China. Their strategic positionings, visions, and development goals provide a new set of urban imaginaries: futuristic, optimistic, and aspirational (table 7.1). The strategic positionings and visions of these top Chinese cities differ, however.

Beijing's four-center (political center, cultural center, international communication center, and sci-tech innovation center) positioning is a reimagining of the capital's role (see chapter 5). This positioning, legitimized in a master plan, signifies a firm departure from the city's previous aspiration for becoming a world city of economic prowess, which was proposed by the city government in 2009.[14] The new positioning is a reaffirmation of the city's primary role as the national capital, which for a long time has been mingled with the impetus of building the city into an economic center rivalling Shanghai and Shenzhen under an overwhelming progrowth ethos and urban regime. Decades of rapid growth—ill-planned and excessive—has generated grave challenges to sustainability and livability (see chapter 2). The new master plan set the vision of a "harmonious, livable city" to counter its big city syndrome in the coming decades.[15] This vision responds to repercussions of the past and expresses a wish for the future.

In contrast to Beijing, the master plan of Shanghai reaffirmed the city's role as China's leading economic center and its gateway city status, through its five-center (economy, finance, trade, shipping, and sci-tech innovation) positioning and its vision of "striving for the excellent global city."[16] Shanghai is already a leading "global city," a buzzword in the global urban discourse that has appealed to city leaders and marketers in recent decades.[17] Shanghai has ascended in the global city system from obscurity to leadership in the first decades of the twenty-first century.[18] The particular use of "excellent global city"—a term carefully considered by Shanghai's planners and advisers—speaks of the city's vision or ambition for the future: Shanghai, a learner and a

TABLE 7.1 MASTER PLANS OF BEIJING, SHANGHAI, AND SHENZHEN

	Beijing 2035	*Shanghai 2035*	*Shenzhen 2035*
Strategic positioning	National political center, cultural center, international communication center, and sci-tech innovation center.	An international center of economy, finance, trade, shipping, and sci-tech innovation.	A national special economic zone and gateway of opening up, an international sci-tech innovation center, and a pilot demonstration zone of socialism with Chinese characteristics.
Vision	A first-class international harmonious, livable city.	An excellent global city.	A global benchmark city.
Goals by 2020	Making significant progress in building a first-class international harmonious, livable city.	Construction of a basic structure for a sci-tech innovation center with global influence; basic construction of an international center of economy, finance, trade, and shipping.	By 2025: becoming a modern, international, and innovative city; basic realization of socialist modernization.
Goals by 2035	Preliminary construction of a first-class international harmonious, livable city.	Basic construction of an excellent global city.	Becoming an innovative, entrepreneurial, and creative city with global influence; becoming a model city of great socialist modern China.
Goals by 2050	Complete construction of a first-class international harmonious, livable capital at a higher level.	Complete construction of an excellent global city.	Becoming a global benchmark city with excellent competitiveness, innovation, and influence.

Source: The author, compiled from the three plan documents.

follower of its counterpart cities like New York, London, Tokyo, Singapore, and Hong Kong, now wants to become a leader. This is a mindset shift not only of the city but probably also of the nation.

Shenzhen, the youngest and the most pioneering major Chinese city, is often dubbed an urban miracle. Planners tend to cite the city as a case of the triumph of planning, but this is a simplistic reading. The city's genesis and rapid growth into an international metropolis is not just a result of top-down decision-making and planning, notwithstanding their crucial roles. Shenzhen is also an unplanned city, growing out of grassroots ingenuity and entrepreneurship—a more important factor in shaping the city's risk-taking culture and its innovation capacity.[19] Shenzhen, essentially a capitalist experiment, is being reideologized and celebrated in the official discourse as a socialist advancement. It was crowned a pilot demonstration zone of socialism with Chinese characteristics by the central government in 2019 (see chapter 6). In its master plan, both an urban vision and a political mission are attached to the city: advancing the Chinese urban development approach and showcasing Chinese socialism. This dual role differentiates Shenzhen's vision from that of either Beijing or Shanghai: it is going to be a Chinese model city and a global benchmark city in the coming decades.[20]

A key recurring notion in the master plans of these three cities is innovation. This is unsurprising in the context of the great innovation leap forward sweeping across Chinese cities (see chapter 4). According to the national vision, China will become an international leader of innovation by 2035.[21] Despite the intercity nuances in setting visions and development goals, they are broadly aligned to the national development vision toward 2035 and beyond. Collectively, the national plan and the urban plans forge a set of imaginaries that stride between confidence and arrogance, between aspiration and ambition, in expressions that are buoyant and optimistic, vague and propagandic. They are illustrative of the new discourse that is attempting to rewrite and reinvent the Chinese city in the coming decades.

NEW WINNERS AND LOSERS

China's social inequality deserves no less attention than its economic growth. The social dimension of China's transformation is more complicated than what statistics often tell us. Social change is rapid and profound. The understanding and interpretation of it must be set in both historical and contemporary contexts. China presents a typical case to illustrate the contradiction and balance among the triple bottom lines of sustainable development, as we have observed in the relationship between its economic development and environmental protection (see chapter 2). Both contradiction and balance also apply to its economic development and social inclusion. Its remarkable progress in increased standard of living and reduced poverty, a direct outcome of economic growth, does not counter the escalating inequality in multiple forms that are not always statistically measured.

In several years at the turn of the 1990s, there was a wave of Maoist nostalgia in China. Those Maoist "red songs" (hong ge)— the revolutionary and patriotic songs for praising and admiring Mao (or the party) mostly propagated and popularized before the end of the 1970s—reemerged. Many people turned to them, not necessarily expressing a wish to return to the Maoist era but expressing discontent with the post-Mao time, in which some people became rich while most did not. The Maoist era was romanticized as one of equality—it is sometimes a human tendency to romanticize the past. The Maoist era was not equal: most ordinary people were equally poor; the bureaucratic class, who could enjoy some luxuries and privileges—in a relative sense—would also suffer from various political movements and struggles. Not many people would genuinely aspire to a Maoist lifestyle. Mao, an icon of the past, has often reemerged, serving a purpose of the present in the Chinese social and political arenas. Both economic growth and social inequality were less prominent in the Maoist era than in the post-Mao era. They have ignited hot debates in social and policy discourses especially since the 1990s, when both indicators were rapidly rising. Anticipating that China would become a middle-income country in the foreseeable future, some expressed justifiable concerns about middle-income trap and Latin Americanization. At the core of the debates was how China could possibly avoid economic stagnation and social inequality and, further, how it could smoothly become a society of both high income and reasonable equality.

As shown in figure 7.3, China's Gini index rapidly increased in the 1990s and 2000s. As it enjoyed unprecedented economic growth, it quickly became one of the most unequal societies in the world. Before the turn of the century, China's Gini index surpassed that of both the United Kingdom and the United States (see figure 7.3). This would sound ironic given that Chinese propaganda had always depicted the capitalist world as one of inequality in contrast to socialist China, which was one of equality.

The growth trend of China's Gini index reversed in 2010; it has been decreasing since then and now sits between that of the United States and the United Kingdom. As cautioned earlier, statistics do not paint a holistic picture of China's social change. The actual shift is multidimensional, and international comparisons do not always capture the complications and nuances established within China's historical and social contexts.

The upward and downward trends of China's Gini index in the past three decades seem to correlate somewhat with the

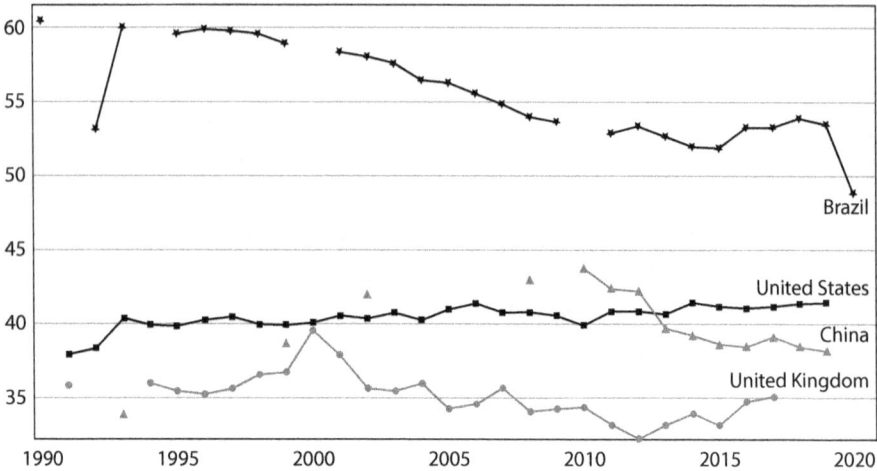

FIGURE 7.3 Gini index (%) of China, Brazil, the United States, and the
United Kingdom, 1990–2020

Source: World Bank, "Gini Index—China, Brazil, United Kingdom, United
States," accessed February 14, 2023, https://data.worldbank.org/indicator/SI.POV
.GINI?end=2020&locations=CN-BR-GB-US&start=1990.

shifts in the Chinese policy discourse about the dichotomy of
"efficiency vs. equality." One of Deng Xiaoping's quotes was
"let some people get rich first." But Deng also stressed that
the ultimate aim of socialism was "common prosperity" (*gong
tong fu yu*); he warned against social polarization, which, in his
view, socialism would help redress.[22] In line with these principles set by Deng, from the 1980s to the 2010s, there has been a
gradual shift from efficiency to equality in the central government's policy discourse about socioeconomic development. The
predominant policy discourse of "efficiency first, considering
equality" in much of the 1980s–1990s was replaced, incrementally and subtly, by one of "more emphasis on equality" in the
twenty-first century. At the nineteenth CPC National Congress

in 2017, common prosperity was formally instituted to characterize Xi Jinping's new era and incorporated into the national development strategy: by 2035—"solid progress has been made toward prosperity for everyone"; by 2050—"common prosperity for everyone is basically achieved."[23] At the twentieth CPC National Congress in October 2022, common prosperity became a major theme and was defined as a hallmark of "Chinese modernization" (further discussed in chapter 8).

The notion of common prosperity has agitated many people and caused various interpretations and worries at home and overseas. Nevertheless, it is not a new notion conceptually or ideologically. It simply echoes Deng Xiaoping's initial proposition for the aim of his reform and relates to the fundamental tenet of socialism—the orthodox ideology of the nation. In the 1980s and early 1990s, facing various ideological accusations and criticism that his reform was capitalist, Deng insisted on its socialist nature and its pursuit of common prosperity.

The Chinese government announced the eradication of absolute poverty in rural areas in 2021. The Chinese criteria for absolute poverty are household-based, not individual-based. They consider average per capita income for a household, the household's guarantees of adequate food and clothing, and its access to compulsory education, basic medical services, and safe housing.[24] Considering personal income only, it is generally believed that China's poverty line—annual income equivalent to around RMB 4,000 (less than US$600) in 2020—is below the international standard and is not commensurate with China's status as an upper-middle-income country measured by GDP per capita. Applying the international poverty line of living on $5.5 a day for upper-middle-income countries, China would have a poor population of roughly 180 million, around one third of whom would be in urban areas.[25]

China has been often in the global headlines about phenomenal economic growth, largely thanks to its large population base,
which elevates its aggregate economy. China remains a poor
country, also largely thanks to its large population, which dilutes
its large economic size. At a press conference in May 2020, then
Chinese premier Li Keqiang admitted that China had 600 million middle- and low-income earners whose monthly income
was just around RMB 1,000 (US$140),[26] refuting illusions of
China as a wealthy country.

Whatever the criteria and standards of a poverty line, China
has made remarkable achievements in poverty reduction and
alleviation. At the same time, it has a long way to go in increasing household income and standard of living, and further in
addressing social inequality, through sustained economic growth
and better socioeconomic policy interventions. Without doubt,
urbanization has been a major factor in China's economic growth
as well as poverty reduction. However, urbanization was also an
explanatory factor for the growing income inequality, which was
empirically measured, for example, for the period 1985–2010.[27]
Urbanization itself should not be a cause—despite being an
explanatory factor statistically—for social inequality; instead,
lack of policy initiatives to offset inequality should be. The concurrent imperatives for growth and equality seem to contextual-
ize and justify the nation's pursuit of common prosperity, as well
as its pursuit of new-type urbanization that is human-centered
and sustainable.

The phrase "unbalanced and inadequate development" in
the new principal contradiction identified for China's national
development through the middle of the twenty-first century
(see chapter 1) well encapsulates the status of China as the largest developing country in the world and the inequalities between

social groups and between regions. The urban-rural divide and the east-west regional inequality in socioeconomic development and access to opportunities are known stories. The *hukou* system, China's unique household registration system that is linked with access to opportunities and public services, has been incrementally liberalized. But *hukou* is not extinct yet, and its influences on China's socioeconomic structure are profound and long-lasting. The urban-rural divide remains the primary divide of the Chinese society. In 2021, China's average disposable income per capita was RMB 35,128: for urban residents, it was RMB 47,412; for rural residents, it was RMB 18,931.[28] A huge urban-rural income gap still exists. This gap has been narrowing, but very slowly.

The urban-rural divide can be continuously narrowed, in a statistical sense, through further urbanization and liberalization of the *hukou* system. But the associated social inequality will not be bridged accordingly and instantly. Urbanization may only transplant the urban-rural divide into cities and transform its representations. Within cities, the divide between migrants and local residents is less prominent in income than in nonincome welfares like housing conditions and social insurance—the rights associated with urban *hukou*.[29] The conventional urbanization in China is described as land-based, materialized in terms of urban development and expansion; the new-type urbanization is expected to be population-based, essentially about citizenization of all urban residents—with or without local *hukou*, migrants, or locals—on an equal basis of accessing rights and services.

Policy design and intervention take time; it takes longer for them to take effect—some may be desired and some may not be. What will take the longest is for the new migrant residents to adapt to and assimilate into an urban society—a journey that

may take more than one generation. For the migrants, legitimized residence in cities may also confer on them vulnerability,
social exclusion, and economic disadvantage that are foreign for
those originally from rural areas. In this sense, the population-
based urbanization, or human-centered new-type urbanization,
is a much longer process than what we have observed as a type of
land-based urbanization in the past decades in China.

Intercity and interregional unbalances present a geospatial dimension of the inequality in China's rapid development.
Broadly speaking, the eastern coastal cities and regions are more
developed and advanced than their inland and western counterparts. But the picture of geospatial inequality is more complicated
and nuanced than the coastal-inland binary. In the booming
urbanization, not all Chinese cities could boast of a growth story.
Urban shrinkage, a phenomenon intuitively linked to developed
societies, is now occurring in China. The shrinking Chinese cities are more than those traditionally resource-based cities that
are now struggling with economic restructuring and diversifica-
tion and, as a result, are suffering population loss. Shrinking cities are identified in the northeast areas, Pearl River delta region,
Yangtze River delta region, and inland provinces like Guizhou
and Shaanxi.[30] They exist in both coastal and inland regions and
in both developed and less-developed regions.

The reasons for shrinking cities are diverse. Resource
depletion and industrial restructuring are the push factors for
small cities in losing people; the opportunities and services in
large cities are the pull factors that attract people moving from
small cities. China's transport infrastructure boom, including
the high-speed rail system, does not counter this trend. On the
contrary, statistically, high-speed rail access has aggravated the
population loss of shrinking cities.[31] Again, as warned earlier, we
need to be cautious about statistics here. High-speed rail itself is

not necessarily the cause of population loss of these cities; structural intercity unbalance is. Urban shrinkage can be read as both a contributor to and a result of intercity inequality—which exists normally between developed large cities and less-developed smaller cities—in China.

The aforementioned new urbanization structure of city clusters and metropolitan circles is established on a central tenet of achieving integrated, coordinated regional development, in great part responding to intercity disparities. Within the city cluster of the Beijing-Tianjin-Hebei region, Xiong'an New Area was imagined; one major consideration was to rebalance the regional structure that is overconcentrated in Beijing (see chapter 5). In contrast to many small cities that suffer urban shrinkage, one planning imperative for megacities like Beijing is to control its growth—urban expansion, densification, or population increase—to achieve so-called reduction-based development (*jian liang fa zhan*) through decentralizing the overconcentrated functions and resources. From 2014 to 2021, the permanent resident population of urban districts in Beijing shrank by 15 percent, and the city's overall construction land decreased by 110 km²—an achievement celebrated at the CPC Beijing Municipal Congress in 2022.[32] While small cities lament urban shrinkage, megacities celebrate it. What can better indicate the unbalanced development between cities?

New policy initiatives and plans for metropolitan circles are surging in recent years. Within a metropolitan circle, the power relationship between the central city and its surrounding cities is structurally unbalanced. This power relationship manifests not only in population and economic sizes but also in administrative status and political influence. Most central cities of the metropolitan circles are provincial capitals. They benefit from better resources and policy favoritism in urban development, often at the expense of other cities in the same metropolitan circle or province.

In this regard, Hefei is a typical example (see chapter 4). The city's rapid growth and innovation-driven economic transformation is more than an endogenous development effort of the city itself. It is situated in a whole-province scenario in which Hefei's growth prevails over that of other cities in Anhui Province, in areas of setting agendas for strategic development, infrastructure provision, and, most importantly, political preferences and policy favoritism at the provincial level. Administrative and political factors have intervened in intercity competition, which, in conventional belief, is supposed to be shaped by market forces. The nonmarket factors are complicating and exacerbating intercity inequalities.

8

THE NATURE OF THE
CHINESE CITY

J iang Kairu is a Chinese songwriter. His songs belong to so-called mainstream themes (*zhu xuan lv*) in the official discourse: these songs are mostly celebratory, praising, and sometimes propagandic. Jiang moved to Shenzhen in May 1992, at the nearly retirement age of fifty-seven, from Heilongjiang Province in northeast China—which was inland, closed, and backward compared with south China then—to pursue a new career and life in the mecca of China's reform and opening up. According to public media, Jiang's move was inspired by the reportage on Deng Xiaoping's Southern Tour earlier that year, during which Deng visited several southern cities, including Shenzhen, and made a series of Southern Talks. The tour and talks were critical in transforming contemporary China. They relaunched Deng Xiaoping's reform and opening-up agenda, which had stalled in the years 1989–1991 after the Tiananmen Square Incident.

In December 1992, Jiang Kairu wrote the song "The Story of Spring" spontaneously, praising Deng Xiaoping and his role in building Shenzhen and changing China. The song mentions neither Deng nor Shenzhen, alluding to "an old man drawing a circle beside the South China Sea," which started the rise of both a city and a nation. Since its formal publicity in 1994, the song has achieved instant popularity and tremendous official endorsement; it is now a classic Chinese song of mainstream themes. Its theme and tune strike a chord with many Chinese, who echo its artistic expressions about Deng and his transformation of the nation.

Deng Xiaoping passed away in February 1997. Later that year, Jiang Kairu wrote another song, "Entering a New Era" (*Zou jing xin shi dai*), acknowledging China's post-Deng transition into a new era under the leadership of Jiang Zemin, who was in office then. This song does not mention Jiang Zemin, referring to him as "a leader inheriting the past and pioneering the future." Was Jiang Zemin's time a new era, as Jiang Kairu extolled in the song? It is out of the question in the predominant discourse of Xi Jinping's new era, since he came into power in late 2012.

Deng Xiaoping selected two generations of top leaders, Jiang Zemin and Hu Jintao, to ensure that his modernization agenda of reform and opening up and political will would be faithfully implemented after his death. Both Jiang and Hu seemed to have fulfilled Deng's expectations during their reigns from the 1990s to the early 2010s. In Xi Jinping's new era discourse, the post-1949 history of China is divided into three broad eras—Maoist, Dengist, and Xi'ist—in which the terms of both of Xi's predecessors, Jiang Zemin and Hu Jintao, are classified in the Dengist era, and Xi claimed a new era of his own.

THE "NEWNESS" IN PERSPECTIVE

In October 2022, the twentieth CPC National Congress was held in Beijing. Following the norms of political power transition established in the Dengist era, such a congress should have been the time when a new generation of leaders would be sworn in. This time, however, people did not expect that to occur. Xi Jinping had, for a long time, paved the way for a third five-year term, after serving two terms beginning in late 2012. There are also signs that he is likely to stay in power—or maintain his power influence—for a longer period than three terms.

On October 23, Xi's reappearance in public after he was "reelected" at the congress as the party head was not a surprise to audiences. However, the composition of his top team—the Politburo Standing Committee—still presented a surprise. All the other members of the committee are Xi's protégés or loyalists. The market responded immediately: on the second day after the unveiling of Xi's team, stocks in Hong Kong, Shanghai, and Shenzhen plunged. On an occasion like this congress, people would expect to see new leadership representing optimism and hope. On the contrary, Xi Jinping and his team brought about feelings of pessimism and doubt. There was a clear ethos of frustration, depression, and a sense of betrayal among the Chinese at home and overseas.

In early 2022, the term "runology" (*run xue*)—an online neologism meaning "the study of running away"—became popular in China. This term expressed many people's frustration with China's draconian dynamic zero-COVID policy (see chapter 3), downward economic trend, and changing political climate, and their wish to escape them by emigrating overseas. The popularity of runology was boosted after this congress. In late November 2022, there were "white paper" protests—a subtle way of expressing defiance by holding white sheets of paper—in major Chinese cities against the COVID policy, rising authoritarianism, and tightening social control. These protests, although they were ad hoc and small in scale, had been rare in China after the Tiananmen Square Incident in 1989. In early December, maybe because of the pressures from the protests, the Chinese government suddenly terminated its zero-COVID policy, unplanned and unprepared.

One criticism of Deng Xiaoping's reform is that it was lopsided: while his reform remade China in an economic sense, it made no attempt to structurally improve China's political system to match its economic and social progress, and further to ensure the country's strategic and comprehensive modernization. In fact, a structural political reform was never on Deng's agenda. Since the Tiananmen Square Incident, political reform has become a taboo topic in the Chinese discourse. But there have been worries that the lack of political reform would someday exact a price.

On March 14, 2012, Wen Jiabao, at his last press conference as Chinese premier, warned that without successful political reform—especially a reform of the leadership system of the party and the nation—China's economic reform and its achievement could be jeopardized, and the historical tragedy of the Cultural Revolution might happen again. Wen also stressed that any reform would require people's enlightenment, support, proaction, and creativity.

The manner of the making of Xi Jinping and the narrative of his new era is not new. It is "reMaoization" mixed with certain elements of "deDengization." Observers tend to approach Xi Jinping's rise and maneuvering of power through the lenses of his personal experiences and qualities. Xi's generation grew up and received early education in the Maoist era. There are explicit Maoist styles in Xi's political language and policy approach. More importantly, the factors for reMaoization are systematic and institutional. The basic system and institution that have enabled Xi's grip on power and its approach and representation are not new. They have been in practice not just since 1949, when the communist regime was established, but for around two millennia of the Chinese empire. China is changing fast, but certain aspects at the very core of the "Chineseness" are enduring. In these senses, Xi Jinping is turning to an old way to aspire to a new era, one whose newness is questionable, and which also maps out a future—despite the grandeur of its narrative—of justifiable uncertainty and unpredictability.

> When Deng stepped aside in 1992 he had fulfilled the mission that had eluded China's leaders for 150 years: he and his colleagues had found a way to enrich the Chinese people and strengthen the country. . . . China continued to change rapidly, but the basic structural changes developed under Deng's leadership have already continued for two decades, and with some adaptations, they may extend long into the future. Indeed, the structural changes that took place under Deng's leadership rank among the most basic changes since the Chinese empire took shape during the Han dynasty over two millennia ago.[1]

Ezra F. Vogel, Deng Xiaoping's biographer, wrote that in his book *Deng Xiaoping and the Transformation of China* (2011). Vogel did not see Deng's transformation of China in the post-1949 history. Rather, he saw Deng's legacy in longer Chinese historical timelines of one hundred fifty years and two millennia, as well as in a broader contemporary international context—China as "an open, urban, national society" and as "a superpower."[2] There is no intellectual or political dispute that Deng created his own era by swerving the direction of the Maoist era—to the surprise and awe of many people inside and outside the nation. Deng was not the only leader within the party elite to endorse and advocate changes at the end of the 1970s. But he seemed destined to steer the titanic, ancient nation onto a new course of modernization. Deng was a pragmatist. He refused any theorization—or ideological mythification—of the changes he was bringing about. His successors did so to justify and legitimize their inheritance of his legacy. Deng also despised personality cult, from which he, his peers, and the Chinese people suffered so much during the Maoist era.

Vogel's selection of historical timelines for comprehending Deng's transformation of China was well considered. It is easy to understand the two millennia of the Chinese empire's history. People who are unfamiliar with Chinese modern history might be puzzled by the timeline of one hundred fifty years, which (roughly calculated at the time of the book's publication in 2011) commenced from 1840 when the British army first invaded China during the Opium War. The colonization of Hong Kong was an outcome of that war (see chapter 6). The year 1840 is a critical dividing line between ancient and modern China in the writing of Chinese history. Ever since, modernity has been imposed, resisted, mingled, and contested, steering the course of an ancient nation, society, and civilization in a new direction.

Set in this historical context of modern China, Deng Xiaoping's reform and opening up is essentially a modernization agenda: the genesis of the "modern" drive can be traced back to 1840, traversing regime changes through the late Qing dynasty (1644–1912), the Republic of China (1912–1949), and the People's Republic of China (post-1949). Deng was not the first Chinese leader to attempt to modernize the nation, but he was the first to have "fulfilled the mission"—in Vogel's words—of finding a way of enriching the Chinese people and strengthening the country through modernization. Set in the longer timelines of post-1840 or the two millennia of Chinese history, post-Deng China is still in the Dengist era. The nation is, by and large, marching on the legacy of Deng despite certain elements of deDengization in the recent decade.

Similarly, there are historical contexts for summarizing an answer to the "new normal or old path" question of the new-type urbanization, which is raised in chapter 1. In the macro context of China's rural-urban transformation, Deng is the dividing line, quantitatively and qualitatively. China's urbanization is ongoing and still evolving, but much of the underlying base was established and instituted in Deng's time. The new normal notion was proposed and advocated in the context of the post-1978 growth and urbanization. Within this shorter timeframe and historical context, there is validated newness in the new-type urbanization discourse and practice arising since the 2010s, as examined in the previous chapters on several transformative urban phenomena.

I see a two-layer structure encapsulating the continuity and change between the old and the new Chinese city: a base layer and a representation layer. Continuity functions more at the base layer, and change manifests more at the representation layer. Comparatively, the base layer is constant, stable, and determining; the representation layer is evolving, dynamic, and responding. This two-layer structure is illustrative and analytical. The purpose here is to construct a structure to make sense of the historicity of the newness in the recent urban transformation and to unravel its continuity and change, which are both differentiated and interlinked. It is important to point out that like any social change, this urban transformation is not a unilinear process; it is cyclical and helical. It involves to-and-fros and complications in progression and regression.

THE GOVERNMENT-MARKET RELATIONALITY

The government-market relationality is the fulcrum of China's reform. Deng Xiaoping's reform and its success are mainly in the economic area, as commonly recognized. It is also lamented or complimented—depending on the perspectives employed—that the reform refrained from encroaching much into the political area. Interestingly, Deng maintained that he did not know much about the economy and that he viewed economic affairs mainly from a political perspective.[3] Deng appointed entrepreneurial and capable aides to implement his economic visions, however.

Zhao Ziyang was a key aide for Deng's economic reform through much of the 1980s. Zhao was the premier in 1980–1987 and secretary-general of the CPC in 1987–1989 before he was deposed for his pro-students stance during the student movement in the spring of 1989 that ultimately led to the tragic Tiananmen Square Incident. According to Zhao's memoir, Deng Xiaoping had advocated for the market economy, explicitly and firmly, since he had been in power beginning in the late 1970s.[4] But ideological and political contests between reformists and conservatives with regard to the planned economy and the market economy ran throughout the 1980s.

In his political finale of Southern Talks in early 1992, Deng brought an end to the debates and disputes, stating that both planning and market are economic means and that they do not define or differentiate socialism or capitalism per se.[5] Deng's resolute endorsement removed the ideological taboo of the market economy—which had been perceived as a hallmark of capitalism in China—in a communist regime. It paved the way for the "socialist market economy," which was enshrined in the orthodoxy of the party in late 1992 and written into the constitution in early 1993. Socialist market economy, like socialism with Chinese characteristics, is open to flexible interpretation, freeing itself from the ideological rigidity.

Two decades later, not long after Xi Jinping came into power, the *Decision of the Central Committee of the Communist Party of China on Some Major Issues Concerning Comprehensively*

Deepening the Reform was adopted at the third plenary session of the eighteenth CPC Central Committee in November 2013. The decision document stated: "We must deepen economic system reform by centering on the decisive role of the market in allocating resources, adhere to and improve the basic economic system, [and] accelerate the improvement of the modern market system, macro-control system and open economic system."[6]

The phrase "the decisive role of the market in allocating resources" was refreshing and encouraging when it was first announced. It was extolled by people who were frustrated by the slow progress of reform in the post-Deng time, especially in the second term of Hu Jintao's leadership in the years around 2010. The decision document was read as a commitment to the Dengist cause made by the new generation of leadership headed by Xi Jinping, who vowed to "deepen reform and expand opening up" at that time. Tribute and commitment to Deng's legacy would strengthen the legitimacy of the new leadership among the Chinese. In the first one or two years of his time in office, there were discussions and expectations that Xi Jinping might become a younger Deng Xiaoping, reflecting people's aspirations and advocacy at a critical moment of leadership transition.

As it has turned out in subsequent years, the market is not yet playing the decisive role in allocating resources, and there is a clear return of the government's intervention in the Chinese economy. In his report to the twentieth CPC National Congress in October 2022, Xi Jinping described the building of "a high-standard socialist market economy" as a cornerstone of underpinning "a new development pattern" and "high-quality development"; and he outlined that "we will work to see that the market plays the decisive role in resource allocation and that the government better plays its role."[7] The philosophy and tactics of reconciling the decisive role of the market and the better role of the government have shaped, and will continue to shape, the trajectory of and debates on market reform.

The market has been firmly established in the Chinese ortho-dox discourse of ideology and policy, but the functioning of the government-market relationality has demonstrated strong path dependence and endogenous rationale and attributes. Compared with the 1990s—the heyday of market reform—there has been a noticeable return of the government's involvement in the economic system in the recent decade. In this regard, the market provides parameters. One catchphrase of the 1990s was "jumping to the sea" (*xia hai*), describing the phenomenon of people leaving government agencies or state-owned enterprises (SOEs) to join the private sector and embrace market forces. Foreign firms were top employment choices for many new graduates, as they offered attractive remuneration and enviable opportunities.

In the recent decade, "civil service examination" (*kao gong*) has become a new trend for many young people; they sit in the competitive examination to seek a career in civil service. The reasons for young people wanting to join the public sec-tor today—in contrast to the 1990s, when they wanted to depart from it—could be complicated, involving social changes and historical and cultural ethos. But one major explanation is eco-nomical. Government jobs provide better security, stability, and long-term reward—despite much lower salaries in terms of cash value—than the private and foreign firms in the new economic circumstance.

This pendulum of choices for young people reflects a shift in the government-market relationality. There has been a clear resurgence of the government, releveraging the relationality toward a prevalence of the government over the market in allocating resources. The decentralization of governance power is often read as an explanatory factor in China's reform and transformation, including urbanization, in the 1980s–1990s, in that it triggered grassroots ingenuity and bottom-up entrepreneurship and innovation.[8] This decentralization trend has been reversed toward a recentralization of power, a salient governance attribute of the new era. Accordingly, "top-level design" (*ding ceng she ji*) has been emphasized as a parallel of—if not a replacement for— "crossing the river by touching the stones" (*mo zhe shi tou guo he*), the famous Deng Xiaoping's motto for his trial-and-error reform. In the official discourse, both are described as the guiding principles for "comprehensively deepening the reform," functioning dialectically. In reality, an elevated belief in and endorsement of top-level design has justified and legitimized the necessity of top-down planning and government intervention into areas where market forces should be at play.

"Whole-state system" (*ju guo ti zhi*)—a strong state role in concentrating resources to achieve prioritized targets—was a hallmark of centralized governance in the Maoist era. It was sidelined, and sometimes criticized in unofficial discourse, in much of the market-oriented reform era of the 1980s–1990s for its explicit imprints of the planned economy and the proven drawbacks of government intervention. Since the late 2000s, there has been a surge of so-called new whole-state system in the official discourse, policies, and practices, as opposed to the old whole-state system of the Maoist era in the 1950s–1970s.

The new whole-state system is not a return to the old one. Rather, it is a recentralized governance approach to expanding the government's role in the economy through new policy tools like "state-led financialization" and "state-private fusion."[9] Rhetorically, the new whole-state system is celebrated as an institutional superiority in pursuing strategic goals like indigenous innovation and in tackling domestic and global crises like the U.S.-China trade war and COVID-19. In his report to the twentieth CPC National Congress in October 2022, Xi Jinping reaffirmed the role of the new whole-state system in advancing scientific and technological innovation, stating that "we will improve the *new system for mobilizing resources nationwide* [italics added; this phrase literally translates as "new whole-state system"] to make key technological breakthroughs."[10]

Yongnian Zheng and Yanjie Huang offer an analytical framework of "market in state" to conceptualize the evolving relations between state and market in contemporary China at three layers: a free market at the grassroots level, mutual interpenetration at the intermediary layer, and state capitalism at the top layer.[11] The three-layer structure and the functioning of state-market relations at each layer are arguable; these are not the focus of discussion here, however. There are merits in the notion of market in state for its endogenous nature of understanding contemporary Chinese political economy, and this nature has historical resonance. In the Chinese context—contemporary and historical— the state's political principles dominate the market's economic principles; the market is not an autonomous, self-regulating order but one that is integral and subordinate to a state-centered order.[12] This notion and its logic seem to respond to and extend Deng Xiaoping's views that he approached economic affairs from a political perspective, and that the market is only an economic means.

Understanding this instrumentality of the market in the Chinese political economy is important for tackling the government-market relationality in China's urban transformation and urban discourse. Fulong Wu posits "planning centrality" and "market instruments" to reconcile planning and market in the political economy of governing China's urban transformation.[13]

A clearer articulation could be "state centrality" and "planning and market instruments" to crystallize their structural relations. From Deng Xiaoping's argument that both planning and market are economic means, it seems reasonable to infer that these means are contradictory as well as complementary—a sort of Chinese *yin-yang* thinking—in serving his mission of economic development. But Wu provides a reinforcing observation on the instrumentality of the market for the state: "Greater orientation towards the market does not automatically lead to the reduction of planning. Rather, it strengthens the politics of using market instruments. . . . Rather than being replaced by market power, state power is reinforced by its use of market instruments."[14]

This government-market relationality helps make sense of the rationale for a combination of capable government and effective market in enabling Hefei's innovation-driven economic growth and urban transformation; it further helps justify the local government's direct participation in economic activities and the local leader's pride in it (see chapter 4). It also helps in understanding the recent regional planning discourse for metropolitan circles. In February 2019, the National Development and Reform Commission released *Guiding Opinions on Cultivating and Developing Modern Metropolitan Circles*. While admitting that the evolving development of metropolitan circles is a "natural" process, the document set the principle of "adhering to the leading of the market and the guiding of the government" in their planning and development.[15] But the regional planning, as illustrated by the case of Chengdu metropolitan circle (see chapter 7), has been led by the government, with limited or token involvement of the market. The crystallized government-market relationality sheds light on many aspects of the recent urban transformation in China.

THE "CHINESENESS"

We have put forward the Chinese Dream of the great rejuvenation of the Chinese nation and proposed promoting national
rejuvenation through a Chinese path to modernization. . . .
Chinese modernization offers humanity a new choice for achieving modernization. . . . Chinese modernization . . . contains elements that are common to the modernization processes of all
countries, but it is more characterized by features that are unique
to the Chinese context.[16]

This statement is excerpted from Xi Jinping's report to the
twentieth CPC National Congress in October 2022. Overall,
this report was lackluster; much of its content had already been
expressed in the official discourse. One of the several notions
that have attracted some attention is "Chinese path to modernization" or "Chinese modernization," which literally means
"Chinese-style modernization" (*zhong guo shi xian dai hua*).
The notion of Chinese-style modernization is not new: Deng
Xiaoping talked about it in the 1980s. But it has been particularly highlighted in the official discourse since 2021 and became
a focal concept in Xi's report.

Chinese-style modernization happens to touch on this book's
conclusive notion of the "Chineseness" in China's urbanization
and modernization. A similar notion was also expressed by the
late John Friedmann, a distant but keen observer of China's
urban transformation, in 2006: "China's urbanization is a result
of forces that in their origins are essentially endogenous. . . .
Chinese cities are evolving in their own ways, and will end up
as cities embodying a *Chinese form of modernity*, regardless of
how many office towers and luxury hotels built in Shanghai are
designed by Western architects. . . . Chinese urbanization must

be studied from within rather than as an epiphenomenon of some vague dynamics bundled together and marketed under the brand name of globalization."[17]

There has been no shortage of writings that graft Western concepts and theories to the Chinese city to "internationalize" an understanding of it, nor has there been a shortage of efforts to seek continuity and change—hidden or expressed—between traditional and modern urban experiences and representations.[18] The encountering of the Chinese and the international (or Western) has run through the reading of the Chinese city in recent decades. Intellectually, the Chinese planning theory—if there is such thing as planning theory—is often presumed as having a "hybrid nature," combining the Chinese and the Western.[19] However, the relationality in this hybridity is subject to reconstruction and reinterpretation. A Western reading of China's urbanization could easily emphasize its uniqueness—falling outside "conventional generalisations" and "standard discussions" about urban development and urban change—that warrants a label of "urbanisation with Chinese characteristics."[20]

Conversely, a Chinese perspective could comfortably identify several Western urban notions and their representations in China, refuting the uniqueness of the Chinese city as a singular urban model.[21] Whether China's urbanization is unique or general may not be a valid question, depending on perspectives, subjects, and issues involved in debates. However, the Chinese-Western relationality in the reading of the Chinese city requires refreshed thinking.

In the first several years of the twenty-first century, I was an urban practitioner in Beijing working on mega development projects. Those years were the golden age of urban planning, design, and development in the city and the nation; they presented unusual opportunities for that generation of urban practitioners both in China and overseas. In 2001, Beijing won the bid for the 2008 Olympic Games, and China was admitted into the World Trade Organization. At the very beginning of a new century, things looked promising and optimistic. Both China and the world (or the West) were keen on closer engagement. The capital city naturally was a hub for the China-world connections. In the area of urban development, numerous international agencies flocked to the city to seek opportunities. I was able to work with a suite of international actors—consultants, investors, managers, engineers, planners, and architects—mostly from the West; I also observed numerous projects that had some form of international involvement.

The scale and importance of many projects would be unimaginable today. These international agents were top-tier names in their fields; they have left their professional imprints in most global cities. Beijing was the newest hotspot then. "Internationalization" was the buzzword—it still is, but in a profoundly different context today—in nearly every aspect of the city's transformation. This internationalization has left obvious legacies in the cityscape and skyline. Beijing's several iconic structures were designed by so-called starchitects from the West: the National Grand Theatre by Paul Andreu from France, China Central Television Headquarters by the Dutch architect Rem Koolhaas, and the National Stadium (Bird's Nest) by Herzog & de Meuron, a Swiss architecture firm. These projects attracted great interest, debate, and controversy at the time; one strong criticism was that the city's architecture was being Westernized.

In thinking about these experiences two decades later, at both temporal and spatial distance, I feel that the very nature of the transformation of Beijing—and of many Chinese cities—is Chinese. It has followed a Chinese logic, purpose, and approach, while internationalization has served an instrumental role, or has expressed a representation.

Reading the Chineseness in the imaginary and practice of the latest Chinese new city Xiong'an (see chapter 5) reminds me of the ethos in the *Greater Shanghai Plan* (1927–1937) and the "Chinese renaissance" of architecture in Shanghai in the 1920s–1930s. The *Greater Shanghai Plan* was not fully implemented due to financial constraints and wars. Technically and professionally, it was the earliest modern plan in China and had strong Western influences on its thinking and approaches. However, it was a nationalist plan, which was essentially about building a new city and a new nation during the period of the Republic of China.[22] Separated by nearly a century, these two benchmark plans—the earliest modern plan of Shanghai and the latest contemporary plan of Xiong'an—contain a dialogue on the Chineseness in urban imaginary and planning. The two plans have profoundly different social, economic, and political settings. However, they seem to converge in historical and cultural senses.

A planning discourse could be highly political, contemporary, and futuristic; the intellectual root could be very traditional and retrospective. In this regard, John Friedmann was insightful in arguing for a "backward into the future" approach to the Chinese city.[23] He also argued that "China has its own urban traditions from which it is fashioning the hybrid cities of the present generation."[24] But his take on the nature of the Chinese city was made in terms of "city identities" and "self-assertion,"[25] which were alien to the Chinese setting, countering many aspects of the urban transformation in recent decades, as examined in previous chapters.

The traditional wisdom of "essence-function" (*ti-yong*) seems to provide an interesting framework for grappling with the nature of the Chinese city. The essence-function paradigm is rooted in ancient Confucianism, Daoism, and Buddhism and in their interaction with and fusion into traditional Chinese and broader oriental philosophy and religion; it has been subject to new meanings, interpretations, contexts, and debates.[26]

The definitions of essence-function vary. Here I draw on the fundamental of the duality in it that refers to two correlative realms of reality in any single entity. Essence (*ti*) means "body": substance, origin, base, and principles. It is the primary, inner, fundamental realm, referring to an absolute reality. Function (*yong*) means "use": application, utility, and phenomenon. It is the secondary, outer, and concrete realm, referring to a relative reality. The terms are not distinct from each other. They are two interrelated aspects of one thing: function is the representation of essence; essence is manifested through function. Thus, a thing's *yong*, or function, is "its characteristic activity in accordance with its nature"—its *ti*, or essence.[27]

In my writings about Shenzhen and Pudong, Shanghai—two signature new cities representative of China's urbanization—I have employed an endogenous development perspective and highlighted a meta-thesis in understanding the Chinese city: urbanization is integral to modernization; city making is instrumental to nation building.[28] Examined through the essence-function paradigm, these relationalities can be further illustrated: urbanization and city making are the function of the essence of modernization and nation building.

This meta-thesis could be universal in a way, but it is especially Chinese in the nation's modern transformation in recent decades, and further in recent centuries. A historical vista matters, although China's urbanization as we know it today normally refers to the post-1978 period. The meta-thesis breaks through the historical phases of modern China classified by regime changes or power restructuring. The pursuit of a "Chinese form of modernity" can be traced back to 1840, when the ancient civilization was first broken open by modern forces, and right through to the latest imagining of Chinese-style modernization toward the mid-twenty-first century. However, underlying the pursuit of modernity and its contexts, the intellectual and cultural roots may be deeper and longer than the modern age—they are traditional and Chinese. This proposition penetrates the massive urbanization in recent decades, which is justifiably the focus of attention and debate, and establishes a dialogue about the reading of the Chinese city that links past, present, and future.

ACKNOWLEDGMENTS

My family has always given me the greatest support in completing each of my books, including this latest one. Support from my wife, Coco, is more than love; she is a collaborator in every book of mine. She assisted with creating several graphics in this book. She was also the first listener and critic of many ideas discussed here. My eight-year-old son, Eddie, has often asked me hard questions about the world and the universe. While I do not have answers to most of the questions, they have educated me about exploring and inquiring into the unknown.

Many friends are in or from China. This book has benefited hugely from my engagement with them. Their first-hand experiences—personal or professional—of China and Chinese cities have informed and inspired the volume's narrative and argument. Numerous colleagues—known and unknown—have contributed to the fruition of this book directly or indirectly, consciously or unconsciously. This book has not come out of the blue; it is part of a borderless intellectual community of the Chinese city. Previous works on this subject have provided the foundation for this book, as well as suggested a need for it.

My editor at Columbia University Press, Lowell Frye, has professionally and patiently guided and supported me through the journey of publication. Justine McNamara copyedited an early draft of the book, making it more accurate and readable. Two anonymous reviewers provided useful comments, which helped sharpen the book's focus and argument. The author is responsible for any errors.

NOTES

1. A NEW URBAN ERA?

1. Xi Jinping, *Hold High the Great Banner of Socialism with Chinese Characteristics and Strive in Unity to Build a Modern Socialist Country in All Respects* (Report, Xinhua, Beijing, October 25, 2022): 18, https://english .news.cn/20221025/8eb6f5239f984f01a2bc45b5b5dboc51/c.html.
2. Xi, *Hold High the Great Banner*, 5.
3. World Bank, "Urban Population (% of Total Population)," accessed January 19, 2023, https://data.worldbank.org/indicator/SP.URB.TOTL .IN.ZS.
4. World Bank, "GDP per Capita (Current US$)," accessed January 20, 2023, https://data.worldbank.org/indicator/NY.GDP.PCAP.CD.
5. Tianyu Wang, "2021: China's GDP Growth Beats Expectations with 8.1 Percent, Fastest in 10 Years," *CGTN*, January 17, 2022, https://news .cgtn.com/news/2022-01-17/China-s-GDP-tops-114-36-trillion-yuan -in-2021-16T64Jtona8/index.html.
6. Nada Hamadeh, Catherine van Rompaey, and Eric Metreau, "New World Bank Country Classifications by Income Level: 2021–2022." *Data Blog, World Bank Blogs*, July 1, 2021, https://blogs.worldbank.org/opendata /new-world-bank-country-classifications-income-level-2021-2022.
7. World Bank, "Population, Total—China, World," accessed January 19, 2023, https://data.worldbank.org/indicator/SP.POP.TOTL?end=2020 &locations=CN-1W&start=1978&view=chart.
8. "China May Soon Become a High-Income Country," *Economist*, February 5, 2022, https://www.economist.com/finance-and-economics/2022/02/05 /china-may-soon-become-a-high-income-country.

9. On inclusive and sustainable urban development in China, see OECD, *All on Board: Making Inclusive Growth Happen in China* (Paris: OECD, May 29, 2015), https://www.oecd.org/economy/all-on-board-9789264218512 -en.htm; World Bank, *Urban China: Toward Efficient, Inclusive, and Sustainable Urbanization* (Washington, DC: World Bank, 2014), http://hdl.handle.net/10986/18865.

10. UN-Habitat, *The State of Asian and Pacific Cities 2015: Urban Transformations Shifting from Quantity to Quality* (Nairobi: UN-Habitat, 2015), https://unhabitat.org/the-state-of-asian-and-pacific-cities-2015.

11. Mao Zedong, "On Contradiction," *Marxists Internet Archive*, August 1937, transcription by the Maoist Documentation Project, last modified 2020, https://www.marxists.org/reference/archive/mao/selected-works /volume-1/mswv1_17.htm.

12. Lingui Xu, "Xinhua Insight: China Embraces New 'Principal Contradiction' When Embarking on New Journey," *XinhuaNet*, October 20, 2017, http://www.xinhuanet.com/english/2017-10/20/c_136694592.htm.

13. Xu, "Xinhua Insight."

14. National Bureau of Statistics, PRC, "Key Data from the 7th National Census on Population" [in Chinese], May 11, 2021, http://www.stats.gov .cn/tjsj/zxfb/202105/t20210510_1817176.html.

15. Richard Hu, "China's Urban Age," in *Connecting Cities: China*, ed. Chris Johnson, Richard Hu, and Shanti Abedin (Sydney: Metropolis Congress, 2008), 153.

16. Yimin Sun and Daria Lisaia, "History Matters: Chinese Urbanisation as an Emergent Space," *Urbanisation* 3, no. 1 (2018): 1, https://doi.org /10.1177/2455747118790422.

17. Angel Gurría, "A 'New Normal' for Urbanisation," OECD, March 21, 2015, https://www.oecd.org/china/china-development-forum-a-new -normal-for-urbanisation.htm.

18. Richard Hu and Weijie Chen, *Global Shanghai Remade: The Rise of Pudong New Area* (Abingdon, UK: Routledge, 2019), 236–39.

2. THE GREEN REVOLUTION

1. IQAir, *2020 World Air Quality Report: Region & City PM2.5 Ranking* (Goldach, Switzerland: IQAir, 2020), 15, https://www.iqair.com/world -most-polluted-cities/world-air-quality-report-2020-en.pdf.

2. IQAir, 2020 *World Air Quality Report*, 6.

3. IQAir, 2020 *World Air Quality Report*, 11.

4. IQAir, 2020 *World Air Quality Report*, 15.

5. Xi Jinping, *Hold High the Great Banner of Socialism with Chinese Characteristics and Strive in Unity to Build a Modern Socialist Country in All Respects* (Report, Xinhua, Beijing, October 25, 2022): 9, https://english .news.cn/20221025/8eb6f5239f984f01a2bc45b5b5db0c51/c.html.

6. Deng Xiaoping, *Selected Works of Deng Xiaoping*, vol. 3 [in Chinese] (Beijing: People's Publishing House, 1993), 81, 113.

7. Wikipedia, s.v. "2013 Eastern China Smog," accessed January 21, 2023, https://en.wikipedia.org/wiki/2013_Eastern_China_smog.

8. Yu Qin and Hongjia Zhu, "Run Away? Air Pollution and Emigration Interests in China," *Journal of Population Economics* 31 (2018): 235, https:// doi.org/10.1007/s00148-017-0653-0.

9. Shuai Chen, Paulina Oliva, and Peng Zhang. "The Effect of Air Pollution on Migration: Evidence from China," *Journal of Development Economics* 156 (May 2022): 1, article 102833, https://doi.org/10.1016/j.jdeveco .2022.102833.

10. Deng, *Selected Works*, 370–83.

11. Hiroshi Onishi, "Superstructure Determined by Base," *World Review of Political Economy* 6, no. 1 (2015): 75–93, https://www.jstor.org/stable /10.13169/worlrevipoliecon.6.1.0075.

12. Richard Hu, *The Shenzhen Phenomenon: From Fishing Village to Global Knowledge City* (Abingdon, UK: Routledge, 2020), 99–101.

13. Hossein Azadi, Gijs Verheijke, and Frank Witlox, "Pollute First, Clean up Later?," *Global and Planetary Change* 78, nos. 3–4 (2011): 81, https:// doi.org/10.1016/j.gloplacha.2011.05.006.

14. Piper Gaubatz and Dean Hanink, "Learning from Taiyuan: Chinese Cities as Urban Sustainability Laboratories," *Geography and Sustainability* 1, no. 2 (2020): 118, https://doi.org/10.1016/j.geosus.2020.06 .004.

15. On Expo 2010 in Shanghai, see Richard Hu and Weijie Chen, *Global Shanghai Remade: The Rise of Pudong New Area* (Abingdon, UK: Routledge, 2019): 219–24.

16. Arup, "Vision of the Future," *A² Magazine*, 2005, 9, https://www.arup .com/perspectives/publications/magazines-and-periodicals/a2/a2 -magazine-issue-1.

17. I-Chun Catherine Chang, "Failure Matters: Reassembling Eco-Urbanism in a Globalizing China," *Environment and Planning A: Economy and Space* 49, no. 8 (2017): 1719–42, https://doi.org/10.1177/0308518X16685092.

18. Li Yu, "Low Carbon Eco-City: New Approach for Chinese Urbanisation," *Habitat International* 44 (2014): 104, https://doi.org/10.1016/j.habitatint.2014.05.004.

19. Federico Caprotti, "Eco-Urbanism and the Eco-City, or, Denying the Right to the City?," *Antipode* 46, no. 5 (2014): 1285, https://doi.org/10.1111/anti.12087.

20. Robert Weatherley and Vanessa Bauer, "A New Chinese Modernity? The Discourse of Eco-Civilisation Applied to the Belt and Road Initiative," *Third World Quarterly* 42, no. 9 (2021): 2115–32. https://doi.org/10.1080/01436597.2021.1905511.

21. Coraline Goron, "Ecological Civilisation and the Political Limits of a Chinese Concept of Sustainability," *China Perspectives*, no. 4 (2018): 40, https://doi.org/10.4000/chinaperspectives.8463.

22. Xi Jinping, *Secure a Decisive Victory in Building a Moderately Prosperous Society in All Respects and Strive for the Great Success of Socialism with Chinese Characteristics for a New Era* (Report, Xinhua, Beijing, October 18, 2017): 20, http://www.xinhuanet.com/english/download/Xi_Jinping's _report_at_19th_CPC_National_Congress.pdf.

23. On China's "eco-civilization," see Sam Geall and Adrian Ely, "Narratives and Pathways Towards an Ecological Civilization in Contemporary China," *China Quarterly* 236 (2018): 1175–96, https://doi.org/10.1017 /S0305741018001315; Mette Halskov Hansen, Hongtao Li, and Rune Svarverud, "Ecological Civilization: Interpreting the Chinese Past, Projecting the Global Future," *Global Environmental Change* 53 (2018): 195–203, https://doi.org/10.1016/j.gloenvcha.2018.09.014; Arthur Hanson, "Ecological Civilization in the People's Republic of China: Values, Action, and Future Needs" (East Asia Working Papers, Asian Development Bank, Manila, 2019), https://www.adb.org/publications /ecological-civilization-values-action-future-needs; and United Nations Environment Programme, *Green Is Gold: The Strategy and Actions of China's Ecological Civilization* (Analysis, United Nations Environment Programme, Nairobi, 2016), https://reliefweb.int/sites/reliefweb.int/files /resources/greenisgold_en_20160519.pdf.

24. United Nations, *Report of the World Commission on Environment and Development: Our Common Future* (New York: World Commission on Environment and Development, 1987), https://sustainabledevelopment .un.org/content/documents/5987our-common-future.pdf.

25. "Economic Growth No Longer Requires Rising Emissions," *Economist*, November 10, 2022, https://www.economist.com/leaders/2022/11/10 /economic-growth-no-longer-requires-rising-emissions.

26. Yonglong Lu et al., "Forty Years of Reform and Opening Up: China's Progress Toward a Sustainable Path," *Science Advances* 5, no. 8 (2019): 1, article eaau9413, https://doi.org/10.1126/sciadv.aau9413.

27. Xi Jinping, "Full Text of Xi's Statement at the General Debate of the 75th Session of the United Nations General Assembly," *Xinhua.Net*, September 23, 2020, http://www.xinhuanet.com/english/2020-09/23/c _139388686.htm.

28. Joanna Lewis and Laura Edwards, *Assessing China's Energy and Climate Goals* (Report, Center for American Progress, Washington, D.C., May 6, 2021): 1, https://www.americanprogress.org/issues/security /reports/2021/05/06/499096/assessing-chinas-energy-climate-goals/.

29. Climate Action Tracker, "China," May 19, 2022, https://climateaction tracker.org/countries/china/2022-05-19/.

30. Hongbo Duan et al., "Assessing China's Efforts to Pursue the 1.5°C Warming Limit," *Science* 372, no. 6540 (2021): 378, https://doi.org/10.1126 /science.aba8767.

31. Ministry of Ecology and Environment, PRC, "The State Council Issues Action Plan on Prevention and Control of Air Pollution Introducing Ten Measures to Improve Air Quality," September 12, 2013, http://english .mee.gov.cn/News_service/infocus/201309/t20130924_260707.shtml.

32. IQAir, *2020 World Air Quality Report*, 6.

33. "Sixty Thousand Staff Became Redundant from Shougang's Relocation; Director of Board Denies Lay-off" [in Chinese], *Sina*, April 5, 2005, http://finance.sina.com.cn/g/20050405/08201487690.shtml.

34. On Caofeidian eco-city, see Simon Joss and Arthur P. Molella, "The Eco-City as Urban Technology: Perspectives on Caofeidian International Eco-City (China)," *Journal of Urban Technology* 20, no. 1 (2013): 115–37, https://doi.org/10.1080/10630732.2012.735411; and Li Yu, "Low Carbon Eco-City: New Approach for Chinese Urbanisation," *Habitat*

International 44 (2014): 102–10, https://doi.org/10.1016/j.habitatint.2014
.05.004.

35. Peng Lin, "Introduction of Tangshan Caofeidian Eco-City," presentation, Tangshan Caofeidian Eco-City Administrative Committee, October 2011, 5, https://www.esci-ksp.org/wp/wp-content/uploads/2016/11
/DrLinPeng.pdf.

36. Gilles Sabrie, "Caofeidian, the Chinese Eco-City That Became a Ghost
Town—in Pictures," *Guardian*, July 24, 2014, https://www.theguardian
.com/cities/gallery/2014/jul/23/caofeidian-chinese-eco-city-ghost-town
-in-pictures.

37. Arup, "Shaping China's First Climate Positive Project," accessed January 23,
2023, https://www.arup.com/projects/shougang-industry-services-park.

38. Hang Chen and Yan Du, "How Does Beijing Have More Days with
Blue Sky?" [in Chinese], *China News*, January 9, 2021, www.bj.chinanews
.com/news/2021/0109/80437.html.

39. Shu Tao, "An Evaluation on Our Country's Air Pollution and Damage
Trends" [in Chinese], September 29, 2021, https://mp.weixin.qq.com/s
/o8qoJJA4PfGio7AgO3rmJg.

40. Jing Huang et al., "Health Impact of China's Air Pollution Prevention and Control Action Plan: An Analysis of National Air Quality
Monitoring and Mortality Data," *Lancet Planetary Health* 2 (2018): e313,
https://doi.org/10.1016/S2542-5196(18)30141-4.

41. United Nations Environment Programme, *A Review of 20 Years' Air
Pollution Control in Beijing* (Report, United Nations Environment Programme, Nairobi, March 9, 2019), 6, https://www.unep.org/resources
/report/review-20-years-air-pollution-control-beijing.

42. IQAir, *2020 World Air Quality Report*, 12.

3. THE SMART CITY MOVEMENT

1. Richard Hu, "The State of Smart Cities in China: The Case of Shenzhen," *Energies* 12, no. 22 (2019): 7, article 4375, https://doi.org/10.3390
/en12224375.

2. Hu, "The State of Smart Cities in China," 6.

3. Chinese Government, *National New-Type Urbanization Plan (2014–
2020)* [in Chinese] (Beijing: Chinese Government, March 16, 2014),
http://www.gov.cn/zhengce/2014-03/16/content_2640075.htm.

4. Xi Jinping, *Secure a Decisive Victory in Building a Moderately Prosperous Society in All Respects and Strive for the Great Success of Socialism with Chinese Characteristics for a New Era* (Report, Xinhua, Beijing, October 18, 2017), 27, http://www.xinhuanet.com/english/download/Xi_Jinping's_report_at_19th_CPC_National_Congress.pdf.

5. Yun Gao and Zhaoyi Pan, "Graphic: Why Guizhou Is Becoming China's Big Data Valley," *CGTN*, December 26, 2019, https://news.cgtn.com/news/2019-12-26/Graphic-why-Guizhou-is-becoming-China-s-big-data-valley-MJyAjWbWtG/index.html.

6. CNN, "Guizhou: China's Finest: The Big Data Valley of China," accessed January 27, 2023, https://advertisementfeature.cnn.com/2018/guizhou/china-big-data-valley/.

7. Shanghai Government, *Shanghai Master Plan 2017–2035* [in Chinese] (Shanghai: Shanghai Government, January 2018), 24, https://www.supdri.com/2035/index.php?c=message&a=type&tid=33.

8. Shanghai Government, *Shanghai Master Plan 2017–2035*, 13.

9. Oscar Holland, "Tencent Is Building a Monaco-Sized 'City of the Future' in Shenzhen," *CNN*, June 16, 2020, https://edition.cnn.com/style/article/tencent-shenzhen-net-city/index.html.

10. Holland, "Tencent Is Building a Monaco-Sized 'City of the Future' in Shenzhen."

11. Katherine Atha et al., *China's Smart Cities Development* (Report, U.S.–China Economic and Security Review Commission, Washington, D.C., April 29, 2020), 2, https://www.uscc.gov/research/chinas-smart-cities-development.

12. Hu, "The State of Smart Cities in China," 1.

13. Hu, "The State of Smart Cities in China," 3.

14. See Richard Hu, "Planning for Economic Development," in *The Routledge Handbook of Planning History*, ed. Carola Hein (New York: Routledge, 2018), 313–18; Hu, "The State of Smart Cities in China," 4–5.

15. Shenzhen Government, *Shenzhen Municipal New-Type Smart City Construction Master Scheme* [in Chinese] (Shenzhen: Shenzhen Government, July 21, 2018), http://cgj.sz.gov.cn/xsmh/zhcg/zcfg/content/post_2017219.html.

16. State Council, PRC, "Premier Urges Use of Internet Plus to Boost Growth," June 25, 2015, http://english.www.gov.cn/premier/news/2015/06/25/content_281475134144826.htm.

17. Richard Hu, *Smart Design: Disruption, Crisis, and the Reshaping of Urban Spaces* (Abingdon, UK: Routledge, 2021), 141.

18. Rana Mitter and Elsbeth Johnson, "What the West Gets Wrong About China," *Harvard Business Review*, May–June 2021, https://hbr .org/2021/05/what-the-west-gets-wrong-about-china.

19. Wuhan Government, *Wuhan Action Plan for Speeding up the Construction of New-Type Smart City* [in Chinese] (Wuhan: Wuhan Government, 2020), http://www.wuhan.gov.cn/zwgk/xxgk/zfwj/bgtwj/202012 /t20201231_1586796.shtml.

20. Alina Polyakova and Chris Meserole, *Exporting Digital Authoritarianism: The Russian and Chinese Models* (Policy brief, Brookings Institution, Washington, D.C., 2019), 2–6, https://www.brookings.edu/wp-content /uploads/2019/08/FP_20190827_digital_authoritarianism_polyakova _meserole.pdf.

21. Atha et al., *China's Smart Cities Development*, 43–54.

22. Andrew Green, "Obituary: Li Wenliang," *Lancet* 395, no. 10225 (2020): 682, https://doi.org/10.1016/S0140-6736(20)30382-2.

23. Alice Ekman and Cristina de Esperanza Picardo, *Towards Urban Decoupling? China's Smart City Ambitions at the Time of Covid-19* (Brief, EU Institute for Security Studies, Luxembourg, May 14, 2020), 1, https:// www.iss.europa.eu/content/towards-urban-decoupling-china%E2%80 %99s-smart-city-ambitions-time-covid-19.

24. Chinese Government, "CPC Politburo Held a Meeting; Xi Jinping Presided Over It" [in Chinese], July 28, 2022, http://www.gov.cn/xinwen /2022-07/28/content_5703255.htm.

25. Xi Jinping, *Hold High the Great Banner of Socialism with Chinese Characteristics and Strive in Unity to Build a Modern Socialist Country in All Respects* (Report, Xinhua, Beijing, October 25, 2022), 3, https://english .news.cn/20221025/8eb6f5239f984f01a2bc45b5b5db0c51/c.html.

26. Hangzhou Bureau of Statistics, *Hangzhou Statistical Yearbook 2020* [in Chinese] (Beijing: China Statistics Press, 2020), 76, http://tjj.hangzhou .gov.cn/art/2020/10/29/art_1229453592_3819709.html.

27. Wikisource, s.v. "The Travels of Marco Polo: Description of the Great City of Kinsay, Which Is the Capital of the Whole Country of Manzi," accessed January 27, 2023, https://en.wikisource.org/wiki/The_Travels _of_Marco_Polo/Book_2/Chapter_76.

28. Hangzhou Bureau of Statistics, *Hangzhou Statistical Yearbook 2020*, 27.

29. Zhu Qian, "City Profile: Hangzhou," *Cities* 48 (2015): 44–45, https://doi.org/10.1016/j.cities.2015.06.004.

30. Hangzhou Bureau of Statistics, *Hangzhou Statistical Yearbook 2020*, 44.

31. *Economist* Intelligence, *China's Emerging City Rankings 2021: Unpacking Opportunities under the 14th Five-Year Plan* (Report, Economist Intelligence, London, 2021), 3, https://www.eiu.com/n/campaigns/china-emerging-city-rankings-2021/.

32. Federico Caprotti and Dong Liu, "Platform Urbanism and the Chinese Smart City: The Co-Production and Territorialisation of Hangzhou City Brain." *GeoJournal* 87 (2022): 1559, https://doi.org/https://doi.org/10.1007/s10708-020-10320-2.

33. Hangzhou Government, "Equip the City with a 'Brain'" [in Chinese], accessed January 27, 2023, http://www.hangzhou.gov.cn/art/2021/3/24/art_812262_59031715.html.

4. THE GREAT INNOVATION LEAP FORWARD

1. Ezra F. Vogel, *The Four Little Dragons: The Spread of Industrialization in East Asia* (Cambridge, MA: Harvard University Press, 1991).

2. Shang-Jin Wei, Zhuan Xie, and Xiaobo Zhang, "From 'Made in China' to 'Innovated in China': Necessity, Prospect, and Challenges," *Journal of Economic Perspectives* 31, no. 1 (2017): 68, https://www.aeaweb.org/articles?id=10.1257%2Fjep.31.1.49.

3. Chinese Government, *Outline Plan for National Innovation-Driven Development* [in Chinese] (Beijing: Chinese Government, May 19, 2016), http://www.gov.cn/zhengce/2016-05/19/content_5074812.htm.

4. Chinese Government, *The People's Republic of China's 14th Five-Year Plan for National Economic and Social Development & Outline Objectives of the 2035 Vision* [in Chinese] (Beijing: Chinese Government, March 13, 2021), 7, http://www.gov.cn/xinwen/2021-03/13/content_5592681.htm.

5. Xi Jinping, *Hold High the Great Banner of Socialism with Chinese Characteristics and Strive in Unity to Build a Modern Socialist Country in All Respects* (Report, Xinhua, Beijing, October 25, 2022), 28–29, https://english.news.cn/20221025/8eb6f5239f984f01a2bc45b5b5dboc51/c.html.

6. Chinese Government, "Bulletin on Statistics of National Investment in Research and Development in 2020" [in Chinese], September 22, 2021, http://www.gov.cn/xinwen/2021-09/22/content_5638653.htm; Dalian

University of Technology, *Report on China's R&D Expenditure* (Beijing: Zhi Shi Fen Zi, May 1, 2021), http://zhishifenzi.com/news/multiple /11239.html.

7. Dalian University of Technology, *Report on China's R&D Expenditure.*

8. "China Wants to Insulate Itself Against Western Sanctions," *Economist,* February 19, 2022, https://www.economist.com/business/2022/02/19 /china-wants-to-insulate-itself-against-western-sanctions.

9. UN-Habitat, *The Story of Shenzhen: Its Economic, Social and Environmental Transformation* (Nairobi: UN-Habitat, 2019), x, https://unhabitat .org/the-story-of-shenzhen-its-economic-social-and-environmental -transformation.

10. The data for both CNETDZs and CNHIDZs are recorded on Baidu Baike, a Chinese-language collaborative online encyclopedia. Baidu Baike, s.v. "China National Economic and Technical Development Zone" [*Guo Jia Ji Jing Ji Ji Shu Kai Fa Qu*] and "China National High-Tech Industrial Development Zone" [*Zhong Guo Gao Xin Ji Shu Chan Ye Kai Fa Qu*], accessed January 31, 2023, https://baike.baidu.com.

11. Edward J. Blakely and Richard Hu, *Crafting Innovative Places for Australia's Knowledge Economy* (Singapore: Palgrave Macmillan, 2019), 19.

12. Richard Hu and Weijie Chen, *Global Shanghai Remade: The Rise of Pudong New Area* (Abingdon, UK: Routledge, 2019), 35–39.

13. Hu and Chen, *Global Shanghai Remade,* 192–94.

14. Richard Hu, "Spatial Disruption and Planning Implication of the Sharing Economy: A Study of Smart Work in Canberra, Australia," *International Journal of Knowledge-Based Development* 10, no. 4 (2019): 315–37, https://doi.org/10.1504/IJKBD.2019.105125.

15. Jonathan Woetzel et al., *China's Digital Economy: A Leading Global Force* (Report, McKinsey Global Institute, August 3, 2017), 2, https://www .mckinsey.com/featured-insights/china/chinas-digital-economy-a -leading-global-force.

16. Manuel Castells, *The Rise of the Network Society,* 2nd ed. (Malden, MA: Blackwell, 2000), 453–59.

17. Baidu Baike, s.v. "Taobao Villages" [*Tao Bao Cun*], accessed January 31, 2023, https://baike.baidu.com.

18. AliResearch, "Research Report on Taobao Villages in China 2020" [in Chinese], October 20, 2020, http://www.aliresearch.com.

19. Weicheng Tang and Jin Zhu, "Informality and Rural Industry: Rethinking the Impacts of E-Commerce on Rural Development in China,"

Journal of Rural Studies 75 (2020): 20, https://doi.org/10.1016/j.jrurstud .2020.02.010.

20. On Taobao villages and e-urbanization, see Juan Lin et al., "Rural E-Commerce in China: Spatial Dynamics of Taobao Villages Development in Zhejiang Province," *Growth and Change* 53, no. 3 (2022): 1082–1101, https://doi.org/10.1111/grow.12560; and Yanliu Lin, "E-Urbanism: E-Commerce, Migration, and the Transformation of Taobao Villages in Urban China," *Cities* 91 (2019): 202–12, https://doi.org/10.1016/j.cities .2018.11.020.

21. Mei Nelson, "Debating China's AI Path: 'Alternative Routes,' or 'Overtaking on the Curve?,'" *DigiChina* (blog), *New America*, November 12, 2019, https://www.newamerica.org/cybersecurity-initiative/digichina /blog/debating-chinas-ai-path-alternative-routes-or-overtaking-on -the-curve/.

22. John Deutch, "Is Innovation China's New Great Leap Forward?," *Issues in Science and Technology* (Summer 2018): 37, http://web.mit.edu/chemistry /deutch/policy/2018-IsInnovChinaLeap-Issues.pdf.

23. On geopolitics and innovation, see Seth G. Jones et al., *Geopolitical Implications of Scientific Innovation Trends in Northeast Asia* (Report, CSIS International Security Program and Chey Institute for Advanced Studies, Washington, D.C., June 24, 2021), https://www.csis.org/analysis /geopolitical-implications-scientific-innovation-trends-northeast-asia; Caetano C. R. Penna, *Geopolitics and the Economics of Innovation* (Policy note, Brazilian Center for International Relations, Rio de Janeiro, 2020), https://www.cebri.org/media/documentos/arquivos/PolicyNote _Geopolitics_and_the.pdf; James L. Schoff and Asei Ito, *Competing with China on Technology and Innovation* (Alliance Policy Coordination Brief, Carnegie Endowment for International Peace, Washington, D.C., October 10, 2019), https://carnegieendowment.org/2019/10/10 /competing-with-china-on-technology-and-innovation-pub-80010; and United Nations, *Technology and Innovation Report 2021: Catching Technological Waves—Innovation with Equity* (Report, United Nations Conference on Trade and Development, New York, 2021), https://unctad .org/webflyer/technology-and-innovation-report-2021.

24. Richard Hu, *Smart Design: Disruption, Crisis, and the Reshaping of Urban Spaces* (Abingdon, UK: Routledge, 2021), 16–21.

25. "China Wants to Insulate Itself Against Western Sanctions."

26. Chinese Government, *14th Five-Year Plan*, 8, 13.

27. Chinese Government, "Bulletin on Statistics of National Investment in Research and Development in 2020."

28. Holly Chik, "China Set to Pass US on Research and Development Spending by 2025," *South China Morning Post*, July 16, 2021, https://www.scmp.com/news/china/science/article/3141263/china-set-pass-us-research-and-development-spending-2025.

29. White House, "Fact Sheet: CHIPS and Science Act Will Lower Costs, Create Jobs, Strengthen Supply Chains, and Counter China" (press release), August 9, 2022, https://www.whitehouse.gov/briefing-room/statements-releases/2022/08/09/fact-sheet-chips-and-science-act-will-lower-costs-create-jobs-strengthen-supply-chains-and-counter-china/.

30. "America Curbs Chinese Access to Advanced Computing," *Economist*, October 13, 2022, https://www.economist.com/business/2022/10/13/america-curbs-chinese-access-to-advanced-computing.

31. "China and the West Are in a Race to Foster Innovation," *Economist*, October 13, 2022, https://www.economist.com/briefing/2022/10/13/china-and-the-west-are-in-a-race-to-foster-innovation.

32. Baidu Baike, s.v. "Qian Xuesen's Question" [*Qian Xue Sen Zhi Wen*], accessed January 31, 2023, https://baike.baidu.com.

33. Philip Ball, "China's Great Leap Forward in Science," *Guardian*, February 18, 2018, https://www.theguardian.com/science/2018/feb/18/china-great-leap-forward-science-research-innovation-investment-5g-genetics-quantum-internet.

34. Anhui Statistics Bureau, "Bulletin of the 7th National Census in Anhui Province (No. 2)" [in Chinese], May 18, 2021, http://tjj.ah.gov.cn/ssah/qwfbjd/tjgb/sjtjgb/145782371.html.

35. Institute for Planets, "What Is Hefei?" [in Chinese], June 2, 2021, https://mp.weixin.qq.com/s/pcvpOylgxTv9AFZ8dfA88A.

36. Chinese Government, "The GDP of 23 Chinese Cities Exceeded RMB 1 Trillion" [in Chinese], January 30, 2021, http://www.gov.cn/xinwen/2021-01/30/content_5583703.htm.

37. Institute for Planets, "What Is Hefei?"

38. Zimu, "Hefei's Counterattack Is Not an Accident, You Will Understand After Reading the Three Stories" [in Chinese], *KK News*, June 17, 2021, https://kknews.cc/zh-cn/finance/n2nxoyq.html.

39. Institute for Planets, "What Is Hefei?"

40. Wanxia Zhao and Yonghua Zou, "Hefei: An Emerging City in Inland China," *Cities* 77 (2018): 164, https://doi.org/10.1016/j.cities.2018.01 .008.

41. Nature Index, "Top 200 Science Cities," *Nature* Index 2020 Science Cities, accessed January 31, 2023, https://www.natureindex.com /supplements/nature-index-2020-science-cities/tables/overall.

42. Zimu, "Hefei's Counterattack Is Not an Accident."

43. CCTV Finance, "Dialogue Hefei" [in Chinese], YouTube, June 13, 2021, https://www.youtube.com/watch?v=Tywowhf8a4g.

44. On SOEs in China, see Karen Jingrong Lin et al., "State-Owned Enterprises in China: A Review of 40 Years of Research and Practice," *China Journal of Accounting Research* 13, no. 1 (2020): 31–55, https://doi .org/10.1016/j.cjar.2019.12.001; and Hong Yu, "The Ascendency of State-Owned Enterprises in China: Development, Controversy and Problems," *Journal of Contemporary China* 23, no. 85 (2014): 161–82, https://doi.org/10.1080/10670564.2013.809990.

45. National Development and Reform Commission, PRC, "Strategic Emerging Industries Had a Good Trend of Clustered Development in Hefei City, Anhui Province" [in Chinese], June 24, 2020, https://www .ndrc.gov.cn/fggz/cxhgjsfz/dfjz/202006/t20200624_1231962.html?code =&state=123.

5. THE XIONG'AN EXPERIMENT

1. Xinhua News Agency, "Millennium Plan, National Initiative" [in Chinese], Xiong'an New Area Management Commission, Xiong'an, April 13, 2017, http://www.xiongan.gov.cn/2017-04/13/c_129769126.htm.

2. Victor F. S. Sit, "Soviet Influence on Urban Planning in Beijing, 1949–1991," *Town Planning Review* 67, no. 4 (1996): 457, https://www.jstor.org /stable/40113418.

3. Beijing Bureau of Statistics, *Beijing Statistical Yearbook 2020* [in Chinese] (Beijing: Beijing Statistics Press, 2021), http://nj.tjj.beijing.gov.cn/nj/main /2020-tjnj/zk/indexch.htm.

4. Beijing Bureau of Statistics, *Beijing Statistical Yearbook 2020.*

5. Beijing Bureau of Statistics, *Beijing Statistical Yearbook 2020.*

6. Beijing Bureau of Statistics, *Beijing Statistical Yearbook 2020.*

7. Beijing Bureau of Statistics, "Beijing Bulletin on the 7th National Census (No. 1)" [in Chinese], May 19, 2021, http://tjj.beijing.gov.cn/tjsj _31433/tjgb_31445/rpgb_31449/202105/P020210519338453665400.pdf.

8. Cong Sun, Siqi Zheng, and Rui Wang, "Restricting Driving for Better Traffic and Clearer Skies: Did It Work in Beijing?," *Transport Policy* 32 (2014): 34–41, https://doi.org/10.1016/j.tranpol.2013.12.010.

9. On Beijing's growth and transformation, see Richard Hu, *Smart Design: Disruption, Crisis, and the Reshaping of Urban Spaces* (Abingdon, UK: Routledge, 2021): 30–42; and Zhenshan Yang et al., "City Profile: Beijing," *Cities* 31 (2013): 491–506, https://doi.org/10.1016/j.cities .2011.07.007.

10. Xiaoma Li, Weiqi Zhou, and Zhiyun Ouyang, "Forty Years of Urban Expansion in Beijing: What Is the Relative Importance of Physical, Socioeconomic, and Neighborhood Factors?," *Applied Geography* 38 (2013): 7, https://doi.org/10.1016/j.apgeog.2012.11.004.

11. Hu, *Smart Design*, 30–42.

12. Wikipedia, s.v. "List of Chinese Prefecture-level Cities by GDP," accessed February 2, 2023, https://en.wikipedia.org/wiki/List_of_Chinese _prefecture-level_cities_by_GDP.

13. Xinhua News Agency, "Millennium Plan." Dayu is an ancient figure in Chinese history who is known for his way of alleviating flooding through diverting water, thus creating the Chinese idiom translated as "Dayu's control of water."

14. Beijing Municipal Commission of Planning and Natural Resources, *Beijing Municipal Master Plan (2016–2035)* [in Chinese] (Beijing: Beijing Municipal Commission of Planning and Natural Resources, January 19, 2018), http://ghzrzyw.beijing.gov.cn/zhengwuxinxi/zxzt /bjcsztgh20162035/202001/t20200102_1554613.html.

15. Xinhua News Agency, "The CPC Central Committee and State Council's Decision on Establishing Hebei Xiong'an New Area" [in Chinese], Xiong'an New Area Management Commission, Xiong'an, April 1, 2017, http://www.xiongan.gov.cn/2017-04/01/c_129769132.htm.

16. Nele Noesselt, "A Presidential Signature Initiative: Xiong'an and Governance Modernization Under Xi Jinping," *Journal of Contemporary China* 29, no. 126 (2020): 838, https://doi.org/10.1080/10670564.2020 .1744378.

17. Anonymous interviewee, June 27, 2021.

18. Hebei Government, *Outline Plan for Hebei Xiong'an New Area* (Xiong'an: Hebei Government, April 21, 2018), http://www.xiongan.gov.cn/2018-04 /21/c_129855813.htm.

19. "Xu Kuangdi on the Planning of Xiong'an New Area" [in Chinese], *The Paper*, June 7, 2017, https://www.sohu.com/a/146813902_260616.

20. Hebei Government, *Outline Plan for Hebei Xiong'an New Area*.

21. Shiuh-Shen Chien and Litao Zhao, "The Kunshan Model: Learning from Taiwanese Investors," *Built Environment* 34, no. 4 (2008): 427–43, https://doi.org/10.2148/benv.34.4.427.

22. Anonymous interviewee, June 24, 2021.

23. SOM, "SOM and TLS Selected to Design Core of Xiong'an New Area, China's Model City of the Future" (press release), June 6, 2019, https://www.som.com/news/som_and_tls_selected_to_design_core _of_xiongan_new_area_chinas_model_city_of_the_future.

24. Zhaowen Liu et al., "Towards Developing a New Model for Inclusive Cities in China—The Case of Xiong'an New Area," *Sustainability* 12, no. 15 (2020): 12–13, article 6195, https://doi.org/10.3390/su12156195.

25. Weina Xu, "NDRC Allocated RMB 1.7 Billion from Central Government Budget to Support the Construction of Xiong'an" [in Chinese], *China Daily*, June 26, 2021, https://cn.chinadaily.com.cn/a/202106/26 /WS60d72984a3101e7ce97573d6.html.

26. Sheng Xu, "CDB Will Provide RMB 130 Billion to Support the Initial Development Zone in Xiong'an" [in Chinese], *Xinhua.Net*, April 27, 2017, http://m.xinhuanet.com/2017-04/27/c_1120886859.htm.

27. Richard Hu and Weijie Chen, *Global Shanghai Remade: The Rise of Pudong New Area* (Abingdon, UK: Routledge, 2019), 56.

6. REORIENTING HONG KONG

1. Kimberly Jin, "Friday Song: Lo Ta-yu Seeks Hong Kong's Roots in 'Pearl of the Orient,'" *China Project*, July 20, 2019, https://thechina project.com/2019/07/20/friday-song-lo-ta-yu-hong-kong-pearl-of -the-orient/.

2. Richard Hu, *The Shenzhen Phenomenon: From Fishing Village to Global Knowledge City* (Abingdon, UK: Routledge, 2020), 111.

3. On the competitions between Hong Kong, Shanghai, and Shenzhen, see Xiangming Chen, "Lost in Competition: Rethinking Hong Kong,

Shanghai, and Shenzhen as a New Triangle of China's Global Cities and Regional Hubs," in *Routledge Handbook of Contemporary Hong Kong*, ed. Tai-lok Lui, Stephen W. K. Chiu, and Ray Yep (Abingdon, UK: Routledge, 2019), 511–30.

4. Country Economy, "Country Comparison Singapore vs Hong Kong," accessed February 13, 2023, https://countryeconomy.com/countries /compare/singapore/hong-kong.

5. Ezra F. Vogel, *The Four Little Dragons: The Spread of Industrialization in East Asia* (Cambridge, MA: Harvard University Press, 1991).

6. Louis Augustin-Jean and Anthea H. Y. Cheung, *The Economic Roots of the Umbrella Movement in Hong Kong: Globalization and the Rise of China* (Abingdon, UK: Routledge, 2018).

7. "A Cartoon on Hong Kong Published in Singaporean Newspaper" [in Chinese], *Hong Kong Discuss*, October 7, 2019, https://news.discuss .com.hk/viewthread.php?tid=28584765.

8. Nancy Pelosi, "Pelosi Remarks at Congressional Executive Commission on China and Tom Lantos Human Rights Commission Hearing" (press release), June 4, 2019, https://pelosi.house.gov/news/press -releases/pelosi-remarks-at-congressional-executive-commission-on -china-and-tom-lantos.

9. Regina Ip, "Hong Kong Is China, Like It or Not," *New York Times*, October 1, 2020, https://www.nytimes.com/2020/10/01/opinion/hong -kong-china-security-law.html.

10. Deng Xiaoping, *Selected Works of Deng Xiaoping*, vol. 3 [in Chinese] (Beijing: People's Publishing House, 1993), 73–75.

11. Deng, *Selected Works*, 220–21.

12. Deng, *Selected Works*, 267.

13. Chinese Government, *The Practice of the "One Country, Two Systems" Policy in the Hong Kong Special Administrative Region* (White paper, Chinese Government, Beijing, June 2014), http://english.www.gov.cn /archive/white_paper/2014/08/23/content_281474982986578.htm# :~:text=According%20to%20Deng%20Xiaoping%2C%20%E2%80 %9Cone,a%20long%20time%20to%20come.

14. On the relationship between Hong Kong and Beijing under "one country, two systems," see Andreas Fulda, *The Struggle for Democracy in Mainland China, Taiwan and Hong Kong* (New York: Routledge, 2020); and Peter W. Preston, *The Politics of China-Hong Kong*

Relations: Living with Distant Masters (Cheltenham. UK: Edward Elgar, 2016).

15. Alvin Y. So, "Hong Kong's Integration with Mainland China in Historical Perspective," in *Routledge Handbook of Contemporary Hong Kong*, ed. Tai-lok Lui, Stephen W. K. Chiu, and Ray Yep (Abingdon, UK: Routledge, 2019): 494–510.

16. Hu, *Shenzhen Phenomenon*, 126–31.

17. Michael Smith, "Low Turnout the True Measure of Hong Kong Voter Sentiment," *Financial Review*, December 20, 2021, https://www.afr .com/world/asia/low-turnout-the-true-measure-of-hong-kong-voter -sentiment-20211220-p59iyn.

18. Chinese Government, *Hong Kong: Democratic Progress Under the Framework of One Country, Two Systems* (Beijing: Chinese Government, December 20, 2021), 51–53, http://www.xinhuanet.com/english/download /2021-12-20/fulltext1220.doc.

19. Michael Shum, "Know Your Place in Chinese Region, LegCo Leaders Told," *Standard*, January 6, 2022, https://www.thestandard.com.hk /section-news/section/4/237730/know-your-plaCE-IN-CHINESE -REGION,-Legco-leaders-told.

20. Chinese Government, *The People's Republic of China's 14th Five-Year Plan for National Economic and Social Development & Outline Objectives of the 2035 Vision* [in Chinese] (Beijing: Chinese Government, March 13, 2021), 136–37, http://www.gov.cn/xinwen/2021-03/13/content _5592681.htm.

21. Gang Wen, "Plan Offers 'Historic' Opportunities to HK," *China Daily*, August 24, 2021, https://global.chinadaily.com.cn/a/202108/24 /WS612429b7a310efa1bd66a989.html.

22. Cat Wang and Danny Mok, "Beijing's Top Man in Hong Kong Visits 'Cage Home' and Medical Service as Part of Drive to 'Listen Directly' to the People," *South China Morning Post*, October 1, 2021, https:// www.scmp.com/news/hong-kong/politics/article/3150810/beijings -top-man-hong-kong-visits-cage-home-and-medical.

23. Jeffie Lam, "Hong Kong Leader Carrie Lam Gets a To-Do List from Beijing's Top Office in the City, as It Reveals Public Outreach Sparked Thousands of Responses," *South China Morning Post*, October 11, 2021, https://www.scmp.com/news/hong-kong/politics/article/3151986 /hong-kong-leader-carrie-lam-gets-do-list-beijings-top.

24. See Barrie Shelton, Justyna Karakiewicz, and Thomas Kvan, *The Making of Hong Kong: From Vertical to Volumetric* (London: Routledge, 2011).

25. Hu, *Shenzhen Phenomenon*, 126–31.

26. Hong Kong Special Administrative Region Government, *Northern Metropolis Development Strategy* (Hong Kong: Hong Kong Special Administrative Region Government, October 6, 2021), 76, https://www.policyaddress.gov.hk/2021/eng/pdf/publications/Northern/Northern-Metropolis-Development-Strategy-Report.pdf.

27. On the history of Hong Kong's urban development, see Pui-Yin Ho, *Making Hong Kong: A History of Its Urban Development* (Cheltenham, UK: Edward Elgar, 2018).

28. Shenzhen Planning and Natural Resources Bureau, *Shenzhen 2035: Territorial Spatial Master Plan of Shenzhen (2020–2035)*, (version for public consultation) [in Chinese] (Shenzhen: Shenzhen Planning and Natural Resources Bureau, 2021), 6, http://pnr.sz.gov.cn/attachment/0/794/794784/8858879.pdf.

7. IMAGINING 2035 AND BEYOND

1. Xi Jinping, *Secure a Decisive Victory in Building a Moderately Prosperous Society in All Respects and Strive for the Great Success of Socialism with Chinese Characteristics for a New Era* (Report, Xinhua, Beijing, October 18, 2017), 24–25, http://www.xinhuanet.com/english/download/Xi_Jinping's_report_at_19th_CPC_National_Congress.pdf.

2. Xinhua News Agency, "CPC Sets Targets Through 2035 to Basically Achieve China's Socialist Modernization," October 29, 2020, http://www.xinhuanet.com/english/2020-10/29/c_139476284.htm.

3. Richard Hu and Weijie Chen, *Global Shanghai Remade: The Rise of Pudong New Area* (Abingdon, UK: Routledge, 2019), 128.

4. Chinese Government, *CPC Central Committee and State Council's Opinion on Standardizing Planning System and Better Playing the Strategic Lead Role of National Development Planning* [in Chinese] (Beijing: Chinese Government, December 2018), https://www.waizi.org.cn/file/64998.html.

5. Chinese Government, *CPC Central Committee and State Council's Opinions on Establishing Territorial Spatial Planning System and Its Supervision and Implementation* [in Chinese] (Beijing: Chinese Government,

May 23, 2019), http://www.gov.cn/zhengce/2019-05/23/content_5394187
.htm.

6. Chinese Government, *The People's Republic of China's 14th Five-Year
Plan for National Economic and Social Development & Outline Objectives
of the 2035 Vision* [in Chinese] (Beijing: Chinese Government, March 13,
2021), 10, http://www.gov.cn/xinwen/2021-03/13/content_5592681.htm.

7. National Bureau of Statistics, PRC, "Key Data from the 7th National
Census on Population" [in Chinese], May 11, 2021, http://www.stats.gov.cn
/tjsj/zxfb/202105/t20210510_1817176.html.

8. Chinese Government, *14th Five-Year Plan*, 63–64.

9. Institute for China Sustainable Urbanization, *Report on the Development of Chinese Metropolitan Circles 2018* [in Chinese] (Beijing: Tsinghua University, 2019): 59–61, http://tucsu.tsinghua.edu.cn/upload_files
/atta/1551401345990_2C.pdf.

10. Chinese Government, *14th Five-Year Plan*, 64.

11. National Development and Reform Commission, PRC, *Guiding
Opinions on Cultivating and Developing Modern Metropolitan Circles*
(Beijing: National Development and Reform Commission, February 21,
2019), http://www.gov.cn/xinwen/2019-02/21/content_5367465.htm.

12. Sichuan Government, *Chengdu Metropolitan Circle Development Plan*
(Chengdu: Sichuan Government, December 1, 2021): 5, https://www
.sc.gov.cn/10462/10464/10465/10595/2021/12/1/e3abe9d6000e47719
fe207ae03d0748b.shtml.

13. Sichuan Government, *Chengdu Metropolitan Circle Development Plan*, 9.

14. Richard Hu, *Smart Design: Disruption, Crisis, and the Reshaping of
Urban Spaces* (Abingdon, UK: Routledge, 2021), 34.

15. Beijing Municipal Commission of Planning and Natural Resources,
Beijing Municipal Master Plan (2016–2035) (Beijing: Beijing Municipal
Commission of Planning and Natural Resources, January 9, 2018), http://
ghzrzyw.beijing.gov.cn/zhengwuxinxi/zxzt/bjcsztgh20162035/202001
/t20200102_1554613.html.

16. Shanghai Government, *Shanghai Master Plan 2017–2035* [in Chinese]
(Shanghai: Shanghai Government, January 2018): 26, https://www.supdri
.com/2035/index.php?c=message&a=type&tid=33.

17. On the concept of "global city," see Saskia Sassen, *The Global City: New
York, London, Tokyo*, 2nd ed. (Princeton, NJ: Princeton University Press,
2001).

18. On the rise of Shanghai as a global city, see Hu and Chen, *Global Shanghai Remade.*

19. Richard Hu, *The Shenzhen Phenomenon: From Fishing Village to Global Knowledge City* (Abingdon, UK: Routledge, 2020): 40–75.

20. Shenzhen Planning and Natural Resources Bureau, *Shenzhen 2035: Territorial Spatial Master Plan of Shenzhen (2020–2035),* (version for public consultation) [in Chinese] (Shenzhen: Shenzhen Planning and Natural Resources Bureau, 2021), 3, http://pnr.sz.gov.cn/attachment /0/794/794784/8858879.pdf.

21. Chinese Government, *14th Five-Year Plan,* 7.

22. Deng Xiaoping, *Selected Works of Deng Xiaoping,* vol. 3 [in Chinese] (Beijing: People's Publishing House, 1993), 373–74.

23. Xi Jinping, *Secure a Decisive Victory,* 24–25.

24. State Council Information Office, PRC, *White Paper: Poverty Alleviation: China's Experience and Contribution* (White paper, State Council Information Office, Beijing, June 2, 2021), http://t.m.china.org.cn/convert/c _2dilkdpp.html.

25. Maria Ana Lugo, Martin Raiser, and Ruslan Yemtsov, "What's Next for Poverty Reduction Policies in China?," *East Asia & Pacific on the Rise* (blog), *World Bank Blogs,* October 15, 2021, https://blogs.worldbank.org /eastasiapacific/whats-next-poverty-reduction-policies-china.

26. Zhou Xin, "Is China Rich or Poor?," *South China Morning Post,* May 29, 2020, https://www.scmp.com/economy/china-economy/article/3086678 /china-rich-or-poor-nations-wealth-debate-muddied-conflicting? module=perpetual_scroll_0&pgtype=article&campaign=3086678.

27. Sonali Jain-Chandra et al., "Inequality in China—Trends, Drivers and Policy Remedies" (Working paper, International Monetary Fund, Washington, D.C., June 1, 2018), 14, https://www.imf.org/en/Publications /WP/Issues/2018/06/05/Inequality-in-China-Trends-Drivers-and -Policy-Remedies-45878.

28. National Bureau of Statistics, PRC, "Residents Incomes and Expenditures in 2021" [in Chinese], January 17, 2022, http://www.stats.gov.cn/tjsj/zxfb /202201/t20220117_1826403.html.

29. Albert Park and Dewen Wang, "Migration and Urban Poverty and Inequality in China," *China Economic Journal* 3, no. 1 (2010): 49, https:// doi.org/https://doi.org/10.1080/17538963.2010.487351.

30. Taotao Deng et al., "Shrinking Cities in Growing China: Did High Speed Rail Further Aggravate Urban Shrinkage?," *Cities* 86 (2019): 213, https://doi.org/10.1016/j.cities.2018.09.017.

31. Deng et al., "Shrinking Cities in Growing China," 216.

32. Cai Qi, "The Report of the 13th Beijing Municipal Congress of the CPC" [in Chinese], *Beijing Daily*, July 4, 2022, https://bj.bjd.com.cn /5b165687a010550e5ddc0e6a/contentShare/5b16573ae4b02a9fe2d558f9 /AP62c21bcde4b0c2cdf0a3825a.html.

8. THE NATURE OF THE CHINESE CITY

1. Ezra F. Vogel, *Deng Xiaoping and the Transformation of China* (Cambridge, MA: Belknap Press of Harvard University Press, 2011), 693.

2. Vogel, *Deng Xiaoping and the Transformation of China*, 703, 713.

3. Richard Hu and Weijie Chen, *Global Shanghai Remade: The Rise of Pudong New Area* (Abingdon, UK: Routledge, 2019), 34.

4. Zhao Ziyang, *The Secret Journal of Zhao Ziyang* [in Chinese] (Hong Kong: New Century Press of Hong Kong, 2009), 107.

5. Deng Xiaoping, *Selected Works of Deng Xiaoping*, vol. 3 [in Chinese] (Beijing: People's Publishing House, 1993), 373.

6. Chinese Government, *Decision of the Central Committee of the Communist Party of China on Some Major Issues Concerning Comprehensively Deepening the Reform* (Beijing: Chinese Government, January 16, 2014), http://www.china.org.cn/china/third_plenary_session/2014-01/16 /content_31212602.htm.

7. Xi Jinping, *Hold High the Great Banner of Socialism with Chinese Characteristics and Strive in Unity to Build a Modern Socialist Country in All Respects* (Report, Xinhua, Beijing, October 25, 2022), 23–24, https://english .news.cn/20221025/8eb6f5239f984f01a2bc45b5b5db0c51/c.html.

8. Richard Hu, "Drivers of China's Urbanisation and Property Development," *Australasian Journal of Regional Studies* 19, no. 2 (2013): 160.

9. Lin Zhang and Tu Lan, "The New Whole State System: Reinventing the Chinese State to Promote Innovation," *Environment and Planning A: Economy and Space* 55, no. 1 (2022): 1, https://doi.org/10.1177 /0308518X221088294.

10. Xi, *Hold High the Great Banner*, 29.

11. Yongnian Zheng and Yanjie Huang, *Market in State: The Political Economy of Domination in China* (Cambridge: Cambridge University Press, 2018).

12. Zheng and Huang, *Market in State*.

13. Fulong Wu, "Planning Centrality, Market Instruments: Governing Chinese Urban Transformation Under State Entrepreneurialism," *Urban Studies* 55, no. 7 (2018): 1383, https://doi.org/10.1177/0042098017721828.

14. Wu, "Planning Centrality, Market Instruments," 1394, 1396.

15. National Development and Reform Commission, PRC, *Guiding Opinions on Cultivating and Developing Modern Metropolitan Circles* (Beijing: National Development and Reform Commission, February 21, 2019), http://www.gov.cn/xinwen/2019-02/21/content_5367465.htm.

16. Xi, *Hold High the Great Banner*, 6, 13, 18.

17. John Friedmann, "Four Theses in the Study of China's Urbanization," *International Journal of Urban and Regional Research* 30, no. 2 (2006): 441, 448, https://doi.org/10.1111/j.1468-2427.2006.00671.x.

18. For the internationalized reading of the Chinese city, see Fenglong Wang and Yungang Liu, "How Unique Is 'China Model': A Review of Theoretical Perspectives on China's Urbanization in Anglophone Literature," *Chinese Geographical Science* 25, no. 1 (2015): 98–112, https://doi.org/10.1007/s11769-014-0713-2; Fulong Wu, *Planning for Growth: Urban and Regional Planning in China* (Abingdon, UK: Routledge, 2015); and Weiping Wu and Piper Gaubatz, *The Chinese City*, 2nd ed. (Abingdon, UK: Routledge, 2021).

For the Chinesized reading of the Chinese city, see Piper Gaubatz, "Understanding Chinese Urban Form: Contexts for Interpreting Continuity and Change," *Built Environment* 24, no. 4 (1998): 251–70, https://www.jstor.org/stable/23289160; Shiqiao Li, *Understanding the Chinese City* (Los Angeles: SAGE, 2014); and Peter G. Rowe and Seng Kuan, *Architectural Encounters with Essence and Form in Modern China* (Cambridge, MA: MIT Press, 2002).

19. Kang Cao and Jean Hillier, "Planning Theory in China and Chinese Planning Theory: Guest Editorial Introduction," *Planning Theory* 12, no. 4 (2013): 331, https://doi.org/10.1177/1473095213493983.

20. Chris Hamnett, "Is Chinese Urbanisation Unique?," *Urban Studies* 57, no. 3 (2020): 690, 697, https://doi.org/10.1177/0042098019890810.

21. See Fulong Wu, "Emerging Chinese Cities: Implications for Global Urban Studies," *Professional Geographer* 68, no. 2 (2016): 338–48, https:// doi.org/10.1080/00330124.2015.1099189; Fulong Wu, "Emerging Cities and Urban Theories: A Chinese Perspective," in *Theories and Models of Urbanization*, ed. Denise Pumain (Cham, Switzerland: Springer, 2019), 171–82.

22. Hu and Chen, *Global Shanghai Remade*, 69–75.

23. John Friedmann, *China's Urban Transition* (Minneapolis: University of Minnesota Press, 2005), 117.

24. Friedmann, "Four Theses," 449.

25. Friedmann, *China's Urban Transition*, 122.

26. On "Ti-Yong," see Chung-Ying Cheng, "On the Metaphysical Significance of *Ti* (Body-Embodiment) in Chinese Philosophy: *Benti* (Origin-Substance) and *Ti-Yong* (Substance and Function)," *Journal of Chinese Philosophy* 29, no. 2 (2002): 145–61, https://doi.org/10.1111/1540 -6253.00074; Sun-hyang Kwon and Jeson Woo, "On the Origin and Conceptual Development of 'Essence-Function' (*Ti-Yong*)," *Religions* 10, no. 4 (2019): 1–9, article 272, https://doi.org/10.3390/rel10040272; and A. Charles Muller, "The Emergence of Essence-Function (*Ti-Yong*) Hermeneutics in the Sinification of Indic Buddhism: An Overview," *Critical Review for Buddhist Studies* 19, no. 6 (2016): 111–52, https://doi.org /10.29213/crbs..19.201606.111.

27. Philip J. Ivanhoe, "Ti and Yong," in *The Routledge Encyclopedia of Philosophy* (London: Routledge, 1998), https://www.rep.routledge.com/articles /thematic/ti-and-yong/v-1.

28. See Richard Hu, *The Shenzhen Phenomenon: From Fishing Village to Global Knowledge City* (Abingdon, UK: Routledge, 2020); Hu and Chen, *Global Shanghai Remade*.

BIBLIOGRAPHY

"A Cartoon on Hong Kong Published in Singaporean Newspaper" [*Kan Deng Zai Xin Jia Po Bao Zhi Yi Fu Feng Ci Xiang Gang De Man Hua*]. *Hong Kong Discuss*, October 7, 2019. https://news.discuss.com.hk/viewthread.php?tid =28584765.

AliResearch. "Research Report on Taobao Villages in China 2020" [*2020 Zhong Guo Tao Bao Cun Yan Jiu Bao Gao*]. October 20, 2020. http://www .aliresearch.com.

"America Curbs Chinese Access to Advanced Computing." *Economist*, October 13, 2022. https://www.economist.com/business/2022/10/13/america -curbs-chinese-access-to-advanced-computing.

Anhui Statistics Bureau. "Bulletin of the 7th National Census in Anhui Province (No. 2)" [*An Hui Sheng Di Qi Ci Quan Guo Ren Kou Pu Cha Gong Bao (Di Er Hao)*]. May 28, 2021. http://tjj.ah.gov.cn/ssah/qwfbjd/tjgb/sjtjgb /145782371.html.

Arup. "Shaping China's First Climate Positive Project." Accessed January 23, 2023. https://www.arup.com/projects/shougang-industry-services-park.

——. "Vision of the Future." *A² Magazine*, 2005, 1–26. https://www.arup.com /perspectives/publications/magazines-and-periodicals/a2/a2-magazine -issue-1.

Atha, Katherine, Jason Callahan, John Chen, Jessica Drun, Ed Francis, Kieran Green, Brian Lafferty, et al. *China's Smart Cities Development*. Report, US–China Economic and Security Review Commission, Washington, D.C., April 29, 2020. https://www.uscc.gov/research/chinas-smart-cities -development.

Augustin-Jean, Louis, and Anthea H. Y. Cheung. *The Economic Roots of the Umbrella Movement in Hong Kong: Globalization and the Rise of China.* Abingdon, UK: Routledge, 2018.

Azadi, Hossein, Gijs Verheijke, and Frank Witlox. "Pollute First, Clean up Later?" *Global and Planetary Change* 78, nos. 3–4 (2011): 77–82. https://doi .org/10.1016/j.gloplacha.2011.05.006.

Baidu Baike. s.v. "China National Economic and Technical Development Zone" [*Guo Jia Ji Jing Ji Ji Shu Kai Fa Qu*]. Accessed January 31, 2023. https://baike.baidu.com.

——. s.v. "China National High-Tech Industrial Development Zone" [*Zhong Guo Gao Xin Ji Shu Chan Ye Kai Fa Qu*]. Accessed January 31, 2023. https:// baike.baidu.com.

——. s.v. "Qian Xuesen's Question" [*Qian Xue Sen Zhi Wen*]. Accessed January 31, 2023. https://baike.baidu.com.

——. s.v. "Taobao Villages" [*Tao Bao Cun*]. Accessed January 31, 2023. https://baike.baidu.com.

Ball, Philip. "China's Great Leap Forward in Science." *Guardian*, February 18, 2018. https://www.theguardian.com/science/2018/feb/18/china-great-leap -forward-science-research-innovation-investment-5g-genetics-quantum -internet.

Beijing Bureau of Statistics. "Beijing Bulletin on the 7th National Census (No. 1)" [*Bei Jing Shi Di Qi Ci Quan Guo Ren Kou Pu Cha Gong Bao (Di Yi Hao)*]. May 19, 2021. http://tjj.beijing.gov.cn/tjsj_31433/tjgb_31445/rpgb _31449/202105/P020210519338453665400.pdf.

——. *Beijing Statistical Yearbook 2020* [*Bei Jing Tong Ji Nian Jian 2020*]. Beijing: Beijing Statistics Press, 2021. http://nj.tjj.beijing.gov.cn/nj/main/2020-tjnj /zk/indexch.htm.

Beijing Municipal Commission of Planning and Natural Resources. *Beijing Municipal Master Plan (2016–2035)* [*Bei Jing Cheng Shi Zong Ti Gui Hua (2016– 2035)*]. Beijing: Beijing Municipal Commission of Planning and Natural Resources, January 9, 2018. http://ghzrzyw.beijing.gov.cn/zhengwuxinxi /zxzt/bjcsztgh20162035/202001/t20200102_1554613.html.

Blakely, Edward J., and Richard Hu. *Crafting Innovative Places for Australia's Knowledge Economy.* Singapore: Palgrave Macmillan, 2019.

Cai, Qi. "The Report of the 13th Beijing Municipal Congress of the CPC" [*Bei Jing Di Shi San Ci Dang Dai Hui Bao Gao*]. *Beijing Daily*, July 4, 2022.

https://bj.bjd.com.cn/5b165687a0105550e5ddc0e6a/contentShare/5b16573ae
4b02a9fe2d558f9/AP62c21bcde4b0c2cdf0a3825a.html.

Cao, Kang, and Jean Hillier. "Planning Theory in China and Chinese Planning Theory: Guest Editorial Introduction." *Planning Theory* 12, no. 4
(2013): 331–34. https://doi.org/10.1177/1473095213493983.

Caprotti, Federico. "Eco-Urbanism and the Eco-City, or, Denying the Right to
the City." *Antipode* 46, no. 5 (2014): 1285–1301. https://doi.org/10.1111/anti.12087.

Caprotti, Federico, and Dong Liu. "Platform Urbanism and the Chinese Smart
City: The Co-Production and Territorialisation of Hangzhou City Brain."
GeoJournal 87 (2022): 1559–73. https://doi.org/https://doi.org/10.1007/s10708
-020-10320-2.

Castells, Manuel. *The Rise of the Network Society.* 2nd ed. Malden, MA:
Blackwell, 2000.

CCTV Finance. "Dialogue Hefei" [*Dui Hua He Fei*]. YouTube, June 13, 2021.
https://www.youtube.com/watch?v=Tywowhf8a4g.

Chang, I-Chun Catherine. "Failure Matters: Reassembling Eco-Urbanism
in a Globalizing China." *Environment and Planning A: Economy and Space*
49, no. 8 (2017): 1719–42. https://doi.org/10.1177/0308518X16685092.

Chen, Hang, and Yan Du. "How Does Beijing Have More Days with Blue
Sky?" [*Bei Jing De Lan Tian Shi Ru He Duo Qi Lai De?*]. *China News*,
January 9, 2021. www.bj.chinanews.com/news/2021/0109/80437.html.

Chen, Shuai, Paulina Oliva, and Peng Zhang. "The Effect of Air Pollution
on Migration: Evidence from China." *Journal of Development Economics* 156 (May 2022): 1–14, article 102833. https://doi.org/10.1016/j.jdeveco
.2022.102833.

Chen, Xiangming. "Lost in Competition: Rethinking Hong Kong, Shanghai,
and Shenzhen as a New Triangle of China's Global Cities and Regional
Hubs." In *Routledge Handbook of Contemporary Hong Kong*, ed. Tai-lok Lui,
Stephen W. K. Chiu, and Ray Yep, 511–30. Abingdon, UK: Routledge, 2019.

Cheng, Chung-Ying. "On the Metaphysical Significance of *Ti* (Body-
Embodiment) in Chinese Philosophy: *Benti* (Origin-Substance) and *Ti-
Yong* (Substance and Function)." *Journal of Chinese Philosophy* 29, no. 2
(2002): 145–61. https://doi.org/10.1111/1540-6253.00074.

Chien, Shiuh-Shen, and Litao Zhao. "The Kunshan Model: Learning from
Taiwanese Investors." *Built Environment* 34, no. 4 (2008): 427–43. https://
doi.org/10.2148/benv.34.4.427.

Chik, Holly. "China Set to Pass US on Research and Development Spending by 2025." *South China Morning Post*, July 16, 2021. https://www.scmp .com/news/china/science/article/3141263/china-set-pass-us-research -and-development-spending-2025.

"China and the West Are in a Race to Foster Innovation." *Economist*, October 13, 2022. https://www.economist.com/briefing/2022/10/13/china-and-the-west -are-in-a-race-to-foster-innovation.

"China May Soon Become a High-Income Country." *Economist*, February 5, 2022. https://www.economist.com/finance-and-economics/2022/02/05 /china-may-soon-become-a-high-income-country.

"China Wants to Insulate Itself Against Western Sanctions." *Economist*, February 19, 2022. https://www.economist.com/business/2022/02/19/china -wants-to-insulate-itself-against-western-sanctions.

Chinese Government. "Bulletin on Statistics of National Investment in Research and Development in 2020" [*2020 Nian Quan Guo Ke Ji Jing Fei Tou Ru Tong Ji Gong Bao*]. September 22, 2021. http://www.gov.cn/xinwen /2021-09/22/content_5638653.htm.

——. *CPC Central Committee and State Council's Opinion on Standardizing Planning System and Better Playing the Strategic Lead Role of National Development Planning* [*Zhong Gong Zhong Yang Guo Wu Yuan Guan Yu Tong Yi Gui Hua Ti Xi Geng Hao Fa Hui Guo Jia Fa Zhan Gui Hua Zhan Lue Dao Xiang Zuo Yong De Yi Jian*]. Beijing: Chinese Government, December 2018. https://www.waizi.org.cn/file/64998.html.

——. *CPC Central Committee and State Council's Opinions on Establishing Territorial Spatial Planning System and Its Supervision and Implementation* [*Zhong Gong Zhong Yang Guo Wu Yuan Guan Yu Jian Li Guo Tu Kong Jian Gui Hua Ti Xi Bing Jian Du Shi Shi De Ruo Gan Yi Jian*]. Beijing: Chinese Government, May 23, 2019. http://www.gov.cn/zhengce/2019-05/23 /content_5394187.htm.

——. "CPC Politburo Held a Meeting; Xi Jinping Presided Over It" [*Zhong Gong Zhong Yang Zheng Zhi Ju Zhao Kai Hui Yi; Xi Jin Ping Zhu Chi Hui Yi*]. July 28, 2022. http://www.gov.cn/xinwen/2022-07/28/content_5703255 .htm.

——. *Decision of the Central Committee of the Communist Party of China on Some Major Issues Concerning Comprehensively Deepening the Reform*. Beijing: Chinese Government, January 16, 2014. http://www.china.org.cn/china /third_plenary_session/2014-01/16/content_31212602.htm.

———. "The GDP of 23 Chinese Cities Exceeded RMB 1 Trillion" [*Zhong Guo 23 Zuo Cheng Shi GDP Chao Wan Yi Yuan*]. January 30, 2021. www.gov.cn /xinwen/2021-01/30/content_5583703.htm.

———. *Hong Kong: Democratic Progress Under the Framework of One Country, Two Systems.* Beijing: Chinese Government, December 20, 2021. http:// www.xinhuanet.com/english/download/2021-12-20/fulltext1220.doc.

———. *National New-Type Urbanization Plan (2014–2020)* [*Guo Jia Xin Xing Cheng Zhen Hua Gui Hua (2014–2020)*]. Beijing: Chinese Government, March 16, 2014. http://www.gov.cn/zhengce/2014-03/16/content_2640075.htm.

———. *Outline Plan for National Innovation-Driven Development* [*Guo Jia Chuang Xin Qu Dong Fa Zhan Zhan Lue Gang Yao*]. Beijing: Chinese Government, May 19, 2016. http://www.gov.cn/zhengce/2016-05/19/content _5074812.htm.

———. *The People's Republic of China's 14th Five-Year Plan for National Economic and Social Development & Outline Objectives of the 2035 Vision* [*Zhong Hua Ren Ming Gong He Guo Guo Ming Jing Ji He She Hui Fa Zhan Di Shi Si Ge Wu Nian Gui Hua He 2035 Nian Yuan Jing Mu Biao Gang Yao*]. Beijing: Chinese Government, March 13, 2021. http://www.gov.cn/xinwen/2021-03 /13/content_5592681.htm.

———. *The Practice of the "One Country, Two Systems" Policy in the Hong Kong Special Administrative Region.* White paper, Chinese Government, Beijing, June 2014. http://english.www.gov.cn/archive/white_paper/2014/08/23/content _281474982986578.htm#:~:text=According%20to%20Deng%20 Xiaoping%2C%20E2%80%9Cone,a%20long%20time%20to%20come.

Climate Action Tracker. "China." May 19, 2022. https://climateactiontracker .org/countries/china/2022-05-19/.

CNN. "Guizhou: China's Finest: The Big Data Valley of China." Accessed January 27, 2023. https://advertisementfeature.cnn.com/2018/guizhou/china -big-data-valley/.

Country Economy. "Country Comparison Singapore vs Hong Kong." Accessed February 13, 2023. https://countryeconomy.com/countries/compare/singapore /hong-kong.

Dalian University of Technology. *Report on China's R&D Expenditure.* Beijing: Zhi Shi Fen Zi, May 1, 2021. http://zhishifenzi.com/news/multiple/11239 .html.

Deng, Taotao, Dandan Wang, Yang Yang, and Huan Yang. "Shrinking Cities in Growing China: Did High Speed Rail Further Aggravate Urban

Shrinkage?" *Cities* 86 (2019): 210–19. https://doi.org/10.1016/j.cities.2018 .09.017.

Deng, Xiaoping. *Selected Works of Deng Xiaoping*, vol. 3 [*Deng Xiao Ping Wen Xuan, Di San Juan*]. Beijing: People's Publishing House, 1993.

Deutch, John. "Is Innovation China's New Great Leap Forward?" *Issues in Science and Technology* (Summer 2018): 37–47. http://web.mit.edu/chemistry /deutch/policy/2018-IsInnovChinaLeap-Issues.pdf.

Duan, Hongbo, Sheng Zhou, Kejun Jiang, Christoph Bertram, Mathijs Harmsen, Elmar Kriegler, Detlef P. van Vuuren, et al. "Assessing China's Efforts to Pursue the 1.5°C Warming Limit." *Science* 372, no. 6540 (2021): 378–85. https://doi.org/10.1126/science.aba8767.

"Economic Growth No Longer Requires Rising Emissions." *Economist*, November 10, 2022. https://www.economist.com/leaders/2022/11/10/economic -growth-no-longer-requires-rising-emissions.

Economist Intelligence Unit. *China's Emerging City Rankings 2021: Unpacking Opportunities under the 14th Five-Year Plan*. Report, *Economist* Intelligence Unit, London, 2021. https://www.eiu.com/n/campaigns/china-emerging -city-rankings-2021/.

Ekman, Alice, and Cristina de Esperanza Picardo. *Towards Urban Decoupling? China's Smart City Ambitions at the Time of COVID-19*. Brief, EU Institute for Security Studies, Luxembourg, May 14, 2020. https://www .iss.europa.eu/content/towards-urban-decoupling-china%E2%80%99s -smart-city-ambitions-time-covid-19.

Friedmann, John. *China's Urban Transition*. Minneapolis and London: University of Minnesota Press, 2005.

——. "Four Theses in the Study of China's Urbanisation." *International Journal of Urban and Regional Research* 30, no. 2 (2006): 440–51. https://doi.org /10.1111/j.1468-2427.2006.00671.x.

Fulda, Andreas. *The Struggle for Democracy in Mainland China, Taiwan and Hong Kong*. New York: Routledge, 2020.

Gao, Yun, and Zhaoyi Pan. "Graphic: Why Guizhou Is Becoming China's Big Data Valley." *CGTN*, December 26, 2019. https://news.cgtn.com/news /2019-12-26/Graphic-why-Guizhou-is-becoming-China-s-big-data-valley -MJyAjWbWtG/index.html.

Gaubatz, Piper. "Understanding Chinese Urban Form: Contexts for Interpreting Continuity and Change." *Built Environment* 24, no. 4 (1998): 251–70. https://www.jstor.org/stable/23289160.

Gaubatz, Piper, and Dean Hanink. "Learning from Taiyuan: Chinese Cities as Urban Sustainability Laboratories." *Geography and Sustainability* 1, no. 2 (2020): 118–26. https://doi.org/10.1016/j.geosus.2020.06.004.

Geall, Sam, and Adrian Ely. "Narratives and Pathways Towards an Ecological Civilization in Contemporary China." *China Quarterly* 236 (2018): 1175–96. https://doi.org/10.1017/S0305741018001315.

Goron, Coraline. "Ecological Civilisation and the Political Limits of a Chinese Concept of Sustainability." *China Perspectives*, no. 4 (2018): 39–52. https://doi.org/10.4000/chinaperspectives.8463.

Green, Andrew. "Obituary: Li Wenliang." *Lancet* 395, no. 10225 (2020): 682. https://doi.org/10.1016/S0140-6736(20)30382-2.

Gurría, Angel. "A 'New Normal' for Urbanisation." OECD, March 21, 2015. https://www.oecd.org/china/china-development-forum-a-new-normal-for-urbanisation.htm.

Hamadeh, Nada, Catherine van Rompaey, and Eric Metreau, "New World Bank Country Classifications by Income Level: 2021–2022." *Data Blog. World Bank Blogs*, July 1, 2021. https://blogs.worldbank.org/opendata/new-world-bank-country-classifications-income-level-2021-2022.

Hamnett, Chris. "Is Chinese Urbanisation Unique?" *Urban Studies* 57, no. 3 (2020): 690–700. https://doi.org/10.1177/0042098019890810.

Hangzhou Bureau of Statistics. *Hangzhou Statistical Yearbook 2020* [*2020 Nian Hang Zhou Tong Ji Nian Jian*]. Beijing: China Statistics Press, 2020. http://tjj.hangzhou.gov.cn/art/2020/10/29/art_1229453592_3819709.html.

Hangzhou Government. "Equip the City with a 'Brain'" [*Gei Cheng Shi Zhuang Shang 'Da Nao'*]. Accessed January 27, 2023. http://www.hangzhou.gov.cn/art/2021/3/24/art_812262_59031715.html.

——. "Statistical Yearbooks" [*Tong Ji Nian Jian*]. Accessed June 17, 2021. http://www.hangzhou.gov.cn/col/col805867/.

Hansen, Mette Halskov, Hongtao Li, and Rune Svarverud. "Ecological Civilization: Interpreting the Chinese Past, Projecting the Global Future." *Global Environmental Change* 53 (2018): 195–203. https://doi.org/10.1016/j.gloenvcha.2018.09.014.

Hanson, Arthur. "Ecological Civilization in the People's Republic of China: Values, Action, and Future Needs." East Asia Working Papers, Asian Development Bank, Manila, 2019. https://www.adb.org/publications/ecological-civilization-values-action-future-needs.

Hebei Government. *Outline Plan for Hebei Xiong'an New Area* [*He Bei Xiong An Xin Qu Gui Hua Gang Yao*]. Xiong'an: Hebei Government, April 21, 2018. http://www.xiongan.gov.cn/2018-04/21/c_129855813.htm.

Ho, Pui-Yin. *Making Hong Kong: A History of Its Urban Development*. Cheltenham, UK: Edward Elgar, 2018.

Holland, Oscar. "Tencent Is Building a Monaco-Sized 'City of the Future' in Shenzhen." *CNN*, June 16, 2020. https://edition.cnn.com/style/article /tencent-shenzhen-net-city/index.html.

Hong Kong Special Administrative Region Government. *Northern Metropolis Development Strategy*. Hong Kong: Hong Kong Special Administrative Region Government, October 6, 2021. https://www.policyaddress.gov.hk /2021/eng/pdf/publications/Northern/Northern-Metropolis-Development -Strategy-Report.pdf.

Hu, Richard. "China's Urban Age." In *Connecting Cities: China*, ed. Chris Johnson, Richard Hu, and Shanti Abedin, 142–57. Sydney: Metropolis Congress, 2008.

——. "Drivers of China's Urbanisation and Property Development." *Australasian Journal of Regional Studies* 19, no. 2 (2013): 156–80.

——. "Planning for Economic Development." In *The Routledge Handbook of Planning History*, ed. Carola Hein, 313–24. New York: Routledge, 2018.

——. *The Shenzhen Phenomenon: From Fishing Village to Global Knowledge City*. Abingdon, UK: Routledge, 2020.

——. *Smart Design: Disruption, Crisis, and the Reshaping of Urban Spaces*. Abingdon, UK: Routledge, 2021.

——. "Spatial Disruption and Planning Implication of the Sharing Economy: A Study of Smart Work in Canberra, Australia." *International Journal of Knowledge-Based Development* 10, no. 4 (2019): 315–37. https://doi .org/10.1504/IJKBD.2019.105125.

——. "The State of Smart Cities in China: The Case of Shenzhen." *Energies* 12, no. 22 (2019): 1–18, article 4375. https://doi.org/10.3390/en12224375.

Hu, Richard, and Weijie Chen. *Global Shanghai Remade: The Rise of Pudong New Area*. Abingdon, UK: Routledge, 2019.

Huang, Jing, Xiaochuan Pan, Xinbiao Guo, and Guoxing Li. "Health Impact of China's Air Pollution Prevention and Control Action Plan: An Analysis of National Air Quality Monitoring and Mortality Data." *Lancet Planetary Health* 2 (2018): e313–e323. https://doi.org/10.1016/S2542 -5196(18)30141-4.

Institute for China Sustainable Urbanization. *Report on the Development of Chinese Metropolitan Circles 2018* [*Zhong Guo Du Shi Quan Fa Zhan Bao Gao 2018*]. Beijing: Tsinghua University, 2019. http://tucsu.tsinghua.edu.cn /upload_files/atta/1551401345990_2C.pdf.

Institute for Planets. "What Is Hefei?" [Shen Mo Shi He Fei?]. June 2, 2021. https://mp.weixin.qq.com/s/pcvpOylgxTv9AFZ8dfA88A.

Ip, Regina. "Hong Kong Is China, Like It or Not." *New York Times*, October 1, 2020. https://www.nytimes.com/2020/10/01/opinion/hong-kong-china -security-law.html.

IQAir. *2020 World Air Quality Report: Region & City PM2.5 Ranking*. Goldach, Switzerland: IQAir, 2020. https://www.iqair.com/world-most-polluted -cities/world-air-quality-report-2020-en.pdf.

Ivanhoe, Philip J. "Ti and Yong." In *The Routledge Encyclopedia of Philosophy*. London: Routledge, 1998. https://www.rep.routledge.com/articles /thematic/ti-and-yong/v-1.

Jain-Chandra, Sonali, Niny Khor, Rui Mano, Johanna Schauer, Philippe Wingender, and Juzhong Zhuang. *Inequality in China—Trends, Drivers and Policy Remedies*. Working paper, International Monetary Fund, Washington, D.C., June 1, 2018. https://www.imf.org/en/Publications/WP/Issues/2018 /06/05/Inequality-in-China-Trends-Drivers-and-Policy-Remedies -45878.

Jin, Kimberly. "Friday Song: Lo Ta-yu Seeks Hong Kong's Roots in 'Pearl of the Orient.'" *China Project*, July 20, 2019. https://thechinaproject .com/2019/07/20/friday-song-lo-ta-yu-hong-kong-pearl-of-the-orient/.

Jones, Seth G., Andrew Philip Hunter, Lindsey R. Sheppard, Park In-kook, Hong Kyu-Dok, Kim Jina, and Lee Geunwook. *Geopolitical Implications of Scientific Innovation Trends in Northeast Asia*. Report, CSIS International Security Program and Chey Institute for Advanced Studies, Washington, D.C., June 24, 2021. https://www.csis.org/analysis /geopolitical-implications-scientific-innovation-trends-northeast-asia.

Joss, Simon, and Arthur P. Molella. "The Eco-City as Urban Technology: Perspectives on Caofeidian International Eco-City (China)." *Journal of Urban Technology* 20, no. 1 (2013): 115–37. https://doi.org/10.1080/1063073 2.2012.735411.

Kwon, Sun-hyang, and Jeson Woo. "On the Origin and Conceptual Development of 'Essence-Function' (*Ti-Yong*)." *Religions* 10, no. 4 (2019): 1–9, article 272. https://doi.org/10.3390/rel10040272.

Lam, Jeffie. "Hong Kong Leader Carrie Lam Gets a To-Do List from Beijing's Top Office in the City, as It Reveals Public Outreach Sparked Thousands of Responses." *South China Morning Post*, October 11, 2021. https://www.scmp.com/news/hong-kong/politics/article/3151986/hong -kong-leader-carrie-lam-gets-do-list-beijings-top?module=perpetual _scroll&pgtype=article&campaign=3151986.

Lewis, Joanna, and Laura Edwards. *Assessing China's Energy and Climate Goals*. Report, Center for American Progress, Washington, D.C., May 6, 2021. https://www.americanprogress.org/issues/security/reports/2021/05 /06/499096/assessing-chinas-energy-climate-goals/.

Li, Shiqiao. *Understanding the Chinese City*. Los Angeles: SAGE, 2014.

Li, Xiaoma, Weiqi Zhou, and Zhiyun Ouyang. "Forty Years of Urban Expansion in Beijing: What Is the Relative Importance of Physical, Socioeconomic, and Neighborhood Factors?" *Applied Geography* 38 (2013): 1–10. https://doi.org/10.1016/j.apgeog.2012.11.004.

Lin, Juan, Han Li, Mingshui Lin, and Chuhai Li. "Rural E-Commerce in China: Spatial Dynamics of Taobao Villages Development in Zhejiang Province." *Growth and Change* 53, no. 3 (2022): 1082–1101. https://doi.org /10.1111/grow.12560.

Lin, Karen Jingrong, Xiaoyan Lu, Junsheng Zhang, and Ying Zheng. "State-Owned Enterprises in China: A Review of 40 Years of Research and Practice." *China Journal of Accounting Research* 13, no. 1 (2020): 31–55. https://doi.org/10.1016/j.cjar.2019.12.001.

Lin, Peng. "Introduction of Tangshan Caofeidian Eco-City." Presentation, Tangshan Caofeidian Eco-city Administrative Committee, October 2011. https://www.esci-ksp.org/wp/wp-content/uploads/2016/11/DrLinPeng.pdf.

Lin, Yanliu. "E-Urbanism: E-Commerce, Migration, and the Transformation of Taobao Villages in Urban China." *Cities* 91 (2019): 202–12. https://doi .org/10.1016/j.cities.2018.11.020.

Liu, Zhaowen, Martin de Jong, Fen Li, Nikki Brand, Marcel Hertogh, and Liang Dong. "Towards Developing a New Model for Inclusive Cities in China—The Case of Xiong'an New Area." *Sustainability* 12, no. 15 (2020): 1–25, article 6195. https://doi.org/10.3390/su12156195.

Lu, Yonglong, Yueqing Zhang, Xianghui Cao, Chenchen Wang, Yichao Wang, Meng Zhang, Robert C. Ferrier, *et al.* "Forty Years of Reform and Opening Up: China's Progress Toward a Sustainable Path." *Science*

Advances 5, no. 8 (2019): 1–10, article eaau9413. https://doi.org/10.1126/sciadv.aau9413.

Lugo, Maria Ana, Martin Raiser, and Ruslan Yemtsov, "What's Next for Poverty Reduction Policies in China?" *East Asia & Pacific on the Rise* (blog). *World Bank Blogs*, October 15, 2021. https://blogs.worldbank.org/eastasiapacific/whats-next-poverty-reduction-policies-china.

Mao, Zedong. "On Contradiction." *Marxists Internet Archive*, August 1937. Transcription by the Maoist Documentation Project. Last revised 2020. https://www.marxists.org/reference/archive/mao/selected-works/volume-1/mswv1_17.htm.

Ministry of Ecology and Environment, PRC. "The State Council Issues Action Plan on Prevention and Control of Air Pollution Introducing Ten Measures to Improve Air Quality." September 12, 2013. http://english.mee.gov.cn/News_service/infocus/201309/t20130924_260707.shtml.

Mitter, Rana, and Elsbeth Johnson. "What the West Gets Wrong About China." *Harvard Business Review* (May–June 2021). https://hbr.org/2021/05/what-the-west-gets-wrong-about-china.

Muller, A. Charles. "The Emergence of Essence-Function (*Ti-Yong*) Hermeneutics in the Sinification of Indic Buddhism: An Overview." *Critical Review for Buddhist Studies* 19, no. 6 (2016): 111–52. https://doi.org/10.29213/crbs..19.201606.111.

National Bureau of Statistics, PRC. "Key Data from the 7th National Census on Population [*Di Qi Ci Quan Guo Ren Kou Pu Cha Zhu Yao Shu Ju Qing Kuang*]." May 11, 2021. http://www.stats.gov.cn/tjsj/zxfb/202105/t20210510_1817176.html.

——. "Residents Incomes and Expenditures in 2021" [2021 *Nian Ju Ming Shou Ru He Xiao Fei Zhi Chu Qing Kuang*]. January 17, 2022. http://www.stats.gov.cn/tjsj/zxfb/202201/t20220117_1826403.html.

National Development and Reform Commission, PRC. *Guiding Opinions on Cultivating and Developing Modern Metropolitan Circles* [*Guan Yu Pei Yu Fa Zhan Xian Dai Hua Du Shi Quan De Zhi Dao Yi Jian*]. Beijing: National Development and Reform Commission, February 21, 2019. http://www.gov.cn/xinwen/2019-02/21/content_5367465.htm.

——. "Strategic Emerging Industries Had a Good Trend of Clustered Development in Hefei City, Anhui Province [*An Hui Sheng He Fei Shi Zhan Lue Xing Xin Xing Chan Ye Ji Qun Fa Zhan Shi Tou Liang Hao*]." June 24, 2020.

https://www.ndrc.gov.cn/fggz/cxhgjsfz/dfjz/202006/t20200624_1231962
.html?code=&state=123.

Nature Index. "Top 200 Science Cities." *Nature* Index 2020 Science Cities,
accessed January 31, 2023. https://www.natureindex.com/supplements
/nature-index-2020-science-cities/tables/overall.

Nelson, Mei, "Debating China's AI Path: 'Alternative Routes,' or 'Overtaking
on the Curve?'" *DigiChina* (blog). *New America*, 12 (November 2019).
https://www.newamerica.org/cybersecurity-initiative/digichina/blog/
debating-chinas-ai-path-alternative-routes-or-overtaking-on-the-curve/.

Noesselt, Nele. "A Presidential Signature Initiative: Xiong'an and Governance Modernization Under Xi Jinping." *Journal of Contemporary China*
29, no. 126 (2020): 838–52. https://doi.org/10.1080/10670564.2020.1744378.

OECD. *All on Board: Making Inclusive Growth Happen in China.* Paris:
OECD, May 29, 2015. https://www.oecd.org/economy/all-on-board
-9789264218512-en.htm.

Onishi, Hiroshi. "Superstructure Determined by Base." *World Review of
Political Economy* 6, no. 1 (2015): 75–93. https://www.jstor.org/stable/10
.13169/worlrevipoliecon.6.1.0075.

Park, Albert, and Dewen Wang. "Migration and Urban Poverty and Inequality in China." *China Economic Journal* 3, no. 1 (2010): 49–67. https://doi.org
/https://doi.org/10.1080/17538963.2010.487351.

Pelosi, Nancy. "Pelosi Remarks at Congressional Executive Commission on China and Tom Lantos Human Rights Commission Hearing"
(press release). June 4, 2019, https://pelosi.house.gov/news/press-releases
/pelosi-remarks-at-congressional-executive-commission-on-china-and
-tom-lantos.

Penna, Caetano C. R. *Geopolitics and the Economics of Innovation.* Policy note,
Brazilian Center for International Relations, Rio de Janeiro, 2020. https://
www.cebri.org/media/documentos/arquivos/PolicyNote_Geopolitics
_and_the.pdf.

Polyakova, Alina, and Chris Meserole. *Exporting Digital Authoritarianism:
The Russian and Chinese Models.* Policy brief, Brookings Institution, Washing-
ton, D.C., 2019. https://www.brookings.edu/wp-content/uploads/2019/08
/FP_20190827_digital_authoritarianism_polyakova_meserole.pdf.

Preston, Peter W. *The Politics of China–Hong Kong Relations: Living with
Distant Masters.* Cheltenham, UK: Edward Elgar, 2016.

Qian, Zhu. "City Profile: Hangzhou." *Cities* 48 (2015): 42–54. https://doi.org
/10.1016/j.cities.2015.06.004.

Qin, Yu, and Hongjia Zhu. "Run Away? Air Pollution and Emigration Interests in China." *Journal of Population Economics* 31 (2018): 235–66. https://doi
.org/10.1007/s00148-017-0653-0.

Ritchie, Hannah, Max Roser, and Pablo Rosado. "CO_2 and Greenhouse Gas
Emissions." *Our World in Data*. Last modified August 2020. Accessed
January 20, 2023. https://ourworldindata.org/co2-and-other-greenhouse
-gas-emissions.

Rowe, Peter G., and Seng Kuan. *Architectural Encounters with Essence and
Form in Modern China*. Cambridge, MA: MIT Press, 2002.

Sabrie, Gilles. "Caofeidian, the Chinese Eco-City That Became a Ghost
Town—in Pictures." *Guardian*, July 24, 2014. https://www.theguardian.com
/cities/gallery/2014/jul/23/caofeidian-chinese-eco-city-ghost-town-in
-pictures.

Sassen, Saskia. *The Global City: New York, London, Tokyo*. 2nd ed. Princeton,
NJ: Princeton University Press, 2001.

Schoff, James L., and Asei Ito. *Competing with China on Technology and Innovation*. Alliance Policy Coordination Brief, Carnegie Endowment for
International Peace, Washington, D.C., October 10, 2019. https://carnegie
endowment.org/2019/10/10/competing-with-china-on-technology-and
-innovation-pub-80010.

Shanghai Government. *Shanghai Master Plan 2017–2035 [Shang Hai Shi Cheng
Shi Zong Ti Gui Hua 2017–2035]*. Shanghai: Shanghai Government, January
2018. https://www.supdri.com/2035/index.php?c=message&a=type&tid=33.

Shelton, Barrie, Justyna Karakiewicz, and Thomas Kvan. *The Making of Hong
Kong: From Vertical to Volumetric*. London: Routledge, 2011.

Shenzhen Government. *Shenzhen Municipal New-Type Smart City Construction Master Scheme [Shen Zhen Shi Xin Xing Zhi Hui Cheng Shi Jian She
Zong Ti Fang An]*. Shenzhen: Shenzhen Government, July 21, 2018.
http://cgj.sz.gov.cn/xsmh/zhcg/zcfg/content/post_2017219.html.

Shenzhen Planning and Natural Resources Bureau. *Shenzhen 2035: Territorial
Spatial Master Plan of Shenzhen (2020–2035), (version for public consultation)
[Shen Zhen 2035: Shen Zhen Guo Tu Kong Jian Zong Ti Gui Hua (2020–2035),
(gong shi du ben)]*. Shenzhen: Shenzhen Planning and Natural Resources
Bureau, 2021. http://pnr.sz.gov.cn/attachment/0/794/794784/8858879.pdf.

Shum, Michael. "Know Your Place in Chinese Region, LegCo Leaders Told."
Standard, January 6, 2022. https://www.thestandard.com.hk/section-news
/section/4/237730/know-your-plaCE-IN-CHINESE-REGION,
-Legco-leaders-told.

Sichuan Government. *Chengdu Metropolitan Circle Development Plan* [*Cheng Du Du Shi Quan Fa Zhan Gui Hua*]. Chengdu: Sichuan Government, December 1, 2021. https://www.sc.gov.cn/10462/10464/10465/10595/2021/12 /1/e3abe9d6000e47719fe207ae03d0748b.shtml.

Sit, Victor F. S. "Soviet Influence on Urban Planning in Beijing, 1949–1991." *Town Planning Review* 67, no. 4 (1996): 457–84. https://www.jstor.org /stable/40113418.

"Sixty Thousand Staff Became Redundant from Shougang's Relocation; Director of Board Denies Lay-off" [*Shou Gang Ban Qian Liu Wan Zhi Gong Cheng Duo Yu Ren; Dong Shi Zhang Cheng Mei Xia Gang Gai Nian*]. *Sina*, April 5, 2005. http://finance.sina.com.cn/g/20050405/08201487690 .shtml.

Smith, Michael. "Low Turnout the True Measure of Hong Kong Voter Sentiment." *Financial Review*, December 20, 2021. https://www.afr.com/world /asia/low-turnout-the-true-measure-of-hong-kong-voter-sentiment -20211220-p59iyn.

So, Alvin Y. "Hong Kong's Integration with Mainland China in Historical Perspective." In *Routledge Handbook of Contemporary Hong Kong*, ed. Tai-lok Lui, Stephen W. K. Chiu, and Ray Yep, 494–510. Abingdon, UK: Routledge, 2019.

SOM. "SOM and TLS Selected to Design Core of Xiong'an New Area, China's Model City of the Future" (press release). June 6, 2019. https:// www.som.com/news/som_and_tls_selected_to_design_core_of_xiongan _new_area_chinas_model_city_of_the_future.

State Council, PRC. "Premier Urges Use of Internet Plus to Boost Growth." June 25, 2015. http://english.www.gov.cn/premier/news/2015/06/25/content _281475134144826.htm.

State Council Information Office, PRC. *White Paper: Poverty Alleviation: China's Experience and Contribution.* White paper, State Council Information Office, Beijing, June 2, 2021. http://t.m.china.org.cn/convert/c_2dilkdpp .html.

Sun, Cong, Siqi Zheng, and Rui Wang. "Restricting Driving for Better Traffic and Clearer Skies: Did It Work in Beijing?" *Transport Policy* 32 (2014): 34–41. https://doi.org/10.1016/j.tranpol.2013.12.010.

Sun, Yimin, and Daria Lisaia. "History Matters: Chinese Urbanisation as an Emergent Space." *Urbanisation* 3, no. 1 (2018): 1–16. https://doi.org/10.1177 /2455747118790422.

Tang, Weicheng, and Jin Zhu. "Informality and Rural Industry: Rethinking the Impacts of E-Commerce on Rural Development in China." *Journal of Rural Studies* 75 (2020): 20–29. https://doi.org/10.1016/j.jrurstud .2020.02.010.

Tao, Shu. "An Evaluation on Our Country's Air Pollution and Damage Trends" [*Wo Guo Kong Qi Wu Ran He Wei Hai Qu Shi Ping Gu*]. September 29, 2021. https://mp.weixin.qq.com/s/o8qoJJA4PfGio7AgO3rmJg.

UN-Habitat. *The State of Asian and Pacific Cities 2015: Urban Transformations Shifting from Quantity to Quality.* Nairobi: UN-Habitat, 2015. https:// unhabitat.org/the-state-of-asian-and-pacific-cities-2015.

——. *The Story of Shenzhen: Its Economic, Social and Environmental Transformation.* Nairobi: UN-Habitat, 2019. https://unhabitat.org/the-story-of -shenzhen-its-economic-social-and-environmental-transformation.

United Nations Environment Programme. *Green Is Gold: The Strategy and Actions of China's Ecological Civilization.* Analysis, United Nations Environment Programme, Nairobi, 2016. https://reliefweb.int/sites/reliefweb .int/files/resources/greenisgold_en_20160519.pdf.

——. *A Review of 20 Years' Air Pollution Control in Beijing.* Report, United Nations Environment Programme, Nairobi, March 9, 2019). https://www .unep.org/resources/report/review-20-years-air-pollution-control-beijing.

United Nations. *Report of the World Commission on Environment and Development: Our Common Future.* New York: World Commission on Environment and Development, 1987. https://sustainabledevelopment.un.org /content/documents/5987our-common-future.pdf.

——. *Technology and Innovation Report 2021: Catching Technological Waves— Innovation with Equity.* Report, United Nations Conference on Trade and Development, New York, 2021. https://unctad.org/webflyer/technology -and-innovation-report-2021.

Vogel, Ezra F. *Deng Xiaoping and the Transformation of China.* Cambridge, MA: Belknap Press of Harvard University Press, 2011.

——. *The Four Little Dragons: The Spread of Industrialization in East Asia.* Cambridge, MA: Harvard University Press, 1991.

Wang, Cat, and Danny Mok. "Beijing's Top Man in Hong Kong Visits 'Cage Home' and Medical Service as Part of Drive to 'Listen Directly' to the People." *South China Morning Post,* October 1, 2021. https://www .scmp.com/news/hong-kong/politics/article/3150810/beijings-top-man -hong-kong-visits-cage-home-and-medical.

Wang, Fenglong, and Yungang Liu. "How Unique Is 'China Model': A Review of Theoretical Perspectives on China's Urbanization in Anglophone Literature." *Chinese Geographical Science* 25, no. 1 (2015): 98–112. https://doi.org/10.1007/s11769-014-0713-2.

Wang, Tianyu. "2021: China's GDP Growth Beats Expectations with 8.1 Percent, Fastest in 10 Years." *CGTN*, January 17, 2022. https://news.cgtn.com/news/2022-01-17/China-s-GDP-tops-114-36-trillion-yuan-in-2021-16T64Jtona8/index.html.

Weatherley, Robert, and Vanessa Bauer. "A New Chinese Modernity? The Discourse of Eco-Civilisation Applied to the Belt and Road Initiative." *Third World Quarterly* 42, no. 9 (2021): 2115–32. https://doi.org/10.1080/01436597.2021.1905511.

Wei, Shang-Jin, Zhuan Xie, and Xiaobo Zhang. "From 'Made in China' to 'Innovated in China': Necessity, Prospect, and Challenges." *Journal of Economic Perspectives* 31, no. 1 (2017): 49–70. https://www.aeaweb.org/articles?id=10.1257%2Fjep.31.1.49.

Wen, Gang. "Plan Offers 'Historic' Opportunities to HK." *China Daily*, August 24, 2021. https://global.chinadaily.com.cn/a/202108/24/WS612429b7a310efa1bd66a989.html.

White House. "Fact Sheet: CHIPS and Science Act Will Lower Costs, Create Jobs, Strengthen Supply Chains, and Counter China" (press release). August 9, 2022. https://www.whitehouse.gov/briefing-room/statements-releases/2022/08/09/fact-sheet-chips-and-science-act-will-lower-costs-create-jobs-strengthen-supply-chains-and-counter-china/.

Wikipedia. s.v. "2013 Eastern China Smog." Accessed January 21, 2023. https://en.wikipedia.org/wiki/2013_Eastern_China_smog.

——. s.v. "GDP in Hefei" [*He Fei Shi Di Qu Sheng Chan Zong Zhi*]. Accessed January 31, 2023. https://zh.wikipedia.org/wiki/%E5%90%88%E8%82%A5%E5%B8%82%E5%9C%B0%E5%8C%BA%E7%94%9F%E4%BA%A7E6%80%BB%E5%80%BC.

——. s.v. "List of Chinese Prefecture-Level Cities by GDP." Accessed February 2, 2023. https://en.wikipedia.org/wiki/List_of_Chinese_prefecture-level_cities_by_GDP.

Wikisource. s.v. "The Travels of Marco Polo: Description of the Great City of Kinsay, Which Is the Capital of the Whole Country of Manzi." Accessed January 27, 2023. https://en.wikisource.org/wiki/The_Travels_of_Marco_Polo/Book_2/Chapter_76.

Woetzel, Jonathan, Jeongmin Seong, Kevin Wei Wang, James Manyika, Michael Chui, and Wendy Wong. *China's Digital Economy: A Leading Global Force.* Report, McKinsey Global Institute, 2017. https://www.mckinsey.com /featured-insights/china/chinas-digital-economy-a-leading-global-force.

World Bank. "CO_2 Emissions (Metric Tons per Capita)." Accessed January 20, 2023. https://data.worldbank.org/indicator/EN.ATM.CO2E.PC.

——. "GDP (Current US$)." Accessed January 19, 2023. https://data.worldbank .org/indicator/NY.GDP.MKTP.CD.

——. "GDP per Capita (Current US$)." Accessed January 20, 2023. https:// data.worldbank.org/indicator/NY.GDP.PCAP.CD.

——. "Gini Index—China, Brazil, United Kingdom, United States." Accessed February 14, 2023. https://data.worldbank.org/indicator/SI.POV.GINI?end =2020&locations=CN-BR-GB-US&start=1990.

——. "Population, Total—China, World." Accessed January 19, 2023. https:// data.worldbank.org/indicator/SP.POP.TOTL?end=2020&locations =CN-1W&start=1978&view=chart.

——. *Urban China: Toward Efficient, Inclusive, and Sustainable Urbanization.* Washington, D.C.: World Bank, 2014. http://hdl.handle.net/10986/18865.

——. "Urban Population (% of Total Population)." Accessed January 19, 2023. https://data.worldbank.org/indicator/SP.URB.TOTL.IN.ZS.

Wu, Fulong. "Emerging Chinese Cities: Implications for Global Urban Studies." *Professional Geographer* 68, no. 2 (2016): 338–48. https://doi.org/10.1080 /00330124.2015.1099189.

——. "Emerging Cities and Urban Theories: A Chinese Perspective." In *Theories and Models of Urbanization*, ed. Denise Pumain, 171–82. Cham, Switzerland: Springer, 2019.

——. "Planning Centrality, Market Instruments: Governing Chinese Urban Transformation Under State Entrepreneurialism." *Urban Studies* 55, no. 7 (2018): 1383–99. https://doi.org/10.1177/0042098017721828.

——. *Planning for Growth: Urban and Regional Planning in China.* Abingdon, UK: Routledge, 2015.

Wu, Weiping, and Piper Gaubatz. *The Chinese City.* 2nd ed. Abingdon, UK: Routledge, 2021.

Wuhan Government. *Wuhan Action Plan for Speeding up the Construction of New-Type Smart City* [*Wu Han Shi Jia Kuai Tui Jing Xin Xing Zhi Hui Cheng Shi Jian She Shi Shi Fang An*]. Wuhan: Wuhan Government, 2020. http://www .wuhan.gov.cn/zwgk/xxgk/zfwj/bgtwj/202012/t20201231_1586796.shtml.

Xi, Jinping. "Full Text of Xi's Statement at the General Debate of the 75th Session of the United Nations General Assembly." *XinhuaNet*, September 23, 2020. http://www.xinhuanet.com/english/2020-09/23/c_139388686.htm.

——. *Hold High the Great Banner of Socialism with Chinese Characteristics and Strive in Unity to Build a Modern Socialist Country in All Respects.* Report, Xinhua, Beijing, October 25, 2022. https://english.news.cn/20221025/8eb6 f5239f984f01a2bc45b5b5db0c51/c.html.

——. *Secure a Decisive Victory in Building a Moderately Prosperous Society in All Respects and Strive for the Great Success of Socialism with Chinese Characteristics for a New Era.* Report, Xinhua, Beijing, October 18, 2017. http://www.xinhuanet.com/english/download/Xi_Jinping's_report_at_19th _CPC_National_Congress.pdf.

Xin, Zhou. "Is China Rich or Poor?" *South China Morning Post*, May 29, 2020. https://www.scmp.com/economy/china-economy/article/3086678 /china-rich-or-poor-nations-wealth-debate-muddied-conflicting? module=perpetual_scroll_0&pgtype=article&campaign=3086678.

Xinhua News Agency. "The CPC Central Committee and State Council's Decision on Establishing Hebei Xiong'an New Area" [*Zhong Gong Zhong Yang Guo Wu Yuan Jue Ding She Li He Bei Xiong An Xin Qu*]. Xiong'an New Area Management Commission, Xiong'an, April 1, 2017. http://www.xiongan.gov.cn/2017-04/01/c_129769132.htm.

——. "CPC Sets Targets Through 2035 to Basically Achieve China's Socialist Modernization." *XinhuaNet*, October 29, 2020. http://www.xinhuanet .com/english/2020-10/29/c_139476284.htm.

——. "Millennium Plan, National Initiative" [*Qian Nian Da Ji, Guo Jia Da Shi*]. Xiong'an New Area Management Commission, Xiong'an, April 13, 2017. http://www.xiongan.gov.cn/2017-04/13/c_129769126.htm.

"Xu Kuangdi on the Planning of Xiong'an New Area" [*Xu Kuang Di Xiang Jie Xiong An Xin Qu Gui Hua*]. Paper, June 7, 2017. https://www.sohu.com /a/146813902_260616.

Xu, Lingui. "Xinhua Insight: China Embraces New 'Principal Contradiction' When Embarking on New Journey." *XinhuaNet*, October 20, 2017. http://www.xinhuanet.com/english/2017-10/20/c_136694592.htm.

Xu, Sheng. "CDB Will Provide RMB 130 Billion to Support the Initial Development Zone in Xiong'an" [*Guo Kai Hang Jiang Ti Gong 1300 Yi Yuan Zhi Chi Xiong An Xin Qu Qi Bu Qu Xiang Guan Gong Zuo*]. *XinhuaNet*, April 27, 2017. http://m.xinhuanet.com/2017-04/27/c_1120886859.htm.

Xu, Weina. "NDRC Allocated RMB 1.7 Billion from Central Government Budget to Support the Construction of Xiong'an" [*Fa Gai Wei Xia Da 17 Yi Yuan Zhong Yang Yu Suan Nei Tou Zi Zhi Chi Xiong An Xin Qu Jian She*]. *China Daily*, June 26, 2021. https://cn.chinadaily.com.cn/a/202106/26/WS60d72984a3101e7ce97573d6.html.

Yang, Zhenshan, Jianming Cai, Henk F. L. Ottens, and Richard Sliuzas. "City Profile: Beijing." *Cities* 31 (2013): 491–506. https://doi.org/10.1016/j.cities.2011.07.007.

Yu, Hong. "The Ascendency of State-Owned Enterprises in China: Development, Controversy and Problems." *Journal of Contemporary China* 23, no. 85 (2014): 161–82. https://doi.org/10.1080/10670564.2013.809990.

Yu, Li. "Low Carbon Eco-City: New Approach for Chinese Urbanisation." *Habitat International* 44 (2014): 102–10. https://doi.org/10.1016/j.habitatint.2014.05.004.

Zhang, Lin, and Tu Lan. "The New Whole State System: Reinventing the Chinese State to Promote Innovation." *Environment and Planning A: Economy and Space* 55, no. 1 (2022): 1–21. https://doi.org/10.1177/0308518X221088294.

Zhao, Wanxia, and Yonghua Zou. "Hefei: An Emerging City in Inland China." *Cities* 77 (2018): 158–69. https://doi.org/10.1016/j.cities.2018.01.008.

Zhao, Ziyang. *The Secret Journal of Zhao Ziyang* [*gai ge li cheng*]. Hong Kong: New Century Press of Hong Kong, 2009.

Zheng, Yongnian, and Yanjie Huang. *Market in State: The Political Economy of Domination in China.* Cambridge: Cambridge University Press, 2018.

Zimu. "Hefei's Counterattack Is Not an Accident, You Will Understand After Reading the Three Stories" [*He Fei De Ni Xi Jue Fei Ou Ran, Kan Wan Zhe San Ge Gu Shi Ni Yi Ding Hui Ming Bai*]. *KK News*, June 17, 2021. https://kknews.cc/zh-cn/finance/n2nxoyq.html.

INDEX

GPSR Authorized Representative: Easy Access System Europe, Mustamäe tee
50, 10621 Tallinn, Estonia, gpsr.requests@easproject.com

www.ingramcontent.com/pod-product-compliance
Lightning Source LLC
Chambersburg PA
CBHW022138020426
42334CB00015B/958